PARIOLI
CORSO D'ITALIA
HQ of German Commandant
Hotel Excelsior
VIA VENETO
VIA DEL 23 MARZO
VIA XX SETTEMBRE
Ministry of Corporations
Pzza. Barberini
Pal. Barberini
S. Maria d'Angeli
QUATTRO FONTANE
VIA DELLE
MESSAGGERO
Piazza Esedra
Staz. Termini
S. Lorenzo fuori le Mura
Tunnel
Koch's Prison
VIA PRINCIPE AMEDEO
VIA NAZIONALE
M. Viminale
VIA CAVOUR
Colle Oppio
M. Esquilino
Terme di Traianeo
Domus Aurea
Piazza Vittorio Emanuele II
DELL'IMPERO
Arch of Constantine
Colosseum
Palatino
VIA TASSO
Gestapo HQ
Villa Wolkonsky German Embassy
VIA CLAUDIA
Partisan hideout
VIA MARCO AURELIO
St. John in Lateran
M. Celio
VIA D. TERME D. CARACALLA
Terme di Caracalla
ROME
1944
to Via Ardeatina and Ardeatine Caves
APPIAN WAY
5 4 3 2 1 0 1/4 1/2
Yards in hundreds
MILES

DEATH IN ROME

Death in Rome

Robert Katz

THE MACMILLAN COMPANY, NEW YORK

Library of Congress Catalog Card Number: 66-23473

Second Printing 1967

The Macmillan Company, New York
Collier-Macmillan Canada Ltd., Toronto, Ontario
Printed in the United States of America

The author wishes to thank the following individuals and publishers for permission to reprint previously copyrighted material:

Eugen Dollmann for the excerpts from *Roma Nazista*, copyright 1949 by Eugen Dollmann; Grove Press, Inc., and Curtis Brown, Ltd., for the excerpt from *The Deputy* by Rolf Hochhuth, translated by Richard and Clara Winston, copyright © 1964 by Grove Press, Inc.; Gaetano Macchiaroli, Editore, for the excerpts from *La Resistenza in Roma* by Renato Perrone Capano, copyright 1963; Simon and Schuster, Inc., and Weidenfeld & Nicolson, Ltd., for the excerpts from *A Spy in Rome* by Peter Tompkins, copyright 1962.

This book
is dedicated to
the people of Rome who resisted

CONTENTS

FOREWORD

On Thursday afternoon, March 23, 1944, a heavily armed column of 156 SS police was attacked by sixteen partisans in German-occupied Rome. The encounter took place in Via Rasella, a narrow, sloping street in the center of the city. The partisans inflicted severe casualties among the Germans and escaped unharmed and unseen, dissolving into the underground of the Roman Resistance.

Notified within minutes of the attack, Hitler, at his headquarters in East Prussia, and Himmler, in Berlin, decided to punish the entire city of Rome. They demanded death and destruction.

The next day the SS rounded up hundreds of Romans. With their hands tied behind their backs, and linked to one another in small groups, the prisoners were herded into sealed meat trucks and driven just beyond the ancient walls of Rome. There, on Via Ardeatina, the trucks stopped at a labyrinth of tunnels among the Christian catacombs of the Appian Way.

Inside these man-made caves, the Germans lighted torches and forced the Italians to get down on their knees and bow their heads. They proceeded then systematically to slaughter them by discharging 9mm. bullets at the base of their necks at an angle that passed through the brain and the top of the skull.

Sixty-seven SS platoons labored into the last hours of that day to complete their work. When they finished, German engineers blew up the entrances to the caves, hoping to seal their contents for all time.

But the secret in the Ardeatine caves could not be concealed for very long. Never in Rome's 2,700-year history had a crime of such enormity been committed, and this one had been carried out on the very ground so sacred to Christianity.

Within hours terrifying rumors began to circulate among the Romans. The following Thursday some boys, scavenging for booty, followed a trail of electric wire and a swarm of flies through a hole blown into the caves by the German mines. They ran for a priest.

After the liberation of Rome by the Allies, June 4, 1944, the Romans opened the caves. They found in two mounds of corpses the remains of 335 individuals from every branch of human society: workers and artists, diplomats and chauffeurs, lawyers and trainmen, municipal clerks and peddlers, physicians and mechanics, professors and students, musicians and shopkeepers, generals, waiters, bankers, industrialists, shoemakers, pharmacists, sailors, farmers, butchers, landlords, postmen, boys, Jews, and a Roman Catholic priest.

Romans and Italians everywhere wanted to know why this crime had occurred. They asked: Who gave the order? Who pulled the trigger? Could it have been prevented? Where was the King? Where were the Allies? Where were the men who claimed to be the representatives of the people? Where was the Pope?

In the late 1940s and throughout the 1950s a series of trials was held in Italy. The passions aroused fired the issue, divided the nation, and shook the foundations of the new postwar republic.

Some people said the massacre was legitimate. Others blamed the Ardeatine crime on the Roman Resistance, claiming that the earlier partisan attack had been a meaningless provocation. Some hinted at a Communist plot. The Germans, throughout, protested their innocence.

Many men were judged in Italian and Allied courts. They were tried, too, in books, in the press, and, in one case—that of an innocent man—by an enraged mob. The details of the crime were more or less established. Those responsible—at least for ordering and carrying it out—were for the most part identified. Some who had been accused were acquitted. Some were convicted. Some were sentenced to be punished; a few of these sentences were carried out. The partisans of the Via Rasella were decorated by the State for military valor in time of war. The victims of the Ardeatine massacre were given a fitting national memorial at the site of their martyrdom. By all rights the events and the hundreds of people involved should have receded into history, as a memory of a tragic time gone by.

In 1966, however, partisans of the Via Rasella were receiving anonymous threats of death. One of them—a woman who had later been elected to Parliament—has been repeatedly vilified on the floor of the Chamber of Deputies for her participation in the attack. To serve political ends the facts of the case have been grotesquely distorted and lies invented. Historians have recorded differing versions. Any of these may be used today by newspapers, politicians, organizations, clergymen, and schoolteachers, depending on their political predilections. Questions raised more than twenty-two years ago have gone unsettled. They are alive today in all of Italy, sometimes setting one man against another. More than ever they demand to be answered.

In March, 1964, on the twentieth anniversary of the events that began in Via Rasella, I was living and working in Rome. On the morning of the 24th, the local newspapers announced the commemoration that day of what is known to all Italians as *Le Fosse Ardeatine*. I was ignorant of its history, but during the week I had become vaguely conscious of the scheduled ceremonies by the posters that come and go from the walls of Rome. Reading the brief newspaper account, the Ardeatine story fit very neatly into the stereotyped images one conjures of good versus evil, and that afternoon I accompanied the procession of thousands of Romans to the caves in Via Ardeatina to honor the memory of the 335 dead.

In the days that followed, further exposure to the background of *Le Fosse Ardeatine* shattered my preconceived notions and revealed the presence of the controversy described above. I found it impossible to accept in its entirety any one or combination of the varying and conflicting "histories" of the incidents in Via Rasella and Via Ardeatina.

In the first place, the partisans of the Via Rasella had been young Communist students, which both explained a great deal and further complicated the matter. In postwar Italy the Communists have grown consistently stronger, at least at the polls, and their party has become the largest and most popular Communist party in the West. It therefore seemed more than likely that the issue had been used or abused by all sides for propaganda purposes. This was another way of saying that it reflected the continuing struggle between communism and political systems from neofascism to social democracy, and—with Rome as the center of 500 million Catholics—this conflict included in a primary role the Roman Catholic Church.

The engagement of powers in a state of relative balance explained why the most important points in the history of the Via Rasella incident have not been resolved. Two examples:

Some say the partisans could have prevented the Ardeatine massacre had they surrendered themselves to the Germans. Others contend that the partisans had no way of knowing what the Germans would do until it had already been done, and then it was too late. What is the truth?

It has been suggested that the Pope could have intervened to prevent the massacre. In defense of Pius XII it is said that he had no way of knowing what the Germans would do until it was too late, and, besides, he could not have done anything. What is the truth?

In the second place, as a result of the conflict, none of the accounts of the events of March 23 and 24 had ever satisfactorily discussed the motivations of the partisans and of those who committed and abetted the Ardeatine crime.

For example, *why* did the Germans respond to the Via Rasella attack with an act of brutality which was unprecedented during the war in all of Italy and was, moreover, an affront to the Pope and the Holy City? Was it, as the Roman Resistance declared some days afterward, "the extreme reaction of the beast that feels itself about to fall"? Or was it a considered political act calculated to produce a predetermined effect? Or was it something else?

Italian right-wing sources have maintained that while deplorable it was simply a legitimate reprisal of war, provoked by the illegal action of criminal, irresponsible extremists and sanctioned by the Hague Convention of 1907. The Church has consistently held that what happened in Via Rasella was a crime and a massacre to be equally condemned with what happened in the caves of Ardeatine.

Despite these well-known attitudes, however, the Italian Supreme Court years ago declared the attack in Via Rasella a legitimate "act of war"; the State proclaimed the partisans national heroes; and British military courts in the two separate trials of the German generals held directly responsible for the Ardeatine massacre rejected the legitimate-reprisal defense, finding all of the accused guilty of a war crime and sentencing them to death.

In the fall of 1964, I had to return to the United States. I tried to learn if there had been any study made of this episode in Italian history by a non-Italian, and, of course, a non-German, since one could not expect impartiality from the offending party. Except for passing mention in a few American and British books and other publications, which are cited in the documentation and bibliography that follow, there was nothing. Moreover, I discovered from further investigation that despite the millions of words that had been written in hundreds of Italian books, pamphlets, periodicals, and newspapers, no one had ever fully reconstructed the events of March 23 and 24, 1944. It also became clear that primary sources of information, such as the captured published and unpublished war documents and the pre-Nuremberg interrogations, had apparently never been consulted; nor had certain relevant secondary material, such as wartime histories and memoirs.

A survey of the German material, although rich in information, confirmed that it was neither disinterested nor complete.

At this point, I was encouraged to proceed with writing this book. I believed that further research and a reexamination of the facts—many of which had appeared after most opinions had been formed and accounts had been written—could cast new light on the controversy. I also felt that an attempt should be made to view the events of those two days from a perspective, at a distance of more than twenty years, that sees the relationship of the issues in Rome of March, 1944, to the issues of today.

The same forces that remain in conflict today—not in Italy alone, but throughout the world—existed before March, 1944, and have, in fact, for most of the twentieth century. Beneath the thick layer of everyday life, they engage one another, sometimes quiescently, sometimes violently, shaping us and our society. On the road from Via Rasella to Via Ardeatina, for a single moment in history—one of many, of course—these forces rose to the surface and clashed openly. In doing so, some of them could be glimpsed in sharp relief. To examine what happened in Via Rasella is to see that clash. To try to understand the former helps in understanding the latter. Obviously, it is this sequential process that has been avoided at all costs for all these years.

I have since been back to Rome. I have been to the archives, the libraries, the ministries, and the newspaper morgues. I have been to the Vatican. Most doors have been open; a few, as will be seen, were closed. I have been to Via Rasella and in the caves of Ardeatine. In search of information, I have been permitted to go down into the cellar of Communist Party headquarters in Via delle Botteghe Oscure and I have met with the sisters of the convent Bambin Gesù. I have stood in the cells of the former Gestapo prison in Via Tasso * and I have seen what had been the Fascist house of torture in Via Principe Amedeo and the old prison on the left bank of the Tiber, the Regina Coeli. I have spoken with men and

* Now a museum dedicated to the Roman Resistance.

women of the Resistance who were inside them and others who were not captured. I have gone to the sites of their battles, to their hideouts, and to their haunts. I have spoken with Romans who lived under the occupation and, among them, those who knew victims of the massacre.

I have met with the partisans of the Via Rasella. Strangely, they told me no one had ever come to them before; no foreigner or Italian who wrote on the subject had ever asked them what they did in Via Rasella, what they thought, and how they felt. At my request, for the first time in all these years they gathered as a group and reconstructed their different roles in the attack. Those who could not attend were interviewed individually, including their former commanders Carlo Salinari, who is now a professor of literature at the University of Rome, and Giorgio Amendola, a vice-secretary of the Italian Communist Party and a former member of the tripartite military directorate of the Roman Resistance.

I have also been to the archives and libraries in Milan, Munich, London, Oxford, New York, and Washington. In Germany, I learned that of the four Germans tried and convicted for the Ardeatine war crime, two have died, one—a ninety-year-old ex-general—lives in seclusion, and the fourth is serving a life sentence in the Italian penitentiary at Gaeta. (Two Italians convicted on charges of having been implicated in the war crime were executed.)

I nevertheless had the benefit of interviews with the man who was head of the SS in Rome, Eugen Dollmann. Dr. Dollmann was an eyewitness and a principal participant in many of the events of March 23 and 24. He provided me with unpublished information, as well as an unpublished manuscript, written by himself, which gives an account of his observations and his actions during those hours.

In Oxford, I was fortunate in having the counsel of F. W. Deakin, Warden of Saint Antony's College and author of one of the most important books on the fall of Italian fascism, *The Brutal Friendship* (New York: Harper, 1963). Professor Deakin holds a collection of copies of captured Fascist documents, the originals of which have been returned to the Italian Foreign Ministry and are now classified. He advised me as to their contents with regard to my research and allowed me to examine the relevant material.

What follows is based on personal interviews, trial testimony, published and unpublished documents, Italian and German memoirs, diaries, and histories, and a wealth of material—albeit fragmented—published in books, pamphlets, and periodicals. Much information has been gathered through correspondence with German military officers, veterans and war-victims organizations, government bureaus, and historians.

As far as possible I have tried to let the participants in this forty-hour drama speak for themselves. The cast of characters, who directly in one way or another influenced the events or were influenced by them, was very long. It included Pope Pius XII, an American spy, two future prime ministers of Italy, a janitor, a deserter from the German Army, a medical student disguised as a garbage man and his fiancée, a drunken German general, Hitler, Mussolini, and many, many others. The parts they played in this story have been examined very closely and set down here, sometimes in great detail. The source of every thought or spoken word, every conversation, every action, and every point that is not an indisputable historical fact has been noted. In every case of conflicting testimony all sides have been recorded either in the text or in footnotes. Hearsay, however melodramatic, has been eschewed or, in every instance, clearly indicated as such. Nothing has been rendered by imagination.

Although I have had help and advice, which are gratefully acknowledged at the end of this book, I alone am fully responsible for the presentation and accuracy of the factual material and for its interpretation.

If the questions of the Via Rasella and the caves of Ardeatine have remained burning, they burn not only for Italians, but for all men. They are the questions of tyranny and antidemocracy and how to confront them. In Rome they were confronted with collaboration, opportunism, submission, indifference, and opposition ranging from passive resistance and civil disobedience to sabotage and guerrilla warfare. Each of these was put to the severest trial in a span of hours from the morning of March 23 to the final moments of the night of March 24, 1944.

This is an account of those hours.

PART ONE

The Eve

March 1–22, 1944

"To the Italian people!
As long as the Germans remain in Italy,
you are condemned to destruction . . .
Sabotage the German! . . .
Out with the Germans!"

—from an Allied leaflet dropped from the air over occupied Rome [1]

I

HE LIVED in an old apartment building. It stood on a corner in the part of Rome between the Spanish Steps, the Trevi Fountain, and Via Veneto. His name was Mario Fiorentini.[1] His code name in the Resistance was Giovanni. Centuries ago his ancestors had been Florentine Jews. With passage of time they had come from Tuscany to Rome, adopting the religion of the Papal States.

The entrance to the building was at number 18 Via di Capo Le Case. The side faced Via Due Macelli. The neighborhood had changed greatly in the last two decades of the nineteenth century. Rome at the beginning of the 1870s had become the capital of a unified Italy. The urbanization of the city that followed had altered the character of the district.[2] But this house in Capo Le Case had only grown older.

On clear March afternoons the sun struck the façade of the third and fourth stories on the Due Macelli side. Residents would go to the windows to close the shutters or, sometimes, to sit by the sill in the warm light. One day early in March, Mario Fiorentini was at the window.

He was rarely home. He had been arrested by the Fascists the previous November in the print shop where the Action Party published the underground newspaper *l'Italia Libera*.[3] After a while, they released him, but three times since then the Germans had come to the apartment in Capo Le Case and three times Fiorentini had eluded them by slipping out the back way.

If they captured him now, he felt certain, it would be for the last time. He and other partisans had on March 2 attacked the barracks on Viale Giulio Cesare. Thousands of Roman men, taken by the SS from the streets and their homes, were being held there. They were awaiting deportation to Germany for forced labor.* The partisans escaped without incident, but Fiorentini dropped and lost his cap and one of the Germans had gotten a good look at his face.

He and his wife, Lucia Ottobrini, slept in a cellar hiding place on Opium Hill, near the Colosseum. But in the rainy first days of March, Lucia had gotten a high fever and sleeping on the damp stone floor of the *cantina* hideout seemed riskier than going home, at least for a while.

At this hour, from the window of the Fiorentini apartment, he could look north with an unobstructed view far beyond the deserted boat-shaped fountain in Piazza di Spagna. In the opposite direction there was almost no one, too, except the refugees sheltered in the tunnel beneath the Quirinal—the palace of the absent King Vittorio Emanuele III. A disquieting silence pressed on the city. It was siesta time, but the stillness was unnatural. Since December it had been forbidden to ride bicycles. The trams and the *filobus* were not operating regularly, and people were reluctant to ride them. Sometimes the Germans would stop a bus, arrest its passengers, and ship them to the north. The streets of Rome had become fearsome, and certain buildings were closed by the Germans to Italians and dogs.[4]

To Mario Fiorentini the silence spoke for the hated war. He was twenty-five years old, a mathematics student at the University of Rome, and newly married. He thought he might become a teacher. The war stood in the way of his future. The

* The partisans struck, killing two Fascist militiamen, a few hours after a German soldier killed a pregnant woman, Teresa Gullace, a thirty-seven-year-old mother of five children. She was shot in the head as she tried to throw a piece of bread to her imprisoned husband. The incident took place in the presence of several thousand women who were protesting the deportation of their men. ("*Le donne e la Resistenza*" in *Noi Donne*, Apr. 25, 1964, p. 45.)

Resistance, it seemed to him, was doing something about it. He believed that it was fighting "a war against war." [5]

The quiet of that afternoon was broken by the Germans. At first he became aware of a sound like that of lightly rolling drums. It came from beyond Fiorentini's line of vision, somewhere north of Piazza del Popolo. Soon he could hear the voices of singing men and the pounding of their boots against the cobbles. They passed the little antique shops and the art galleries of Via del Babuino. Their singing and their cadence thundered closer all the while. He could see them clearly now. The column marched through Piazza di Spagna, beside the Spanish Steps—so naked this wartime month of March without the carpet of azaleas that would have stretched as far as the church of Trinità dei Monti. The Germans passed the house where Keats and Shelley once had lived. They passed American Express and the Vatican Collegium Propaganda Fide, then crossed Via di Capo Le Case and continued on beneath Fiorentini's windows.

The column was escorted by about half a dozen troops with submachine guns leveled straight ahead. An armored truck with a machine gun mounted on a platform brought up the rear. The formation was a hundred yards long—more than 150 men harnessed with belts of ammunition. Each carried a rifle and a pistol. On the lapels of their gray uniforms and on the front of their helmets, as Fiorentini could see, they bore the double lightning bolt, symbol of the SS. [6]

It occurred to him that this was not the first time he had seen the column go by. It had passed yesterday, too, but he had not given it further thought. Perhaps it had even come by the day before—always just about this time. He looked at his watch. It was almost two o'clock.

He watched the marching men continue on toward the tunnel. It had recently been closed to traffic by the German commandant of the city. Almost at the black mouth of the passageway, the troops turned left and disappeared into one of the narrow streets that climbs the slope toward the Palazzo Barberini. The sound of hammering footsteps and chanting soldierly voices faded quickly.

Mario Fiorentini made a mental note of which street they entered. It was Via Rasella. The thought of attacking them had already crossed his mind.[7]

II

In the last days of winter, March, 1944, Rome was a city of tension and frustration. For eight months it had been strained by momentous events that had promised an early end to the war. Now, for everyone, everything had gone wrong.

Fascism had fallen in July, only to be restored in September. The King had arrested Mussolini, only to have him taken from his hands by Hitler's agents and carried to the north to head the neo-Fascist regime. For forty-five days that summer the King's government had maneuvered for a favored armistice from the Allies, only to be offered unconditional surrender. Italy had finally conceded, only to be too late: the Germans drove into Rome, while both King and Government fled in the dead of night, abandoning the city in chaos and leaving no one in charge.[1] The Allies had invaded Italy three times to drive out the Germans, only to be stopped south of Rome at Cassino and Anzio. The Pope had sought in vain to negotiate a peace in the West, only to pay the price of silence at the spectacle of Nazi inhumanity before his eyes.[2]

Rome was an "open city" whose walls shook under the waves of German military movements and the thunder of Allied bombs.[3] Swollen to nearly twice its usual size by refugees from the countryside, Rome was a city of spies, double agents, informers, torturers, escaped war prisoners, hunted Jews, and hungry people.

Yet at this late date in the war, Rome to a great extent clung to an illusion. Rome was the Holy City and, people still believed, was therefore protected from the "excesses" the Germans had visited upon other great cities of Europe.[4]

In this atmosphere a resistance movement had arisen, only to become racked and split by internal crises. After being silenced for more than twenty years, the six anti-Fascist parties in Rome had come together in a timid, clandestine union called the *Comitato di Liberazione Nazionale* (CLN).*

In its midst were representatives of the monarchy and republicanism; the aristocracy and socialism; industry and labor; the Army, the state bureaucracy, the Church, and communism. Mistrustful of one another, incapable of bold decisions, and virtually paralyzed, they were strung together by a single thread: the will to liberation. Toward this end they had created the Military Junta † and the Corps of Freedom Volunteers. But it was an almost powerless junta; it was a corps with-

* National Liberation Committee: Led by Ivanoe Bonomi, pre-Mussolini, democratic Prime Minister, and its members were De Gasperi of the Christian Democrats (*Democrazia Cristiana*); Ruini, Democratic Labor (*Democrazia del Lavoro*); Casati, Liberals (*Partito Liberale Italiano*); La Malfa, Action Party (*Partito d'Azione*); Nenni, Socialists (*Partito Socialista Italiano di Unità Proletario*); Scoccimaro, Communists (*Partito Comunista Italiano*).

There was also a number of splinter underground movements outside the CLN. The most influential was the right-wing *Fronte Militare Clandestino della Resistenza* and its intelligence service, *Centro* X. It maintained liaison with the CLN and was in continual radio contact with the King's government in the Allied-liberated zone of Italy. Unswervingly loyal to the monarchy, it believed the King's flight from Rome in the face of German aggression was justified. At the other end of the Resistance's political spectrum were the *Cattolici Comunisti* (Catholic Communists) and the extremist *Movimento Comunista d'Italia*, better known as *Bandiera Rossa* (Red Flag), a Trotskyite-anarchist movement which enjoyed a certain popularity in the periphery of Rome.

† Nominally each of the six CLN parties had representation in the Military Junta. But in practice it functioned under the leadership of the left-wing members: Action Party (the embodiment of an earlier liberal-socialist-republican movement), represented by Riccardo Bauer; Socialists, Sandro Pertini; Communists, Giorgio Amendola.

out unity. Only the men and women of the political parties themselves seemed capable of striking militarily against the German occupiers.

They were called *partigiani.*

Some had fought the Germans on September 9, 1943, at the foot of the 2,000-year-old pyramid near the south wall of the ancient city. There, at Porta San Paolo, the armed Resistance in Rome and in all of Italy was born. A motley army of civilians and scattered units of the regular forces tried to block the German takeover of the city. But with the occupiers seated in power and a semblance of calm restored, the *partigiani*, or partisans, were in the beginning hesitant and uncertain.[5]

Who, after twenty years, would be the first to hurl a hand grenade? In October, one among them answered this question. With a bomb in his pocket, he mounted a bicycle and attacked.[6] The Germans banned the use of bicycles, but by the new year, partisan units were operating in the streets and in the countryside.* On January 22, 1944, when the Allies landed at Anzio, thirty-three miles south of Rome, they called on the partisans to lead the population in rising up against the Germans.† The Anzio beachhead failed to move and the insurrection never got started, but the partisans and the Military Junta by now were determined not to wait for the *anglo-americani* to rescue the city. They still sought to prepare the people for insurrection. A participation in their own liberation would

* The Allied-liberated sector of Italy, south of Cassino, declared war on Germany on Oct. 13, 1943.

† While amphibious elements of the American and British armies were landing on the Anzio and Nettuno beaches, Resistance forces in Rome received the following radio message: "From Allied Command–stop–the hour has arrived for Rome and all Italians to fight in every possible way and with all forces–stop– . . . sabotage the enemy . . . block his roads of retreat destroy his communications to the last wire . . . strike against him everywhere continuing the fight indefatigably without thought of political questions until our troops have arrived–stop– . . . notify all bands and parties." (Quoted in E. Piscitelli, *Storia della Resistenza romana*, Bari: Laterza, 1965, p. 259.)

help regain the dignity of the people of Rome, many of whom felt tarnished by the Fascist past.*

"We make no truce with the enemy," the Junta directed the Freedom Volunteers. "We will strike them in their men and in their things. . . . We will not lay down our arms and we will continue the battle at the side of the armies of freedom until all of Italy is liberated, and Nazism and fascism is overcome." [7]

By March there was more than a directive; there was a strategy that sought to weaken the German lines of communication to the fronts at Cassino and Anzio. The Junta hoped to divert to the periphery of Rome the movement through the city of reinforcements and supplies to the German battlefields. This area was under intensive Allied bombardment. It was a zone of further partisan activity and had a population extremely hostile to the Germans. Further, the Junta wanted to create an armed, insurrectional threat within Rome to discourage the Germans from attempting to hold the city. There was a danger that with the eventual arrival of the Allies the Germans would engage them in street-by-street combat. For a city with its nerves worn thin and already desperately short on food, this would bring havoc, destruction, and a tremendous loss in civilian lives. It could mean the end of everything treasured and beautiful about Rome.[8]

The plans of the Junta called for armed conflict, sabotage, and terrorism. In the weeks following Anzio, the partisans destroyed gasoline depots and munitions dumps; the supply

* In this connection the Junta was at odds with the right wing of the CLN and the monarchists outside the liberation committee. These groups saw a threat to their power in postwar Italy—especially to the discredited King and the House of Savoy. Counting on support from the Western Allies, themselves fearful of a shift to the left, they argued in and out of the CLN that it was useless to fight the Germans, at least militarily, when liberation was "just around the corner." It was wiser, they said, to express one's antifascism in carrying out intelligence for the Allies and fighting the Nazis with the clandestine press, etc.

roads were showered with homemade four-pointed nails; enemy trucks, buildings, and war equipment were assailed and blown up; armed German soldiers were fought in the outlying areas of the city; assassination attempts were made on high Nazi and Fascist officials.[9]

But until now they had not gained any decisive victories, and not everyone agreed this was the best way to fight.

III

THE ONE man who most vigorously opposed both the strategy and the tactics of the Junta and the partisans was Pope Pius XII.

Eugenio Pacelli was sixty-eight years old on March 2, 1944. That same day, he completed his fifth year as the 262nd Pope of Rome. He was preoccupied with the fate of his native city. Many mornings, at about six-thirty, he would go to the window of the austere *appartamento privato*. Below him the Tiber was turgid from the heavy rains of February 29 and March 1. He would look out on a city he loved, on a people he had felt close to but now could no longer trust.

The war came closer to Rome every day. Allied aircraft that March were bombing the city relentlessly. The unrest among the Romans was explosive. For the Pope, the present precarious situation had not existed the previous summer. The relative pacification of the Italians as a result of years of Fascist dictatorship; the great *Conciliazione* of 1929, wrought by the Lateran treaties, reconciling the long-standing questions between the Papacy and the State; a distant war that at least until the battle of Stalingrad seemed to have doomed the forces of atheist communism; all of these conditions—whatever else they might have meant to the 2,000-year-old Church

—had created for the Vatican the illusion of a measure of stability.

The air attacks on Rome had begun on July 19, 1943, some days after Allied troops landed in Sicily. The war had come home to Italy. On July 10 President Roosevelt had written to the Pope. He said that "the soldiers of the United Nations have come to rid Italy of fascism and all its unhappy symbols, and to drive out the Nazi oppressors who are infesting her soil." [1]

The Pope was not pleased.[2] He was above political systems. His enemies were upheaval and the uncertainties of change. He replied on the 20th with an appeal that Rome, "the patrimony of Religion and Civilization," be spared from British and American military operations.[3] Five days later Mussolini fell. Spontaneous demonstrations of joy broke out in the piazzas. In Rome and elsewhere people were saying that the Pope had intervened mediating an imminent peace between Italy and the Allies.[4] But events had taken place too fast for such a possibility to have developed.

In reality Pius XII was fearful of the new situation in Italy. He interpreted the fall of fascism as a victory for communism. He was suspicious of the new government appointed by the King and headed by the old monarchist Army Marshal Pietro Badoglio. Vatican diplomats told Washington that "the recent demonstrations accompanying the fall of fascism are sufficient evidence that the Communists are well organized in Italy . . ." [5]

The Pope's position, according to the German Ambassador to the Holy See, was outlined in a document drawn up by Vatican Undersecretary of State Monsignor Montini.* Referring to the Montini note, the Ambassador cabled Berlin: "In the Vatican the Italian situation is considered very threatening; no one any longer believes in an Axis victory . . . Bolshevism

* Now Pope Paul VI.

really represents a main preoccupation." [6] The German, Baron Ernst von Weizsäcker, followed this with a report on the Vatican's reserve toward the Badoglio government. The Holy See believed that "the so-called freedom it promised has opened the door to Communist movements . . . In reality the Church today is worried. Communism is and remains its most dangerous enemy both in foreign and domestic policy." [7]

In the meantime the Allies had decided to put maximum political and military pressure on the King's government to surrender.[8] The Vatican, however, warned Washington of the "grave consequences of such a military campaign."

"Vatican City," it said, "would inevitably become involved in, and perhaps even engulfed by, any serious disorder which might arise." [9] It depicted as "a consideration of paramount importance . . . the favorable reaction of such a war policy in the interests of communism." [10]

The Pope apparently believed that an Italy freed from Fascist dictatorship and left to govern itself was desirable only for Communists. He seemed unsure of the Vatican's place in an anti-Fascist country. He feared, as these despairing and exaggerated Vatican statements would indicate, the physical, and perhaps ultimately the spiritual, destruction of the Roman Catholic Church.

To prevent this, the Pope worked to restore order. The aim of the Vatican was a negotiated armistice in Italy. This would be a first step in a general settlement in the West, which would then be free to deal with the Bolshevik East. Vatican diplomacy sought to enlighten the British and the Americans to the notion that the greatest danger to the world was not Nazi Germany but their ally Russia.* [11] "The Curia detests the

* To convince the British and the Americans of this danger, Vatican diplomats, by design or by error, consistently overestimated the strength of the Communists and equated the complex, often conflicting forms of antifascism with monolithic procommunism. Sometimes these views bordered on hysteria. In a diplomatic note to the US Department of State, the Holy See cited the demonstrations following Mussolini's fall—which were

Anglo-American alliance with the Soviet Union," Weizsäcker reported.[12] In September he told Berlin that it was "the dream of the Vatican that the Western Powers will recognize their true interests while there is still time and will act in common with the Germans to save European civilization from bolshevism . . ."* [13]

---

surprising in their passivity—as evidence that the Italian Communists "*have at their disposal both financial means and arms.*" (Italics in original) It added, "Information reaching the Holy See also shows that communism is making continual progress also in Germany. These facts are a clear warning of the grave peril that Europe will find itself overrun with communism immediately on the cessation of hostilities." (Memorandum of Aug. 20, 1943, *Foreign Relations of the United States, 1943*, Vol. II, Europe, Washington: Government Printing Office, 1964, p. 946.) The Italian Communists were actually very weak and disorganized at this date. Suppressed and outlawed for almost twenty years, the party had but a few thousand members. (*Cf.* Piscitelli, *op. cit.*, p. 73.) Its founder had died in a Fascist prison, and its leader, Palmiro Togliatti, had been living in exile for the past seventeen years. Seven months after the Vatican's memorandum, in a document prepared by the Roman Communists and dated Mar. 2, 1944, the party described its contemporary condition in occupied Rome. In a city with a population of nearly 2,000,000, it had only 3,000 members. "We will not be in a position for a long time to sustain a battle" against the Germans, it said in noting a shortage of weapons and a greater shortage of ammunition. "The most serious weak point is and remains the lack of experience" in underground life. (This document, unpublished for twenty-one years, appeared in the party's theoretical journal *Critica Marxista*, Mar.–Apr., 1965, p. 118.)

* Defenders of the Vatican's wartime policies say the Weizsäcker telegrams are not to be taken seriously. The Ambassador, it is said, was only telling Berlin what it wanted to hear, especially of the Vatican's interest in an Axis-Western Allies settlement followed by a Euro-American crusade against the Soviets. If this were true, it would not explain that at the same time German diplomats in Lisbon and Paris were cabling exactly the same information—said to come from high Vatican sources—to the Foreign Office. (The texts of these telegrams of Aug. 1943, are published in S. Friedländer, *Pio XII e il Terzo Reich*, Milan: Feltrinelli, 1965, pp. 171–172.) Weizsäcker, furthermore, was considered by the Vatican and others, including himself, to be secretly anti-Nazi. Since it is true that Berlin did indeed like to hear what was reported from the Vatican, one may assume that Weizsäcker was not inventing such good news. After the war, Weizsäcker never repudiated his telegrams, which were captured by the Allies and did not come to light until after his death. In his memoirs he wrote that the Pope's dearest wish was for peace in the West. "And the Vatican could have no wish to see Germany, the barrier against the Bolshevist invasion from the East, totally destroyed . . ." (E. Weizsäcker, *Memoirs*, Chicago: Regnery, 1951, p. 297.)

In September this diplomacy received a severe setback when the Italians were forced to surrender unconditionally to the Allies and the Germans occupied Rome. The Pope's belief in the possibility of the Church's being "engulfed" as an outcome of the Allied and native opposition to the Nazis and the Fascists was thus heightened immeasurably. It left him with only one alternative. He had to rely solely on the military strength of the German occupiers for the protection he sought for the Vatican and its property.

When the Germans marched into Rome, he was wary as to what they might do with regard to the Church. He immediately asked for assurances that the Vatican's rights would be safeguarded.[14] Hitler gave an affirmative reply.[15] The German Foreign Office had always considered Pius XII *sehr deutschfreundlich.** On direct authorization from Nazi Foreign Minister Ribbentrop, the Pope was personally informed by Weizsäcker that "the sovereignty and the territorial integrity of the Vatican will be respected and . . . furthermore the Germans for their part undertake to conduct themselves in such a way as to protect Vatican City from the fighting." [16]

The German Command in Rome ringed Vatican City with Wehrmacht troops.† The Vatican's anxiety, according to a telegram to the Department of State from an American diplomat in the Holy See, Harold Tittmann, was allayed by the

* A Germanophile. This is how the Reich Foreign Ministry described Pacelli, who had lived twelve years as a Papal Nuncio on German soil, on the day following his election as Pope. (Memorandum of Mar. 3, 1939, *Staatssekretär: Vatikan;* text published in Friedländer, *op. cit.*, p. 21.) Almost five years later, during the German occupation of Rome, Weizsäcker was able to report that the Pope "has done all he could not to strain relations with the German Government and the German authorities in Rome." (Letter to Berlin of Oct. 28, 1943, text in *ibid.*, p. 186.)

† The presence of the cordon of German soldiers gave rise to Allied propaganda that the Pope was being kept prisoner by the Nazis. Vatican Radio on Oct. 29 broadcast a statement "to put an end to unfounded rumors, especially abroad, regarding the conduct of German troops towards the Vatican City . . ." (*Keesing's Contemporary Archives,* Vol. V, London, 1943–46, p. 6166.)

Germans to the extent that the atmosphere in the Curia could be "described as optimistic." The Germans, he said, had created a "sensation of relative security." [17]

At about the same time, Weizsäcker reported: "The Curia has by now put aside its Italian sentiments. Now one plays for all or nothing . . ." [18]

Buying German protection, the Pope found himself compelled to close his eyes to the face of Nazism in the Holy City, including the brutalities of the SS and the mass roundup of the Jews of Rome on October 16, 1943.* But the presence of a harsh foreign occupier only intensified the unrest in the city and the high degree of antifascism among the Romans. This gave rise to a resistance movement.

Now the moral contradictions in the Church deepened. With the emergence of the Roman Resistance, the Pope, by the logic of his own policies, was forced to interpret every blow against the German occupiers as a threat to the security of the Holy See. He feared that the military activities of the partisans might kindle the despair of the Romans and their hatred of the Nazis and the Italian Fascists. This could ignite a popular uprising that would get out of the control of the occupiers and, of course, the Allies, who were still far from Rome. It could bring the Italian anti-Fascists to power. In the process and in the accomplished fact, this would create the very situation the Pope months before had sought to avoid. Accordingly, in spite of whatever compassion he might have had for the Romans, he had now placed himself in the dubious position of having to favor increased police measures against them, or at least against those among them who opposed the Germans.

* Three days after the Germans had emptied the Jewish quarter of Rome for deportation to Auschwitz the Pope gave an audience to Tittmann, the US diplomat. Pius said nothing about what the Germans had done beneath his window, but he worried, according to Tittmann, about "little Communist bands stationed in the environs of Rome." (Telegram to Secretary of State Hull of Oct. 19, 1943, *Foreign Relations of the United States, op. cit.*, p. 950.)

He was especially worried about what might happen if the Germans were forced to withdraw. In a police state teeming with Italian Fascist and German police organizations and unspeakable police terror, Pope Pius XII began to call repeatedly for more police.

On October 14, according to Weizsäcker, the Vatican Secretary of State, Cardinal Maglione, spoke to him of the "Communist danger that threatens the clergy of Rome in the event the city passes from the hands of the Germans to those of the English, if the police forces and public authorities were to demonstrate themselves ineffective . . ." [19]

On October 19 the Pope, in an audience with Tittmann, "seemed preoccupied that, in the absence of police protection, irresponsible elements . . . might commit violence in the city during the period between the German evacuation and the arrival of the Allies." [20] The term "irresponsible elements," as will be seen, was the Pope's way of referring to the armed Resistance.

According to a report sent to Ribbentrop from the very high SS official Kaltenbrunner about a private and secret audience the Pope had granted an agent of the Gestapo, Pius expressed his alarm that the situation in Rome and in the north of Italy tended more and more to the left. "We fear the worst," the Pope was said to have declared to the Gestapo man, "if Germany finds herself forced to evacuate those regions." [21]

The Germans, for reasons of their own, obliged by continually increasing the SS police forces in Rome and elsewhere in Italy.[22]

To reduce the threat of insurrection, the Pope—within the bounds of the assurances given him by the German occupiers —tried to ease the tremendous pressure on the population. The Vatican opened its soup kitchens to the hungry and the refugees. The churches, convents, and monasteries of Rome opened their doors to succor political suspects and Jews who had escaped the SS net.*

The Pope himself worked tirelessly in the "open-city" negotiations. When the Germans occupied Rome, they agreed to respect an earlier proclamation that Rome was an open city, a political neutral.[23] The Vatican cited this proclamation as evidence that Rome should not be subjected to the Allied air attacks.[24] But as of March, 1944, the "open city" was still nothing but an empty phrase. The Pope looked away when the Wehrmacht abused the city, but he protested angrily when the British and Americans bombed it. He never once called for the withdrawal of the Germans. Open-city status for Rome was never recognized by the Allies.

In March, 1944, the number and importance of German military movements through the "open city" had tripled since the Allied landing at Anzio, according to a dispatch by a Swiss correspondent reported in *The New York Times*.[25] The eyewitness account continued:

> On the Ponte Milvio, which is perpetually clogged throughout the hours of darkness, down the Via Flaminia and the Corso in the heart of Rome proper, the stream pours in unending waves of tanks, motorized artillery and trucks loaded with munitions which filter through the maze of streets to disappear into the Pontine Plains or southward to the escarpments of Cassino. During the daytime, of course, none of this is visible . . . for there is the perpetual danger of American aerial machine gunning along the roads north and south of the capital.

* There were 2,775 Jews in convents, 992 in churches and monasteries. An additional 680 persons were given temporary shelter in religious institutions, and an unestimated number "very difficult to establish" was refuged in the Vatican and its extraterritorial buildings. (*La Civiltà Cattolica*, Mar. 4, 1961, p. 451.) In all, including political suspects this represented only a small percentage of the total number of 200,000–300,000 persons in Rome who were in hiding from the Germans. (*Cf.* for the total figures, M. Meneghini, *Roma "città aperta,"* Rome: Magi-Spinetti, 1946, p. 84; C. Delzell, *Mussolini's Enemies*, Princeton: Princeton University Press, 1961, p. 276.)

Nazi services of the rear, the dispatch concluded, have been "set up practically under the shadow of the Vatican." [26]

IV

DUILIO GRIGION walked across the courtyard of a house in Via Marco Aurelio.[1] The 7 P.M. curfew had driven everyone from the streets hours ago, but to Grigion, the building's *portiere*, it seemed safe enough to move from one wing of the house to the other. He carried a parcel of food in his hand. In his desk drawer he kept a letter given to him by a young woman called Elena.[2]

"If you don't see me for seven days in a row, Duilio," Elena had told him, "that will mean I am dead. Deliver the letter to my mother." [3]

The caretaker climbed the stone steps at entrance B. He was fifty-five years old and graying. Among his friends and the middle-class tenants of 42 Via Marco Aurelio, some knew he had learned to read and write in a Fascist prison. To others he was simply Duilio, who had a pleasant family and an enduring smile, especially at Christmas, Easter, and *Ferragosto*, when custom brings a tip to the *portieri* of Rome.

In the dark hall, he descended the three short flights around the shaft of the elevator, which was not in use for lack of electricity. He walked about twelve feet to his right and stopped at the heavy steel door that closed off the coal bin. Partisans were hiding inside. Grigion had brought them something to eat. They were members of GAP Central, the Communist military command that operated in the center of Rome.*

* GAP: *Gruppi di Azione Patriottica*—Patriotic Action Groups. Each of the six CLN political parties had military commands theoretically under the Military Junta. In practice they were autonomous partisan bands led by

Duilio Grigion greeted his young friends. He left his parcel of food and departed. He felt he was one of them. They shared with him secrets of the Resistance the Germans would pay almost any price to learn. He was their lookout. They were hunted by the SS and the Fascist police, who said the reward for even the "slightest clue" that would reveal their identity began at 50,000 lire (almost $500) and was graduated upward "according to the importance and the substance of the information." [4] Hidden in the tiny *cantina*, the partisans passed their nights beside the coal bin. They slept on the scant square feet of stone floor or stacked one above another on long narrow wooden shelves that looked like a bookcase against the concrete wall.

Mario Fiorentini and his wife, Lucia, had come back this night to the *cantina* hideout.[5] He had seen the column of SS police go by for several consecutive days now. Always, they passed at two o'clock in the afternoon. He had followed them. Their route was always the same. They came down toward the tunnel, turned left in Via Rasella, then right at the top of the street into Via Quattro Fontane; they turned left again at the next corner and went straight ahead past the Ministries of Defense, Agriculture, and Finance, through the Roman wall of Porta Pia, and on to the Macao barracks in the compound Castro Pretorio.[6]

He had gone to his commander, Carlo Salinari, the *gap-*

---

a party commander and operated under the generic order of the Junta to strike against the German occupiers. Only after the liberation of Rome did the partisans come under a unified command. As a uniformed resistance army, they fought alongside the Allies in the war against the German forces who occupied northern Italy until Apr. 25, 1945. In Rome the most active partisan bands were the Communists, the Actionists, and the Socialists; toward the end of the occupation the Christian Democrats built up an extensive military structure, while the military activities of the Democratic Laborites (a party which became defunct shortly after the war) and the Liberals were far more limited. On the other hand, the parties of the center-right apparently had better links than the left to the underground supply of explosives and ammunition and played a key role in supplying this material.

pista known as Spartaco. He had proposed a partisan action against the Germans. Salinari was cautious and noncommittal. He asked for a plan.[7]

In the hiding place, Fiorentini now told his comrades about the column of Germans. Among the partisans to whom he spoke were a young man and a young woman, both twenty-one years old, who would become and remain the principal figures of the Via Rasella history—first as a couple in love, later as man and wife.

They were known as Paolo and Elena. In the *macchia*—the underground—the code names were always used, even between lovers, even in moments of tenderness or anguish. For them that rule would foil a traitor in their midst and save their lives.

Her real name was Carla Capponi.[8] She was born in Rome and raised in a house just across the street from the famous balcony of Mussolini's Palazzo Venezia. Part of her family had come from Poland. Her face was oval and fair, there was a touch of red in her auburn hair, and she used her eyes to punctuate and underline whatever she said. She could speak well, and there was persuasive energy in her voice. The night that Fiorentini's wife, Lucia, had been sick with a high fever, Carla had gone out to get her some medicine, breaking the strictly enforced curfew law. She was stopped by the Fascist police. The penalty was immediate arrest. Violators of the curfew were often shot at first and questioned later. But Carla, although she lacked identity papers and there was always a pistol in her purse, had managed to talk her way free.[9]

Before the occupation she worked in a chemical laboratory and was engaged to a young Yugoslav in the diplomatic corps. But when the Germans came, she became a partisan. On March 7 she single-handedly blew up a German fuel truck at a depot in Via Claudia, exploding 2,500 gallons of gasoline.[10] The scorch marks on the bricks can still be seen.

Paolo's name was Rosario Bentivegna.[11] He had completed

three years as a medical student and was near the top of his class. On January 17, the day examinations were to be held at the medical college, students of the University of Rome deserted the halls. They demonstrated against the Germans and the Fascists and in protest closed down almost all of the schools.[12] Most of the students went to fight in the underground. In many cases, they were joined by their professors.[13]

Carla and Bentivegna were hoping to marry soon. They would wait for Rome to be liberated. His love for her, he would recall, was deeper than an infatuation. "She was an exceptional girl, and very dear." [14] She said she loved him because he was gay, intelligent, and sensitive. Always, though she knew he had committed them to memory, he carried in his pockets two battered books of the poetry of Quasimodo and Montale.[15]

Fiorentini outlined his plan.[16] The apparently invariable routine of the column of Germans made them vulnerable. If the partisans could count on them to be at a certain point at a certain time, it would be relatively easy to strike suddenly and escape swiftly and cleanly. Three partisans, he proposed, would be positioned at the top of Via Rasella, behind the corner of Via Quattro Fontane. When the first troops of the column neared the turn, two of the three would run into Via Rasella, launching grenadelike explosives. The third partisan, armed with a pistol, would be the cover and lookout for the first two. In the confusion all would escape.

The partisans that night in the *cantina* hiding place agreed that Fiorentini and his wife would lead the attack.

In the following days the plan was discussed with Spartaco. He was in contact with the Military Junta. He was skeptical. So small an attack on so large a column seemed uneconomical and unimaginative. Nevertheless it was approved.[17]

Early one afternoon in the second week of March two men

and a woman stood on the corner of Via Rasella and Via Quattro Fontane. They were armed and in wait for the Germans. Two o'clock passed in silence. The Germans did not come that day—nor the next day, nor the day after. The column had disappeared from the streets of Rome.[18]

V

THE 11th Company of the 3rd Battalion, SS Polizeiregiment Bozen was new in Rome.* The regiment had been formed in October, 1943, of recruits from South Tyrol, which that month had been incorporated into the Greater German Reich as the Alpenvorland. Its headquarters was in Innsbruck. In Rome it was under the command of the Higher SS and Polizeifuehrer for Italy, Obergruppenfuehrer Karl Wolff.†

Since February, the 3rd Battalion, headed by Major Hellmuth Dobbrick, had been in the process of being transferred from Gossensass to Rome. It was not yet up to full strength.[1]

The mission of the 3rd Battalion was to provide manpower for the increasingly repressive police measures against the Romans. Since the beginning of the year the Germans and the Fascists had been determined to break the will of the Romans and all Italians who resisted the occupation and Mussolini's new regime.[2] Strikes by industrial workers in the north and the emergence of partisan bands in the cities and in the mountains revealed the threat to the Fascist restoration. In Rome, as in other cities, the majority of the people did not collaborate

* The Bozen SS was to earn a reputation of being "notoriously cruel." A Swiss national, in Apr., 1944, after visiting with the German Ambassador in Italy, was horrified. "Karl Wolff's SS troops were behaving in Italy as if it were Russia," he said. (E. Wiskemann, *The Rome-Berlin Axis*, Oxford: Oxford University Press, 1949, p. 333.)

† The rank Obergruppenfuehrer was the SS equivalent of a general in the German armed forces.

with the authorities. Men did not respond to call-ups for military service or the German demands for labor in the Reich. Instead they hid. In Rome and in central Italy more than 90 per cent did not present themselves for the draft calls.[3]

The answer to this defiance was the proliferation of police forces. General Wolff, police plenipotentiary for Italy, undertook to crush the partisans and arm the Fascists.[4] Strikers were to be arrested by the thousands, the organizers shot. Men were to be rounded up for forced labor. To fight the war against the Allies in the south, law and order had to be maintained.[5]

The 11th Company of the 3rd Bozen Battalion, consisting of 156 men, had come to Rome to prepare for this work. About the second week in March the training exercises that had brought them on a daily march through the streets of the city were called to a halt. Very soon they would begin again.

VI

In his office in Piazza Colonna, Giuseppe Pizzirani, vice-secretary of the Fascist Republican Party, was planning a celebration.[1] March 23, a holiday for fascism, was less than a fortnight away. On that day in 1919 Mussolini, with nothing specific in mind, met with about 150 of his friends in Milan's Piazza San Sepolcro. They ended the afternoon by founding the Fascist Movement. March 23 was especially historic this year of 1944. It was the twenty-fifth anniversary of the ideology that had inspired not only the Duce, but Hitler and Nazism as well.

Pizzirani only a month before had been appointed by Mussolini to his new post in Rome.[2] The entire party had been reorganized and renamed with the proclamation of the neo-Fascist Government. He was eager to commemorate the anniversary date with an imposing day-long series of events. As he envisaged it, a solemn morning Mass would be held to honor those who had fallen for fascism on the battlefields. This would be followed, he planned, by swearing-in ceremonies for Roman members of the new party. There would be a great parade through the streets of Rome, culminating in a massive demonstration at the traditional Fascist assembly hall, Teatro Adriano, in Piazza Cavour.[3]

That the people of Rome believed fascism was the cause of their being starved, bombed, and brutalized scarcely dimmed Pizzirani's enthusiasm. He seemed oblivious to the reality that the Italians had already once deposed Mussolini and that the Duce was disliked now even more than before. He failed to read even the smaller signs. On February 18, while he was being driven near his office, a bullet aimed unsuccessfully at his head came close enough to punch a hole through his car.[4] On March 10, the last time the Fascists had paraded through Rome, they were attacked by partisans in Via Tomacelli.[5]

But the Fascists, apparently hoping to gain prestige for the regime, persisted in celebrating.* For so important an occasion, Pizzirani was determined to stage a big show. He knew he could rely on Padre Redento Zannoni to lead the Fascists in prayer. Undersecretary of Aviation Carlo Borsani, who had been blinded in the Albanian war, could be trusted to make an emotional speech at the Adriano.† By the beginning of the third week in March the party leader had plunged into the morass of details that went into the making of the great *mani-*

* They persisted even at the risk of being ridiculous. In Via Tomacelli they were commemorating the seventy-second anniversary of the death of Italian *Risorgimento* leader Giuseppe Mazzini. A few weeks before, they had marked, with great fanfare, the ninety-fifth anniversary of the first Republic of Italy.

† More than an impassioned speaker for the Fascist cause, Borsani was also a poet. In "Song of Nettuno" he wrote: "Rise up, my Italy, to conquer the world/ Serene and strong as the new and innocent soul/ Of the heroes who in Republican arms/ Went to Nettuno to die for love." (*L'Ora*, Feb. 11, 1945, quoted in R. Capano, *La Resistenza in Roma*, Vol. II, Naples: Macchiaroli, 1964, p. 237.)

festazione. Communiqués had gone to the press; he had called in the printers, the banner hangers, and the placard makers.

VII

WHEN Eitel Friedrich Möllhausen, head of the German Embassy in Rome, learned of Pizzirani's plans, he decided they were politically inopportune.[1] After the March 10 incident in Via Tomacelli, the German Command had banned all Fascist parades, and Möllhausen knew he would find support for his view. He called a conference of the principal German rulers of the city.[2]

At thirty, Möllhausen was the youngest chief of a diplomatic mission in Europe, holding the rank of consul. He had formerly served in occupied Paris as an editor of *La Gerbe*, a French-language weekly that sought to attract the intellectuals of France to the National Socialist cause.[3] Tall and slender, the Nazi diplomat was called by his friends and colleagues the Byzantine Christ, because of his physical appearance.[4]

Möllhausen, his youth and inexperience notwithstanding, was not averse to taking diplomatic initiatives. In October he had opposed as impolitic the deportation of the Jews of Rome. Making reference to their planned extermination, he had cabled Berlin that "it would be better to use the Jews for fortification works." [5] This idea was rejected, and he received a reprimand from the Foreign Office for using the word "liquidate" in an official telegram to Foreign Minister Ribbentrop.[6]

The meeting on Pizzirani and March 23 was held at the German Embassy in Villa Wolkonsky, a five-acre estate in the southern part of Rome. It was a favorite gathering place for Nazis and Fascists. There, as Möllhausen recalls, they would sit by the fireplace in the not overly large Red-and-White room, smoking cigars, drinking fine Cognac from occupied France, and examine the problems of a war some still hoped they could win.[7]

As for the question of Pizzirani's holiday, Consul Möllhausen developed his argument that, considering public opinion, "to file through the city with music and Fascist banners was nothing but a useless provocation." [8]

Standartenfuehrer (Col.) Eugen Dollmann spoke for the SS. He was the personal representative in Rome of Heinrich Himmler. He cultivated his image as a political man of the Machiavellian school and he had a taste for intrigue. Blond, gracious, elegantly tall, he looked a decade younger than his forty-four years. He was an accomplished student of Italian culture and spoke the language flawlessly. He drove around Rome in a Mercedes and charmed the women of Roman aristocracy with sophisticated epigrams in a flow of conversation that seemed as inexhaustible as it was, to them, bright and witty. He was equally a delight to his Fuehrer and was a confidant of Eva Braun. All that, according to Consul Möllhausen's estimation of him, "was nevertheless an artifice, because when he was not in society he lapsed easily into a state of melancholy. His only true affections were for his mother." [9]

Dollmann's proposal for the March 23 ceremonies was that they be condensed. He agreed with Möllhausen's point of view. He said he wanted the festivities to end before dark.[10]

SS Obersturmbannfuehrer (Lt. Col.) Herbert Kappler, head of the SD in Rome, represented the Gestapo.*

He spoke in a monotone: "Politics is not my field," he said, "but if I were asked I would say that neofascism has to disappear so that we can hold on to the last vestige of German prestige in Italy. This requires the elimination of Mussolini, and if

* The SD—*Sicherheitsdienst*—was set up by Reinhard Heydrich as the Security Service of the SS. By 1944, under Kaltenbrunner, who replaced the assassinated Heydrich, the SD had become indistinguishably merged with the Secret State Police—the Gestapo. (*Cf.* E. Crankshaw, *Gestapo,* New York: Viking, 1956; paperback ed., 1961, p. 8.)

I were charged with that task, I would know just how to carry it out." [11]

Kappler was not given to boasting. He was thirty-seven years old and a native of Stuttgart, but he considered Italy his "second home" and he liked to collect Etruscan vases. He had a bony face and penetrating eyes that were the color of lead. Trained in espionage and security, he had come to Rome in 1939 as a consultant to the Fascist police and the German Embassy. He studied Italian history and he loved Rome so much that he sent for his parents to join him. Despite his modesty, he was far more politically astute than both Dollmann and Möllhausen. He had foreseen the weaknesses in Italian fascism long before his superiors, including the Fuehrer. When Mussolini fell, Kappler, on orders from Hitler, located the secret mountaintop lodge where the King was holding the Duce prisoner. He told Himmler that if Mussolini were freed "he would not be able to return to power, unless he ruled by the strength of German bayonets." [12] Nevertheless, on further orders, he helped organize the dramatic rescue of the Duce.

Kappler had few friends. He had a difficult wife, whom he was trying to divorce. He loved roses, photography, dogs, and his adopted son of the *Lebensborn*, the SS institution where "experimental" children were procreated by Germans of pure Aryan blood. It was Kappler who, on orders, planned and led the mass arrests and deportation of the Jews of Rome.[13]

General Kurt Mälzer, an old Falstaffian alcoholic who was known by both Germans and Romans as the "King of Rome," [14] solved in a single stroke the problem that had evoked Möllhausen's meeting. Formerly of the Luftwaffe, he was the German Commandant of Rome. He liked to keep orchids in his office and wear his beret at a rakish angle over his right ear. Among his associates he was considered a colossal boor, and he governed the city like a warden. He simply overruled Pizzirani. The parade was canceled. The meeting at Teatro Adriano was shifted to the heavily guarded Ministry of Corporations in Via Veneto. If he cared to, the party vice-secretary could still have his church services.[15]

Pizzirani, when he learned of Mälzer's fiat, complained bitterly to the general and finally protested to Mussolini. It was a question of saving face. But his importuning was to no avail.[16] It was Germany's Italy now.

VIII

THE JUNTA and the partisans were also discussing March 23.[1] A stunning blow against the Fascists on their most sacred day would go beyond being militarily valuable. It would electrify the people of Rome, almost all of whom were united in their opposition to fascism but were divided and unsure on how to oppose it. The presence of a strong Resistance felt throughout the city as an answer to the Fascists and to the Nazi occupation would cut across at least some of the lines that separated the highly stratified population. It would tend to unify the Romans. This, of course, was an indispensable prerequisite if there were ever to be an insurrection in the capital. The partisans knew that powerful forces in Rome—the Pope, as well as some anti-Fascists who in many cases gave lip service to the contrary—were against insurrection. For a mandate, the partisans could look to the despair of the Romans, never so profound as in those first weeks of March.

One Roman chronicler of the times recorded early that month:

> The Anzio bridgehead has bogged down and it is not to be spoken of. *Addio* to the liberation of Rome. When? More than ever it appears as a dream. That they should be so near, at our doorstep, and to have to suffer this way. The people by now do not even speak of them and resign them-

selves to recognizing the military valor of these Germans . . .[2]

People were lamenting in song:

The invasion doesn't come
And the days go by
The pain gets worse
It seems we will die . . .[3]

Having read of Pizzirani's plans in the Fascist-controlled Roman newspaper *Il Messaggero*, the *gappisti* were preparing a large-scale attack on Teatro Adriano.[4] The partisans of the Socialist band Matteotti were mobilizing an assault on the Fascist parade.[5] They were unaware that Consul Möllhausen's meeting in Villa Wolkonsky had already neutralized their plans.

IX

In the meantime the column of SS began to march again. The 11th Company of the 3rd Bozen Battalion picked up the routine it had broken a few days before.

The Fiorentini plan for the Via Rasella action was restudied. It was decided now that this attack required a more complex operation. A second plan was drawn up. Fiorentini, his wife, Carla Capponi, and Rosario Bentivegna would be stationed in Via Rasella. Two hidden cases of explosives would go off at the moment the column passed.[1]

GAP commander Salinari rejected this proposal. Since the beginning of February, when Kappler and men of the SD had raided the underground's Santa Barbara chemical workshop in Via Giulia, there had been an extreme shortage of explosives, especially TNT. Perhaps there would be enough material for one bomb, but not two, Salinari said. He told the *gappisti* to use more men.

Two GAP detachments consisting of four squads were made available for the attack.[2] If it took place, it would be by far the biggest action yet. Until now the partisans had rarely operated in groups larger than three or four; most often they acted as individuals or in pairs.

They now began to follow the column every day. Via Rasella remained the best site for the battleground. It was narrow, sloping, and quiet. It was like the neck of a funnel between Traforo and Quattro Fontane. The column would move slower on the ascent than normally. It would be more concentrated than on a wider street and thus subject to greater damage and less freedom of counteraction. They timed the movements of the Germans, who each day now, with *pünklichkeit*, would go by at 2 P.M. They counted the number of paces in the march through Via Rasella. It took 140 seconds to cross from bottom to top. At about one-third of the way up the street, Via Rasella is bisected by the still-narrower Via Boccaccio. From there, it was 90 seconds to the corner of Quattro Fontane. At some point in that minute and a half when the full length of the column would be enclosed in Via Rasella the attack would have to begin.

A new, intricate plan took shape. On paper, it looked like this (see diagram on opposite page).[3]

The attack would be in two stages.[4] A bomb would be placed at number 156 Via Rasella—a building known as Palazzo Tittoni* about one-third down from the higher end of the street. This part of Via Rasella was chosen because the building was known to be semiabandoned, there were no shops, and people rarely walked by, especially during the siesta hours. These factors would lower the possibility of

* Palazzo Tittoni, at 156 Via Rasella, was the home of the pre-Mussolini Foreign Minister Tommaso Tittoni, who later, as a senator, supported the Fascist regime. He died in 1931.

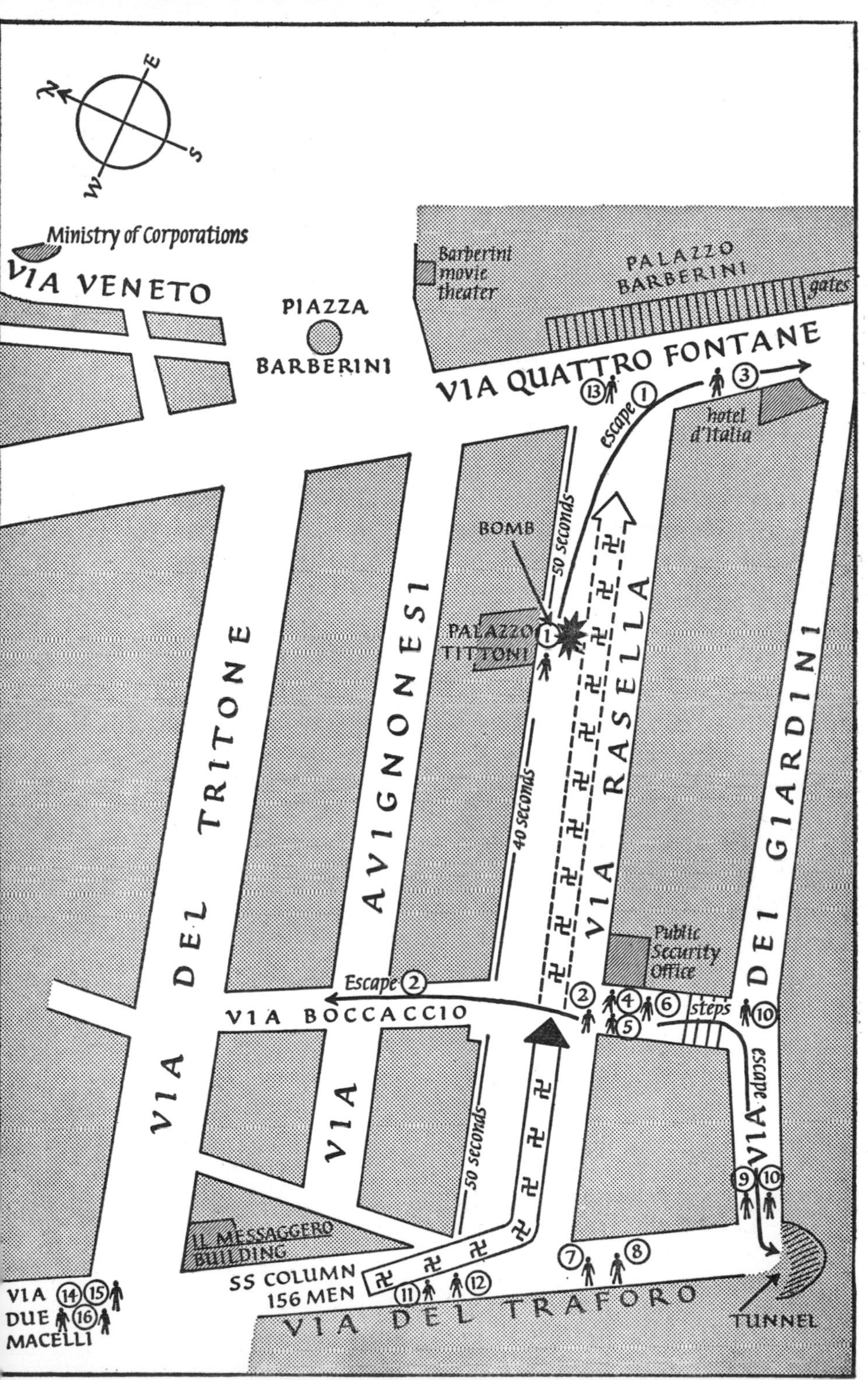

N
E
S
W
Ministry of Corporations
VIA VENETO
PIAZZA
BARBERINI
Barberini movie theater
PALAZZO BARBERINI
gates
VIA QUATTRO FONTANE
escape 1
hotel d'Italia
BOMB
50 seconds
PALAZZO TITTONI
VIA RASELLA
VIA DEL TRITONE
VIA AVIGNONESI
VIA DEI GIARDINI
40 seconds
Public Security Office
Escape 2
VIA BOCCACCIO
steps
escape
VIA
50 seconds
IL MESSAGGERO BUILDING
SS COLUMN 156 MEN
VIA DEL TRAFORO
TUNNEL
VIA DUE MACELLI

arousing suspicion in the period before the arrival of the column and reduce the risk of civilian casualties during the actual attack.

Partisan number 1 (see diagram) would be near enough to the bomb to ignite it at the proper moment. Partisan number 2 would be at the intersection of Via Boccaccio. When the head of the German column arrived at this point, he would lift his cap to signal partisan 1 to light the fuse. His signal would also alert partisans 4, 5, 6, and 10, who would participate in the second stage. Partisan 2 would then cross in front of the column and escape, continuing north along Via Boccaccio. Partisan 1, having lit the fuse, would withdraw to safety behind the stone building at the southeast corner of Quattro Fontane and escape. This walk, from Palazzo Tittoni to the corner, would take 45 seconds. The fuse would be designed to expend itself in 50 seconds. At that moment, when only the Germans would be in Via Rasella and the first troops of the column would have passed Palazzo Tittoni, the bomb—if everything functioned properly—would explode.

The secondary stage of the attack would now take place. Partisans 4, 5, and 6, stationed in Via Boccaccio, would descend on the rear flank of the column. They would launch four 45mm. mortar shells, converted to be set off by a lighted cigarette.* They would escape by scaling the few steps that lead to Via dei Giardini and continuing on through the tunnel. In the meantime partisans number 7, 8, 11, and 12 would converge from Via Traforo at the bottom of Via Rasella and block the retreat of the column. They would continue the rearguard attack, finally escaping through the tunnel or dispersing into the streets west of Traforo.

* These were Italian-made Brixia shells. They weighed about nine pounds, were red and gray in color, and were supplied by men of the disbanded Army who had gone over to the Resistance. The partisans refitted these shells with a two- to three-second fuse. When they exploded they made a great deal of noise but did little damage. This was one of the reasons it was decided to use a specially constructed bomb in Via Rasella.

A lookout system employing other partisans would signal the approach of the column from beyond Piazza di Spagna. The key men would be covered by others. Partisan 1 would be guarded by partisan 13, positioned at the gates of Palazzo Barberini in Via Quattro Fontane. Partisans 9 and 10 would first cover the men in Via Boccaccio, then those in Via Traforo.

Throughout the drafting of these plans, one unanswered questioned persisted: how to place and detonate a bomb before the eyes of an armed formation of SS police? Mario Fiorentini contributed the solution. He had been ruled out of participation in the attack by Salinari when he learned that Fiorentini had an uncle living in Via Boccaccio and thus risked being recognized at some crucial moment, endangering not only himself but everyone.

Fiorentini suggested that the partisan at the bomb be disguised in the uniform of a city street cleaner. The bomb itself would be hidden in an ordinary rubbish cart, used by the municipal sanitation services. To aid the street cleaner's escape, partisan number 2 would wait at the corner of Quattro Fontane with a raincoat to cover the uniform and they would flee together in the direction of Via XX Settembre.

In all, sixteen partisans of the GAP Central squads Garibaldi, Pisicane, Sozzi, and Gramsci would take part in the attack. The younger men would be given the active roles and their seniors—those over the age of twenty-three—would carry out the supportive tasks. Everyone would be armed. Though they had only 10 per cent of the numerical strength of the German column and far less in terms of weaponry, they counted on two factors to militate in their favor. The first was the element of surprise; the second was the support of the people, most of whom could be relied on, if necessary, to help them escape, hide, or conceal their identity.

When it became known at the last moment that the schedule of Fascist celebrations had been changed and the sites shifted, the earlier-planned attack at Teatro Adriano had to be canceled. The operation in Via Rasella was now of primary importance. It was set for March 23, 2 P.M.

X

ON MARCH 22 Rome was bristling with rumors. People were saying that through the efforts of the Pope the open city would shortly become a reality. The Germans at any moment would pack up and leave. The Allied bombers would never again be seen over Rome.[1]

Ten days earlier, on the 12th, Pius had addressed an audience of 150,000 Romans gathered in Saint Peter's Square. He spoke out against the horrors of an "air war that knows neither law nor limit," [2] but said nothing of the German military use of Rome. He appealed to the "wisdom of the responsible men of both belligerent parties" not to bring the land war to Rome.[3] The following day the United States replied that if the Germans were not using Rome militarily there would be no problem of air attacks.[4] On the 14th President Roosevelt declared at a press conference in Washington that "Germany has used the Holy City of Rome as a military center." [5] At the same time, four waves of American bombers were hitting the south and east parts of the city.[6] Allied aircraft struck again on the 16th, 18th, and 20th.[7]

Now, at noon on the 22nd, *Il Messaggero* came out with a startling piece of news that reawakened the hopes of the discomfited Romans and set the excited rumors in motion. *Il Messaggero's* Fascist director, Bruno Spampanato, had written an article entitled "Why Rome Is Bombed." [8] He maintained that Rome was an open city and only the Allies were its violators. Then he stated:

> In order that the enemy may bear the full responsibility of the harm he is doing, the German Command will, in the

coming days, scrupulously withdraw from Rome anything that might furnish a pretext for air raids and will avoid still more carefully the transit of troops through the Eternal City.[9]

It was a cruel lie. In the first place, if the Germans were respecting the open city, how could they "withdraw" and "avoid" what was allegedly nonexistent? In the second place, they had no intention of doing any such thing.

The Germans immediately confiscated the first edition of *Il Messaggero* and the subsequent press run of that day's paper was printed without the Spampanato editorial.[10]

But the rumors would not be quelled. They were based on something very real. The Pope was continually acting on his appeal to the wisdom of the Nazis and the Allies. In open-city negotiations with the Germans, considered by the Vatican to be extremely delicate, Pius sought to convince them to demilitarize Rome to the extent that the Allies might halt their air raids. This would be the first step of an orderly departure of the Germans at the moment of the inevitable arrival of the Allies.[11] At no time, however, did he want the Wehrmacht to fully withdraw before that moment. Vatican diplomacy aimed to avoid at all costs a situation in which the Nazis would leave before the entry of the Allies, taking with them police protection and leaving the city to those whom Pius felt were the unpredictable Romans.*

* Ambassador Weizsäcker, who was the principal Nazi negotiator in the Vatican during the occupation, says in his memoirs that the inevitable withdrawal of the German troops had been under discussion in the Vatican months before the liberation of Rome. "The question was," he wrote, "who would protect the population from mob violence?" (Weizsäcker, *op. cit.*, p. 292.) "Mob violence," of course, being the Resistance.

What these open-city negotiations meant to the Pope was reported in a cable from the American diplomat Tittmann. According to the Vatican, he said, "open city would appear to mean simply this: . . . During the interval between the withdrawal of the Germans and the arrival of the Allies the latter would provide police protection for the city." This would be arranged "through agreement with the belligerent parties," and the Allies would provide food supplies during the interval and afterward. (Telegram to Secretary of State Hull of Dec. 1, 1943, in *Foreign Relations of the United States, op. cit.*, p. 925.)

As for the Germans, they had as yet no thought of leaving the Holy City, and, in fact, their police were continually bearing down on the population. Hitler had ordered the measures against the traitorous Italians to be "very hard." [12] He and the generals of the Italian theater of war were still undecided whether to hold off the Allies in the streets of Rome or to destroy strategic parts of the city before retreating—or both.[13] The Fuehrer would not make his final decision until eight days before the liberation, and then it would be purely on military grounds.[14] With Berlin and other German cities being bombed off the map, he certainly could not have been very much concerned that Rome, too, was feeling the lash of Allied air power. On March 22, 1944, the open-city talks with the Holy See, so important to Pius XII, meant little to Hitler, or to any other German outside the Vatican.

On March 23, however—that is, the day of the Via Rasella—these negotiations would take on a new light for both the Germans and the Pope.

XI

In the *cantina* hiding place on Opium Hill, Carla Capponi sat in the warmth of the black iron furnace. It had been an overcast day. But at sunset the sky had opened and turned gold and red and to Carla that was an omen that augured well for the following day.[1]

The night, clear of heavy clouds, carried to her ears the drone of the distant guns at Anzio. They were German guns, shelling the Allied beachhead, blocking the road to Rome. Over 2,000 American soldiers and 1,000 British had already lost their lives in the combat on the beaches of Anzio.[2]

Outside, in a corner of the courtyard just beyond the black matting that covered the high cellar windows, an empty rubbish cart rested in the gravel. A partisan named Raoul Falcioni had stolen it that day from a city depot behind the Colosseum.[3] Tomorrow, packed with forty pounds of TNT, it would stand in Via Rasella.

Carla would be there, too. She would wait on the corner of Quattro Fontane with a raincoat over her arm, ready to cover a fleeing, counterfeit street cleaner. Rosario Bentivegna, the young man she loved, had been given the street cleaner's mission. Now he lay beside her, trying to fall asleep on the stone floor.

Commander Salinari had wanted to place either Raoul Falcioni or GAP member Guglielmo Blasi in this critical role. Carla had gone to him and asked him to choose Bentivegna. It was a feeling she had. She had been in actions with Falcioni and Blasi that had failed. With Bentivegna everything always seemed to work right, such as the attack on the Hotel Flora, where General Mälzer had his headquarters, and the action against Pizzirani's Fascist parade in Via Tomacelli. Bentivegna had been in more than thirty GAP operations and they had all gone well. She had pointed this out to Salinari and he had been persuaded.[4]

Later, her initiative would be welcomed. Falcioni might have carried out the mission well; Guglielmo Blasi, on the other hand, would very shortly betray them all to the SS.

Carla, who like everyone else was unable to foresee Blasi's betrayal, had only trusted to instinct the prevalent desire to reduce the risks. In the *macchia* anything could go wrong. The war matériel, which usually came from the underground links with the disbanded units of the Italian Army, was shoddy. Explosives failed to explode. Fuses would not ignite or, worse, they would burn too rapidly. One night only recently Carla and five others had attacked two German trucks in Via Tor de' Schiavi. Every one of the partisans had been armed with a submachine gun. All six jammed.

She thought of other hazards, too. Everyone did. A split-second delay could make an attack miscarry—a child coming along and asking the time . . . a chance meeting with a friend . . . a schoolmate calling from across the street.[5]

The underground life was anything but adventurous and exciting. There was no glory then. There was hunger. To eat on four out of every seven days was a good average. There was fatigue. "We were always dead tired," Bentivegna would recall. "The clandestine fight took place on foot. The Germans had prohibted the use of bicycles, the trams often were not running, and more often we didn't have the money for the fare. So we walked, covering tens of kilometers every day." [6]

There was boredom, isolation, discomfort, gloom, self-deception. "Because of the violence of the fight," Carla says, "there arose in all of us, constantly, a human need to reshape all things and strip them of their cruel reality." [7] The moments of pleasure, gaiety, exhilaration, and love had to be clasped and enjoyed with a passion, even to an excess.

There was hatred for the enemy; but it was not boundless or uncomplicated, which would have been easier. One partisan wrote, "The Fascists or the Germans don't look like dogs or beasts. They are men: tall, short, dark, blond, and they walk or sit and they laugh, play, smoke, talk; they have arms and legs, a head—like all men . . . For a moment one feels lost, one feels small, alone, lawless . . ." [8]

Bentivegna says, "Even if he was a Fascist, even if he was a German, I could never forget that he was a man . . ." [9]

And there was fear—fear of violence, fear of betrayal, fear of torture, fear of death. Carla says that her fear grew in intensity on the eve of an attack. Bentivegna felt greater fear afterward than before. "Always, there was fear," he says. "It was felt as pain." [10] Every time it arose it had to be conquered.

"I have come to the conclusion," a captured Resistance leader wrote in a final letter to his wife, "that our only enemy was my fear. The times that I, for various reasons, have been assailed by fear, required all of my energy to transcend it. Is it not then true that my duty was my only source of strength?" *

Not everyone fought in the Resistance. Not everyone was opposed to Nazism and fascism. For those who fought, it was the only alternative. All others had been exhausted. They came from every social class, from different backgrounds and occupations, from different histories and different futures. The common goal gave birth to a common bond. "We felt very close to one another," says Bentivegna. "Strangely, we felt free, near to everything." [11] If there was a lack of unity in action and methods, there was nevertheless an intensely felt camaraderie and a naïve belief in the goodness of the coming postwar world. No one, given the circumstances, would fight for anything less.

In another corner of the tiny *cantina*, a young physicist named Giulio Cortini and his wife worked on the bomb and the fifty-second fuse.[12] He weighed off twelve kilograms of TNT. He packed it tightly into a steel case, which had been stolen by workers at the Rome plant of Italgas. This was set into a bag with six kilograms of loosely packed TNT mixed with pieces of iron tubing, each of which was itself filled with an explosive charge.

The delicate package was put aside until morning. There was enough TNT in the *cantina* to blow out half of the five-story building. Encased the way it was, the bomb would explode into a million bullets of steel shrapnel, with death riding on each one.

* His name was Leone Ginzburg. Thirty-four years old, he was a leader of the Action Party and director of the clandestine newspaper *L'Italia Libera*. He was arrested at the same time as Mario Fiorentini in the print shop in Via Basento. He was tortured to death by the Germans. An Italian Jew, he had been a professor of Russian literature at the University of Turin and a founder of the Einaudi publishing house. (Letter quoted in R. Battaglia, *Storia della Resistenza italiana*, Turin: Einaudi, 1953. *Cf.* also Capano, *op. cit.*, Vol. II, p. 491.)

XII

ACROSS THE night, across the Tiber and behind the north wall of Vatican City, the Resistance was hurtling into a deep crisis.

Ivanoe Bonomi, the seventy-one-year-old head of the CLN who wore a white goatee and round, horn-rimmed glasses too small for his face, was concealed tonight from the Germans in his nephew's apartment in the Trionfale district. To avoid capture he often moved from one hiding place to another. Some hours earlier he had been brought a message from one of the CLN parties. Now he could not see how the coalition of the six anti-Fascist parties would hold together for another day. He had gone as far as he could, he believed, to maintain a degree of unity in the underground organization.[1]

In a lifetime of political struggle, the most crucial moment seemed at hand. As former Prime Minister, he had watched Mussolini pass him by and climb to the heights of absolute power. Unlike so many of his colleagues, he had remained anti-Fascist. He had helped to convince the King at last to overthrow the Duce.* Then, in the turmoil that followed Mussolini's fall, he had joined the opposition to the King and the Badoglio government. Badoglio had assumed the impossible and foolhardy mission of making a deal with both Axis and Allies to get Italy out of the war unscathed.

Early in the morning of September 9, 1943, while the

* The King, unfortunately, did not take Bonomi's advice to denounce at the moment of the *coup d'état* the Italian alliance with Germany. At this point Italian military strength on its own soil was superior to that of the Germans, and presumably the occupation could have been prevented. Instead, the King and Badoglio, hoping to gain time to negotiate a surrender to the Allies "on terms," announced that the war would continue at the side of the Nazi ally. Unimpressed, Hitler used this delay to move twelve new divisions down the Italian peninsula. When Badoglio, aware that the Allies would not back down from the unconditional-surrender policy, finally capitulated, the Germans were in a military position to swoop down and grab most of Italy from the Italians and the Allies.

King and Badoglio were running from Rome and the Germans were battling their way into the city, Bonomi and other leaders of the six parties met in a house in Via Adda. They set up the CLN. Bonomi was voted president.[2]

Bonomi was a kind and generous person, but he was irresolute as a leader. He could not reconcile the differences in the CLN. He had tried to balance the opposing forces rather than harness them to the fight against the common enemy.

The Resistance parties were continually trying to break a deadlock over domestic questions regarding the future life or death of the monarchy. They met on March 18 in a daylong plenary meeting.* Outside, Rome was trembling under one of the heaviest bombings of the war. The meeting ended, Bonomi said on that day, "100 per cent inconclusive." [3]

They had sought to adopt a resolution that would have delayed the issue until the liberation of Rome. This measure had won but five of the six votes; three on the right, two on the left. The Action Party had hesitated, postponing its response for four days. Now the Actionists had sent one of their representatives, Sergio Fenoaltea,† to Bonomi with their

* The matter was further complicated by a sharp disagreement on this issue between Roosevelt and Churchill. The British Prime Minister, while noting the "usual arguments against having anything to do with those who worked with or helped Mussolini," felt himself "bound to work with the King" and openly supported the Badoglio government. He considered the CLN a coalition of intriguers of "six or seven Leftist parties." (W. Churchill, *The Second World War,* Vol. V, Boston: Houghton Mifflin, 1951, p. 188.) Churchill says that Roosevelt, who had not yet publicly expressed his views, "disappointed" him by cabling a recommendation that "we give immediate support to the program of the six Opposition Parties. . . . American public opinion would never understand our continued tolerance and apparent support of [King] Victor Emmanuel." (Telegram of Mar. 13, 1944, in *ibid.,* p. 503.) The entire matter was thrown up in the air on that very day, however. Stalin, surprising everyone, including Churchill and Roosevelt, extended diplomatic recognition to Badoglio. The Russians believed that by strengthening the authority of the King's government they were obstructing "British and American imperialists [who] were out to saddle the European nations with their own administration . . ." (G. Deborin, *The Second World War,* Moscow: Progress Publishers, 1962, p. 323.)

† Presently Italian Ambassador to the United States.

reply. It was no. Hoping to be the beneficiary of the popular resentment held for the King and the House of Savoy, they proposed a formula that excluded the monarchy from any new government until the matter could be settled by the people in free, national elections.* Further, they invoked their unity pact with the Socialists and the Communists, persuading them to withdraw their support of the March 18 resolution.[4]

Bonomi, at the end of this day, was ready to quit. He wrote in his diary: "I remain very surprised by this move, which was truly unexpected, and I replied that its acceptance will be very difficult . . ."[5]

* The CLN had adopted such a formula on Oct. 16, 1943. This ultimately led to the deadlock the Mar. 18 resolution sought to overcome by delay. (*Cf.* I. Bonomi, *Diario di un anno*, Milan: Garzanti, 1947; Piscitelli, *op. cit.*, p. 293.)

PART TWO

The Attack in Via Rasella

March 23, 1944

"I loved the Italians too much. Now I hate them."

—Field Marshal Albert Kesselring, *Oberbefehlshaber Sud West* (OBSW)—Commander in Chief, German Armed Forces in Italy [1]

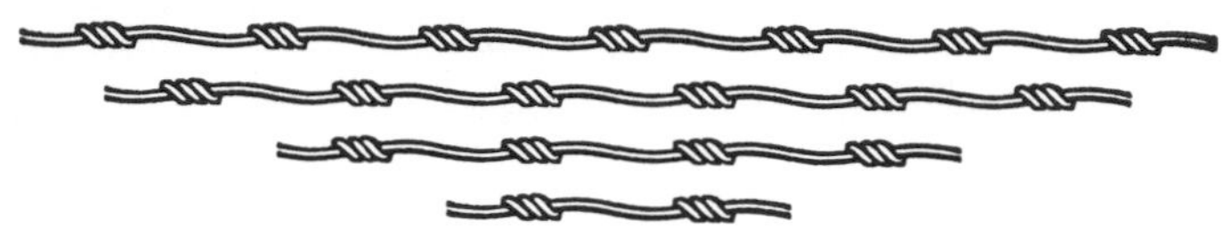

I

A LITTLE before nine o'clock on the bright sunny morning of March 23, 1944, an armed platoon of the Fascist Republican National Guard surrounded the church of Santa Maria della Pietà in Piazza Colonna. No one could enter it without a pass.

Inside the tiny church the balustrades were draped in black and striped with gold. A tumulus in the center aisle was ringed with flickering candles and covered with a satiny quilt. Before this solemn setting lay a giant laurel wreath. Tied with a ribbon of the colors of Rome, it bore the words "*Il Partito Fascista Repubblicano*."

The Fascist flags hung limply from the altar. Some showed the blazoned fasces, power symbol of ancient Rome. Before long the *repubblicani* began to gather: party leader Pizzirani; Chief of the Province of Rome Edoardo Salerno; Prefect Moresi, who had been with Mussolini in Piazza San Sepolcro twenty-five years before; and the lesser party faithful. Padre Redento Zannoni, assisted by the rector, the brethren, and a small choir, opened the sacred rites. The twenty-fifth anniversary of fascism—the last ever to be commemorated in Rome—had begun.[1]

II

THE COMMUNIST underground newspaper *l'Unità* that day ran the headline "On Toward the Armed Insurrection of the

Masses and the Expulsion of the Germans and the Fascists." [1] But the news that Thursday morning was anything but good.

For most Romans the only accessible source of information was the Fascist-controlled press. On the morning of the 23rd, *Giornale d'Italia* was reporting in the official daily communiqué from Berlin that at the Anzio and Cassino fronts "enemy losses were much greater than those of the Germans." [2] This was substantially correct. The Allies for weeks had been unable to gain a single inch of ground. The scribblings on the walls of the Roman working-class Trastevere district spoke with bitter irony: "Americans, hold on. Soon we'll come to liberate you." [3] The German Fourteenth Army that very morning was positioning at Anzio its giant 280mm. railroad gun. It would be fired for the first time the following day and would very soon be called Anzio Annie by the GIs. [4] It would help block the liberation of Rome for two more tragic months.

The news from other parts of the world—as the Romans received it that morning—was equally depressing. A dispatch from Lisbon reported that the Allied Command believed that the war was going badly. Another Lisbon story was headed "Americans Accuse England of Starving Europe." The Japanese were said to be making advances in the Pacific, and the British were reported in retreat on the Burma front. The Germans had "victoriously counterattacked" the Russians; London had been bombed by the Luftwaffe.[5]

The war news, however, was overshadowed by a natural disaster in Italy that made world headlines. Mount Vesuvius, for the second time that week, had erupted, spewing rushing rivers of lava 150 feet wide and 40 feet deep over the villages above the Bay of Naples.[6]

The local news told of the destruction caused by the most recent Allied bombing of Rome, three days before, and printed a "very noble letter" from a woman whose mother had died after having lived in a cave for forty days because of the "Anglo-American terrorist bombings." She was a "fervent admirer of the Duce . . . and in honor of her memory, I would like to remit the sum of 1,000 lire to add to the armaments fund of the resurging Republican Army. *Viva l'Italia!*" [7]

There were few advertisements to read; the Germans were running the only display ad. It offered "Work for Everyone!" "Come in full confidence to Germany . . . Immediate work at the same excellent conditions, salary, and benefits as your German comrades . . ." [8]

Two classified notices expressed the deep contradictions of the times:

"Bombed-out bank official seeks small furnished apartment one or more rooms. Central, Prati, Parioli, Vatican districts. Telephone after curfew. 862-823."

"Villa near Florence, luxurious, furnished, all comforts; park, garden, adjacent farm, free immediately. Asking 400,000 lire. Write Cassetta 723 Pubblicità Italiana, Florence." [9]

The Roman Stock Exchange was holding steady, and in some cases—such as Fiat (up .25 lira)—shares were climbing. In sports, Rome was playing Latium for the soccer championship. There were sixty-one theaters showing films, and Radio Rome the night before had broadcast a concert of seventeenth-century Italian music—live.[10]

III

THE FIRST thing Duilio Grigion, the *portiere* at 42 Via Marco Aurelio, did that morning was to see if the stolen rubbish cart was still in the courtyard. It stood, as it had been left, beside the concrete steps that led to building B. If tenants going off to work had wondered why a piece of city-owned equipment was parked at their front door, their curiosity had failed to get the better of them.

The iron garbage barrels of the rubbish cart rested on a four-wheel, carriagelike structure. It looked like a baby's stroller with two silver-colored smokestacks. There were racks to hold the street cleaner's tools. On one side, an iron ring gripped the broom. The other ring was empty. It suddenly occurred to Duilio Grigion that the shovel was missing. For a garbage man who was an impostor with forty pounds of TNT in his cart to be caught without the shovel would certainly mean the death penalty. There would be no attack in Via Rasella.

Grigion alerted his wife. He rushed off to the Colosseum, covering the few blocks as swiftly as he could without provoking suspicion. He stopped at the part of the Flavian amphitheater where the outer walls had centuries ago been removed by spiteful popes. There, on the open pavement, was a city storage area for sanitation equipment. This time of morning most of the street cleaners were already making their rounds. Nevertheless Grigion found a suitable shovel and hurried away with it at once.

Now the rubbish cart lacked only the bomb.[1]

IV

AT ABOUT 10:30 A.M. Pietro Caruso, a forty-four-year-old Neapolitan, stood at attention beneath a giant portrait of Mussolini. With his thick right hand raised high, Caruso faced Pizzirani. The vice-secretary was swearing in the Fascists to the new Republican Party. The scene of the twenty-fifth-anniversary celebration had shifted to the great *Salone* in the Ministry of Corporations in Via Veneto.[1]

Pietro Caruso was not new to fascism. A member of the

celebrated La Serenissima Action Squad, he had participated in the March on Rome in October, 1922. Twenty-one years later he returned to Rome as Questore—chief of the city's police. A bungler and a dullard, Caruso was an apish-looking man who had a history of mental illness in his family.[2] He was one of the most hated Fascists in occupied Rome. He was reviled by the people, held in low regard by his men, and mocked by his Nazi superiors. He had earned all of these sentiments on the very day he came to Rome, early in February, 1944. Minutes after being sworn in as Questore, he was ordered to lead a roundup of men for slave labor in Germany. The busy Via Nazionale was blocked off by the police and whoever they trapped was seized. When Caruso arrived on the scene, he was promptly rounded up himself, loaded into a truck and taken off to Macao barracks to await deportation. It required the intervention of an Italian general to gain his release some hours later.[3]

One by one Pizzirani administered the Fascist oath and signed party cards. Cucco, Cerruti, Salerno, Orgera, now Caruso:

"In the name of God and of Italy . . ."[4]

Some 400 miles to the north—at a place known to all Italians only as X—the Duce himself was receiving party card number 1 from Pizzirani's boss, Alessandro Pavolini. The secret ceremony was taking place in the Villa Orsoline, at Gargnano on the left bank of Lake Garda. A group of *sansepolcristi* was there to express gratitude to Mussolini.[5]

"Duce!" one among them named Sandro Giuliani cried. "We are here in the name of those comrades who have had the good fortune of participating in the historic meeting of March 23, 1919, in Piazza San Sepolcro, to renew our pledge to you of absolute devotion. After the inauspicious days of last summer we remain, with inextinguishable faith in the destiny of Italy, with the Fascist Republican Party. As we did twenty-five years ago, Duce, we beseech you to regard us, now and forever, at your orders for life and for death." [6]

Mussolini exhorted them to work for the rebirth of Italy.[7] But he himself had little faith in that cause. He was a broken, shrunken shell of the man he had been only a few months before. On the eve of his fall the previous July, he had said to his ministers, "At this moment I am certainly the most disliked, or rather, hated man in Italy." [8] In the eight months that had gone by since then there had been nothing to change his mind. For the Duce of fascism this twenty-fifth-anniversary day was to be very long and hard—longer and harder than he could at this hour imagine.

Pietro Caruso completed the party oath:

". . . I swear to execute the orders of the Duce and to serve with all my strength and, if necessary, with my blood the cause of the Fascist Revolution." [9]

In a few hours he would be called upon to live up to every letter of his faith.

Now Pizzirani stepped before the huge image of Mussolini. He held his arm high in the Fascist salute, the flat of his palm reaching for the eyes of the leader.

"Duce!" he cried. And a chorus of Blackshirts, who had filled the hall, responded mightily, "For us!" [10]

V

In a musty room in number 2 Via Principe Amedeo, Lieutenant Maurizio Giglio lay writhing in pain. With eight other men and a twelve-year-old boy, he was in a nine-foot-square cell in the Fascist house of torture. Giglio had been arrested six days earlier.[1] The twenty-three-year-old Italian was an officer in the Public Security branch of the Rome police and a spy for the United States wartime intelligence agency, the Office of Strategic Services. His code name in the OSS was Cervo. He was working with an American agent who had infiltrated Rome, Major Peter Tompkins.[2]

On March 17 Giglio had gone to a hiding place near the Risorgimento Bridge over the Tiber to move the transmitter used to contact US Fifth Army Headquarters in the south of Italy. The radio operator, Vincenzo Bonocore, was an informer.[3] Giglio and his orderly were captured by the notorious sadist Pietro Koch, a German-Italian who liked to be called "doctor" and was the head of a squad of political police. He was taken to Koch's personal prison in Via Principe Amedeo.[4]

It was located on the top floor of a yellow, six-story building on the corner of that street, two blocks from Stazione Termini, the main railroad station. It had been an old boarding house called Pensione d'Oltremare. Now the muddy-brown shutters of the rooms were tightly closed. They were blocked by newly installed iron bars. The air was thick with the odor of urine and feces.

Since Friday, Giglio and his orderly, Giovanni Scottu, had been beaten and tortured at regular intervals. There were interrogations conducted by Koch and his men, sometimes in the presence of Questore Pietro Caruso and Koch's mistress, Marcella Stoppani,[5] a stenographer who laughed at the sight of blood, liked to kick men in the groin, and wrote sadistic poetry.*

* In a long series of couplets dedicated to the Koch band, she describes 21 of its 67 members, 10 of whom were women. Here is an excerpt: "All those who are in Rome/ to harm our nation's home/ To plot against the Duce/ who guides the Fascist future/ Must confront a band/ under Piero Koch's command/ . . . Against a punch from Masè/ there's no remedy in any way/ From the room next door you can hear the sound/ of how the pleasures of a captured partisan abound/ If he persists and will not squeal/ and if there's nothing he'll reveal/ Even Zangheri, strange thing,/ will lose his temper and make him sing/ But just what are those screams?/ the work of Brilli, as it seems?/ Or do they come from the fists/ of Pallone's big

Giglio had not been interrogated for two days. His ribs were broken, some of his teeth had been knocked out, and he could barely move his head.[6] He had been a pale but handsome, strongly built man. The son of an officer in the secret police organization OVRA, he had been raised on Fascist ideology. But on September 9 he had fought the Germans at the Porta San Paolo pyramid. He had gone behind the Allied lines and was recruited by the OSS. He then had returned to Rome with a radio hidden in a suitcase and a mission: to establish an intelligence network among the partisans.[7]

There was a double bed in Giglio's cell, two cots with mattresses of wool and dried grass, and a waterless basin to be used by nine men as a toilet. Yesterday there had been a special treat: a plate of spaghetti sent with the compliments of Caruso. Thus far today, there was only the single flask of water for the next twenty-four hours.

During the morning the twelve-year-old boy, who had been thrown into the cell last night, was released. The others sat quietly now, waiting. Giglio, Scottu, who had been crushed against a board of nails, a tailor, a shoemaker, a merchant, a professor—all with swollen eyes and bloody faces—waited.[8]

VI

IN A top-floor Parioli apartment overlooking the gardens of Villa Borghese, the young American Major Peter Tompkins was listening to a report from a Roman partisan named

---

mitts?/ Run, they're from the hands of Nucci!/ or else I think it is Gabrucci/ Who has laid out a man/ for as long as one can/ . . . This is Koch's squad/ men, strong-minded and hard/ Who work for the glory of Italy/ and for the Fascist victory/ And I, having been granted your trust/ cry, with all my heart, 'Duce for us!'—Marcella" (published in *l'Italia Libera*, June 24, 1944, p. 2).

Franco Malfatti. The Italian had located the building where Giglio was being held. He and his men, he told Tompkins, had had the house in Via Principe Amedeo under surveillance for the past few days. They had seen what was believed to be three dead bodies removed from the premises. The pensione-prison was well guarded, he said, by heavily armed men. But Tompkins felt he had to make an attempt to free his comrade from the Fascist torturers.[1]

Giglio had been one of his first contacts when he slipped into Rome on the eve of the Anzio invasion. He had trusted him almost immediately. They were about the same age. Tompkins had spent his first night in the enemy city in the Prati apartment where Giglio lived with his parents and his sister.[2] His own mission in Rome, Tompkins later recalled, was somewhat vague and went under the generic phrase of "coordinating intelligence and partisan activities." [3] With the help of Giglio and other anti-Fascist Italians, he had been collecting important data on German military movements in and around the city and radioing this information to the US Fifth Army in the south. This effective intelligence operation was ended by the capture of the transmitter on March 17.

Tompkins had lived in Italy as a youth and spoke the language fluently. Before the war he had been a correspondent for the Rome bureau of the New York *Herald Tribune*, and he knew the city as well as any Roman. As an American spy he operated under the cover of an Italian identity.

Tompkins and Malfatti now decided to consider an attack on Koch's prison. It was agreed that if at any time there were less than fifteen men in the Pensione d'Oltremare, Tompkins, Malfatti, and the partisans under his command would attempt a raid in order to rescue Giglio. Malfatti had already assigned men to plan the bold assault.[4]

VII

ELSEWHERE IN the city, while this morning of the 23rd slipped away, journalist Luigi Barzini was meeting for the first time with his staff. He had been appointed the new chief of the Fascist news agency Stefani.[1] The post had been vacant since the morning following Mussolini's arrest on July 25, 1943. On hearing the news, the former director, Manlio Morgagni, had committed suicide in a supreme show of loyalty to the Duce; he had been the only casualty of the fall of fascism.[2]

With Barzini at the head of the wire service there would be no change in the policy of calculated distortions. Barzini's Stefani would be the first to tell the world about the Via Rasella.

Beyond the sloping walls of Vatican City, Pope Pius XII was receiving his financial adviser from the Holy Office, Monsignor Alfredo Ottaviani.[3] This morning, copies of the Pope's March 12 speech, "New Concern for the Safety of Rome," just off the Vatican printing presses, became available to the public. Number 56 in the series "The Voice of the Pope," its advertised price would be "seven lire per hundred." [4]

In another part of the Holy See, funeral services were being conducted for Vincenzo Fastellini, a chauffeur for the Vatican. He had been killed by an Allied bomb while driving a truck full of flour from the countryside to Rome. His vehicle bore Vatican City registration plates.[5] These facts would be highly publicized by the Vatican in the continuing campaign against the Allied bombings.

Meanwhile, at the first-run movie theater Barberini—just around the corner from Via Rasella—the feature film went on at 11:40 A.M. It was the premiere of *The Lover in the*

Shadows, a Swedish production, with a deceptive title, about the difficulties that face a young and dedicated surgeon.[6]

VIII

At noon, Rosario Bentivegna, the partisan known as Paolo, sat at a table in the *trattoria* Dreher. He was having lunch with Carla Capponi and the scientist Giulio Cortini and his wife. They had taken the long walk from the *cantina* because Dreher's was the safest restaurant they knew. It was a noisy place in Piazza dei SS Apostoli that looked like a big marble kitchen. Just a block from the house Carla had grown up in, it had been a favorite for a long time.[1]

Today, there was meat on the menu. It was ground and broiled and served like a hamburger. It may have come from a horse. It may have come from a dog. But it was meat and no one asked questions. The normal ration was never more than a taste each month. There was also the black-market meat—at 1,000 lire a kilogram, a price only the *Pariolini* could afford.[2] Restaurants served meat sometimes. Often they broke the rationing rules, imposed but not observed by the German occupiers. When they were caught they were punished. That morning Caruso's police had closed down a number of restaurants for rationing violations, among them Alfredo's in Via della Scrofa.[3]

After lunch the four *gappisti* returned to Via Marco Aurelio. Quietly, each of them got ready. Soon it would be time to go to Via Rasella. GAP commander Carlo Salinari came by to see if everything was set.[4] It was. Raoul Falcioni and Guglielmo Blasi arrived. Their first task would be to linger about seventy-five feet behind Bentivegna as he pushed the rubbish cart to Via Rasella. They would cover him in the event of trouble on the way.[5]

Inside the cellar, Cortini went over the bomb apparatus. It was then carried outside and eased into one of the garbage barrels. Bentivegna changed clothes. He dressed in the street cleaner's uniform, which had been acquired by Blasi.[6] He put on a pair of old patent-leather shoes, lacing them with red string. He thought that would make him look more like an authentic street cleaner. He checked his pockets. Did he have matches? He would light the fuse with his pipe. Did he have his pipe? Tobacco? He removed his glasses. He was ready. It was one o'clock.

The sun was high now and the sky was clear. The temperature, this third day of spring, was in the eighties. Bentivegna rolled the rubbish cart out of the courtyard. Slowly, he lowered it over the curb into Via Marco Aurelio. He began to push and, almost immediately, to sweat profusely. The cart, with its weighty load, was far more difficult to maneuver than he had imagined it would be, and the hills of Rome lay before him.

With Falcioni and Blasi following behind, he came out into Via Claudia, climbing toward the Colosseum and, beyond, the ruins of ancient Rome. A girl he knew suddenly came down the street. His heart quickened, but she walked by without recognizing him. The street cleaner had passed the first test.[7]

He walked slowly, fighting an instinct to run, to be done with it. He wanted to be rid of the fear and the hatred. Guiding the hidden bomb around the Colosseum, he moved on to the wide boulevard known in those days as Via dell'Impero.* He passed the forums of the Romans, of Caesar, of Trajan. Before him was the Vittoriano, the great mass of botticine marble that formed a monument to a united Italy. In its ugly white power and the lie of its symbolism, it was cruel irony in March, 1944.

He was near Dreher's again. He climbed the hill to the

* Today known as Via dei Fori Imperali.

Quirinal Palace, guarded by the muscled stone horse tamers of Monte Cavallo. At the palace gardens an unexpected thought crossed his mind: Rome was beautiful and he might never see it again.

Now he was nearing Via Rasella; suddenly there was trouble.

"Hey you!" someone cried, breaking the afternoon silence of the streets.

He looked around. Two street cleaners—real street cleaners—were coming from Via XX Settembre, heading his way.

"What are you doing around here?" one of them asked. "This is not your district."

"Nothing," he stammered, "nothing. I'm carrying a load of cement."

"Oh, I get it," said the street cleaner with a knowing smile. "You're in the black market. Go on, go on." [8]

He turned into Via Quattro Fontane, slowly letting the rubbish cart down the steep grade, passing alongside the gates of Palazzo Barberini and, on the other side, the Hotel d'Italia.

Now he was at Via Rasella. The sun was just a few minutes over the zenith. Its light hit behind the rooftops on the north side of the street and flooded the furrowed façades of the other. A carpet of shadow lay lengthwise down one-half the cobbled street. The houses on the bright side were sienna in color and uniform in appearance. On the dark side, that of the Palazzo Tittoni, they were of gray stone and they varied in width and height.

He could see clearly to Via Traforo at the bottom of the street. His line of vision was broken only by a single truck parked close to where he would place the bomb.[9] In the hazy distance, reaching above the seven-story building at the bottom of the hill, he could see the tower of Montecitorio, the palace Bernini had built for the Ludovisi family.

He passed the parked truck and stopped at number 156, at the entrance to Palazzo Tittoni. He edged the heavy rubbish cart against the curb to prevent it from slipping and rolling away. He looked to Via Boccaccio and saw Franco Calamandrei, the partisan who would command the action and who would signal the moment to light the fuse. Now, he felt, everything was in order. It was only a matter of waiting for the Germans. Waiting—if all went well—until two o'clock. He checked his watch. There were ten minutes to go.

Between 1:50 and 1:55, Carla Capponi arrived in front of the *Il Messaggero* building in Via del Tritone. On the most beautiful, cloudless day of the year, she was carrying a man's raincoat over her arm. She was two blocks from Via Rasella. She would wait here until receiving further word from a lookout, a partisan named Pasquale Balsamo. Then she would proceed to her position on the corner of Quattro Fontane. Her movement through the streets would be a signal to the others that the Germans were coming.

Now, as she neared the entrance to the *Il Messaggero* building, two plainclothes Fascist detectives were waiting there.[10]

IX

At two o'clock Walter Di Franco, a member of the Koch band, entered Lieutenant Giglio's cell.[1] Di Franco was twenty-eight years old, short, and olive skinned. He had a heavy-bearded, expressionless face. Marcella Stoppani, the poetess of the gang, had rendered him as "feeling his heart consumed by love." [2] He gave Giglio a cigarette. He had once been a friend of the lieutenant's. But in the past few days he had knocked out his teeth and smashed his face until it was pulpy.

Now he promised Giglio that if he talked, if he identified

the American spy and the Italians who were in contact with the Allies, he could go free. He offered Giglio some chocolate.

There was, of course, a great deal Giglio could say. Besides his OSS mission, he had links with the King's government in the south. He knew the names of scores of partisans and Allied agents in Rome. They had met in his home. He knew their hiding places, how they communicated, the codes, and where the guns and money came from.

"Walter," he said, "you are like Judas." [3]

X

LIEUTENANT COLONEL Herbert Kappler and General Kurt Mälzer, the "King of Rome," had succeeded in avoiding the Fascist ceremonies scheduled for the afternoon. They were enjoying a leisurely luncheon in the dining room of the Hotel Excelsior. They had been joined by the Fascist Minister of Interior, Guido Buffarini-Guidi.[1] He was a cunning and corrupt Tuscan lawyer whose principal task in the neo-Fascist regime was, at this stage, strengthening the Italian police forces and leading the administration of the antipartisan operations. Mussolini, who had only reluctantly appointed him, had recently said of Buffarini-Guidi, "He is hated even more than me." [2]

Today the Minister was less fortunate than his hosts. He would soon have to make an appearance at Pizzirani's celebration. He had come down from the north to lend prestige to the event and was staying at the Excelsior; the hotel in Via Veneto was favored among the hierarchy of Nazism and fascism. It was situated directly across the street from the complex of villas, gardens, and palazzi that would shortly become the Embassy of the United States.

Once each week Kappler would meet personally with

Mälzer and report on the activities of the Gestapo.[3] If this came up at the luncheon, there was very little new to discuss. At the moment, Obersturmbannfuehrer Kappler was holding some 290 Roman men and women as political prisoners.[4] They were incarcerated at SD headquarters in Via Tasso and in the Third Wing of Regina Coeli, the Italian penitentiary across the Tiber. The Third Wing had been set aside by the Fascists for exclusive use by the German police. Among his prisoners were fifty-seven Jews, who had been recently arrested in Rome. They were to be shipped to the extermination center at Auschwitz to share the fate of the more than 2,000 Roman Jews Kappler had already deported.[5]

One item of unusual news Kappler had for Stadtkommandant Mälzer was that on the previous day the *Feldgericht*—the German Military Tribunal in Rome—had acquitted an Italian by the name of Pietro Paolucci.[6]

He had been arrested by the SD in January on the word of an informer and charged with political crimes. The Germans had failed to learn that Pietro Paolucci, whose true name was Paolo Petrucci, was in fact an agent trained by the Allies for a spying mission in Rome. He was being held in Regina Coeli pending his release.[7]

The old Luftwaffe general could hardly have been interested in this detail. As usual, halfway through this quiet luncheon, Mälzer was drunk.[8]

XI

Carla Capponi was perfectly aware of the two plainclothesmen in front of the *Il Messaggero* building. And she knew precisely why they were there. They were the bodyguards of Bruno Spampanato, director of the newspaper. She was frightened nonetheless.[1] They were watching her very closely.

Two o'clock had come and gone. The column of SS police was nowhere in sight. She tried to avoid the eyes of Spampanato's men. But they came up to her.

"Signorina," one said, "don't you know you're not supposed to be standing here?"

"Who are you waiting for?" the other asked. "Do you have your documents?" [2]

She had no identification papers in her purse; only a loaded gun. But they seemed almost friendly. Perhaps they were only flirting, she thought. "I smiled," she would remember, "and flirted a little myself; all the while I thought I would die of anxiety." [3]

She walked to the glass case on the building front, where the latest edition of Spampanato's newspaper was displayed, and pretended to read.

Il Messaggero had come out two hours earlier. The news in the window offered more of the usual: a new "government" in Fascist Hungary; the enemy at Cassino "once again was subjected to grave losses"; another eruption of Vesuvius; and although Berlin had been bombed last night, the Americans had done little damage due to the effectiveness of German artillery.[4]

It was now 2:20. Still no Germans. No sound of marching boots. Suddenly, Carla saw Pasquale Balsamo coming toward her. He lingered for a moment at the displayed newspaper and hummed nonchalantly. Then, almost unexpectedly, he whispered something to Carla and hurried away. But she had heard only a muffle of air she did not understand. "It could only mean the Germans are coming," she thought.[5] It was surely the signal to go through Via Rasella to Quattro Fontane.

As she walked, Carla sensed she had been wrong. She looked behind. One of the Fascists, about fifty feet back, was following her. She could see the partisans come alert. She knew they were thinking that the Germans were coming.

She sought to somehow signal them that she had made a mistake. But how? She kept moving, climbing Via Rasella. She walked in the shadow of the north sidewalk. She was still being followed.

Carla saw Bentivegna. She looked away. How could she let him know that this was a false alarm? [6]

Bentivegna thought this was the moment. He lit his pipe. But where was Calamendrei? he wondered. Where were the Germans? He saw only Carla—then, the man who was following behind her.[7]

Carla looked anywhere but at Bentivegna. When she passed him she blindly brushed against the rubbish cart, almost stumbling. At the top of Via Rasella, she crossed Quattro Fontane and stopped at the gates of the Palazzo Barberini. She paused to catch her breath from the steep climb. The man who had pursued her, she saw now, had been joined by the other detective, and both of them were coming toward her.

"Signorina," said one, "why are you carrying a man's raincoat?"

"It's for my boy friend," Carla said.[8] At that moment she saw an old friend of her mother's coming down the street. Carla rushed up to her with the warmest greeting she knew how to give.

The older woman was pleased. She spoke endlessly in light conversation. "How's your mother?" she asked. "What are you doing around here?" "What's new?" "What have you been doing lately?" Carla smiled, without hearing anything. Out of the corner of her eye she could still see the two Fascist policemen. They were waiting for her.[9]

XII

Less than 600 feet away, in the great Hall of Ministers of the State in Via Veneto, Pizzirani's celebration was reaching its highest moments. He had just led the "Salute to the Duce." Now he gave the floor to the blind war hero Carlo Borsani.[1]

The Ministry of Corporations was a huge imposing building that curved with the graceful bend in the street. Everyone who had entered that afternoon had been given a security check and searched, as a precaution against any incidents. But the atmosphere inside was anything but relaxed. For days now the Fascists had been whispering among themselves that the Resistance would strike hard on this memorable day.[2]

Consul Möllhausen, in charge of the German Embassy, said that the air was "charged with electricity." [3] He was there making his first—and last—appearance in public. He was seated with Colonel Dollmann, Himmler's personal representative in Rome, and Buffarini-Guidi, who had left the luncheon with Kappler and Mälzer at the Excelsior. Buffarini-Guidi, who was very close to *il Signor* Himmler, was also a good friend of Dollmann's. The two men had not seen one another for some time. To Möllhausen they seemed delighted with each other's company.[4]

When Borsani rose to speak, the applause was warm and loud. He was a popular man and a passionate orator. But today he was received by his fellow Fascists with unusual enthusiasm and the laudatory interruptions were too fervent to be credible. They were lurid and indulgent; one man continually clapped frantically and in the wrong places, and he made strange noises with his lips.[5]

Borsani began:

> Comrades of Eternal Rome, it has often happened in the history of your city that the misfortunes of war and internal conflict have given rise to such calamity and such grave dangers as to threaten even the hope of salvation. All the same, that very history demonstrates that our forefathers were never as great in their glory as they were in their misfortunes, precisely because they did not despair —in neither the future nor the Fatherland.[6]

This depressing rhetoric was cheered wildly. Borsani, in his pompous language and his crippled body, personified the hollowness of fascism and a blind hope in a shapeless future. The Fascists knew in March, 1944, that their world would soon be crushed, yet they clung to a belief in some kind of victory.

Borsani went on grandiloquently:

> The spring that renews the warmth of the heavens and of the earth, and the hopes of men of good will, reawakens from the sleep of the unrecognized and the outraged the memory of our past solely because our future will be grander and more joyful. Whosoever, in the trial and in bitterness, no longer feels the courage to reaffirm his claim to the nobility of his origins, relinquishes the struggle and excludes himself from life and from history . . .[7]

The armed paratroopers of the Storm Division and the legionnaires of the Rome or Death Battalion, who formed the color guard, stared attentively at the speaker. Consul Möllhausen was deeply touched by the "beautiful, sensible, and moving" things about which Borsani spoke.[8] But he had difficulty following him; he was being continually distracted, he said, by Dollmann and Buffarini-Guidi. They were joking with each other at the expense of the blind man and his speech.

"At the most pathetic moment," according to Möllhausen, "Dollmann made the pupils of his eyes disappear beneath the lids and Buffarini pushed my jacket under the table." [9]

Borsani concluded:

> All of Italy is here. Not the Italy made to forever serve the conqueror, but the Italy purified by pain and humiliation, reconciled with past glories, drawn near to the heaven of God and of heroes, reconsecrated to the dignity of the future! [10]

The hall erupted in a thunderous ovation. It was said to be a demonstration of faith to the Duce, the Fuehrer and the resurging Italian armed forces of "8 million bayonets,"[11] which as of that moment numbered 169,373 untrained and unwilling soldiers.[12]

XIII

ROSARIO BENTIVEGNA searched his pockets for tobacco crumbs and bits of paper. Three times he had lit his pipe, thinking the Germans were coming; and three times it had been a false alarm and he had had to put out the fire. Now, at past three o'clock, he was out of tobacco.[1]

He stuffed some odd scraps into the bowl of the pipe. And again he waited. The shadow cast by the falling afternoon sun had crept almost across the street. Nothing else moved. Nothing happened.

In a quiet room inside number 156 Via Rasella an old woman sought rest among the memories of a celebrated past. Her name was Donna Bice Tittoni, the octogenarian widow of the Fascist senator whose house this had been.[2]

Mussolini himself had lived in a five-room flat in the old palazzo. For Christmas, 1926, Donna Rachele had come down from Milan to Via Rasella to visit with her Benito. Four years earlier he had installed himself in Rome as the youngest prime minister in Italian history. She was surprised to find that her husband, the Duce of fascism, lived in so small an apartment. "The bedroom was the only decent-size room," she said later, "but even there the lighting was poor."[3] There was no kitchen and the Duce's meals were sent up by Baron Alberto Fassini, an industrialist who lived on the floor below. An Umbrian spinster named Cesira did the housekeeping. "For us," Donna Rachele would remember years later, "the memory of Via Rasella was linked to the sad period" of her husband's life.[4] But Mussolini had other memories of Via Rasella. According to one of his biographers, the Duce in the mid-twenties was compulsively sexual:

> He assaulted the various women who came to . . . his flat on an upper floor of a palazzo in Via Rasella with a frenetic passion which was always exciting and often frightening. . . . He liked all women indiscriminately, provided they were not too thin; and his only requirement was that they should smell strongly either of scent, if their bodies had little natural smell, or preferably of sweat. He did not mind if they were not clean and often dabbed his own body with *eau de Cologne* instead of washing. Totally uninhibited and wholly egocentric, he gave little thought to his lovers' comfort or their pleasure, often choosing the floor in preference to the bed, removing neither his trousers nor his shoes. The whole uncontrolled process was usually over in a minute or two.[5]

These were the dynamic days of fascism. It was a time when many liberal scholars and statesmen had begun to understand that the dictatorship was here to stay. For them, despite the assassinations, the armed violence of *squadrismo*, and the scandals, fascism was not as bad as some people said. They were men like Tittoni. That year, 1926, he donned the ostrich feather of the academic costume and became the first president of the Fascist Academy of Arts and Sciences. Men like the philosopher Giovanni Gentile and the radio scientist Guglielmo Marconi were wooed firmly to the Fascist side with titles from Mussolini, who made each a *marchese*, thereafter to be addressed as *sua eccelenza*—your excellency.

Donna Rachele and Donna Bice had seen and known these *dirigenti* of fascism, who now were dead, or, like the Duce, hopelessly fallen.

Across the city to the southeast, a man who had often been a guest in the Palazzo Tittoni apartment of the Duce was locked in a cell in the Via Tasso prison of the Gestapo. His name was Aldo Finzi. He was unaware that at this moment he had about twenty-eight hours to live.

In those early days in Via Rasella he had met Donna Rachele and sent her an enormous bouquet of flowers. He was the Duce's Undersecretary of Interior. He fell early in the Fascist period. In the first years that followed the March on Rome, fascism was still opposed. The regime had had to deal severely with its most outspoken critic, Socialist Giacomo Matteotti. He could not be silenced; he was therefore murdered.* But the outcry that followed was regarded as threatening to Mussolini's political future. The Duce needed a scapegoat. Finzi, who had been accused in economic scandals, was dropped from the Government.

If he had ever thought of returning to public life, by the late 1930s it was impossible. He was a Jew. In 1938, after Hitler's visit to Rome, the Fascist racial laws were decreed.

Finzi had retired to his beautiful villa in the Castelli Romani, the vineyard hills south of Rome. When the Germans came, he took up the underground fight against them. He supplied bands of Latium partisans–including a small formation of escaped Russian war prisoners–with food, tobacco, and information about Wehrmacht troop movements. The Germans had set up a command post in his home. He lived with them. "If I escaped it would be worse," he had told a partisan in February. "I don't think they will find out about my activities." [6]

In March the Germans found out. He was arrested and brought to Kappler's prison. Now he was waiting. Tall, fifty-

* At the very least Mussolini gave his tacit approval to the crime, which was committed in Rome on June 10, 1924. In any case in his infamous "ultimatum speech" of Jan. 3, 1925, he assumed full responsibility for the killing. (*Cf.* D. Mack Smith, *Italy, A Modern History,* Ann Arbor: University of Michigan Press, 1959, pp. 380–387.)

three years old, Aldo Finzi was a sad, defeated man. But he wanted to survive this war. He wanted to confess and to expose his past, especially details about the Matteotti crime. "After the liberation," he had said a few days before his capture, "I will be able to publish what really happened. I am completely innocent." [7] Now he waited.

XIV

AT THE top of Via Rasella, Carla Capponi had returned to the front of Palazzo Barberini. She had left her mother's friend. Spampanato's men stayed about a block away. They watched her with patient suspicion. In the garden just beyond the Barberini gates three children were playing. Carla began to fear for their safety. She had never seen forty pounds of TNT explode. She had no way of knowing what it might do.

"Why must you play over here?" she called to them softly. "Move farther in. It's better over there." [1]

The children regarded her strangely. But they slowly drifted deeper into the gardens.

Carla looked around. Something else was wrong. Guglielmo Blasi was not at the gates. He was to have covered Bentivegna. He was gone. She had not seen him at all.

The time was 3:15. The only one coming up Via Rasella was another street cleaner. He was walking straight to Bentivegna.

"You'd better watch yourself," he said to the partisan. "There's an inspector from the Sanitation Department around here. What are you doing? You'd better get a move on, if you don't want to catch a fine." [2]

Bentivegna began to sweep the street around his rubbish

cart. The partisan-medical student had never held a broom in his life. He did not know what to do, and what he did was clumsy and awkward. They had thought of everything but this. The other man walked away. He must have been convinced his fellow street cleaner was headed for trouble.

3:30. The punctual Germans were an hour and a half late. At the Excelsior Kappler and Mälzer were finishing their lunch. Kappler was preparing to return to his office in Via Tasso. The general, thoroughly intoxicated, would retire to his suite in the hotel, perhaps to nap.

In the Ministry of Corporations, Pizzirani was making the closing remarks. Consul Möllhausen and his aide, Press Attaché Herbert von Borch, went out on the balcony overlooking Via Veneto for a breath of fresh air.[3]

Giorgio Amendola, the Communist member of the Military Junta, was observing the Via Rasella operations from a point in Via Due Macelli. The tall, heavy-set Resistance leader had a four o'clock appointment with Sergio Fenoaltea of the Action Party.[4] They were to go to Christian Democrat De Gasperi to discuss the crisis in the CLN. De Gasperi was in hiding only a block away in the Vatican-owned Propaganda Fide, which faced Piazza di Spagna. With the approach of the hour of the meeting, Amendola was growing impatient. He wondered if the Germans would ever come. He looked down the straight and empty street. Beyond the Spanish Steps, as far as his eye could see, the way was still clear. Then, from somewhere along the distant Via Flaminia, he could hear a faint rumble. The Germans were coming.

In Via Rasella, Bentivegna could not yet hear the marching Germans. He was convinced the action had failed. It was obvious, he thought, they were either not going to show up today or they had changed their route. It would be better to leave now before any more time was lost. His comrades were thinking likewise. At 3:35, Pasquale Balsamo came by with a message from the attack commander. He mumbled as he passed Bentivegna, "If they don't come in ten minutes, leave." [5]

"Sure," Bentivegna thought. "And now what do I do with the rubbish cart?" [6] Did he have to push it across all of Rome again? This time he would certainly be stopped. Suddenly, however, he too could hear the rhythmic thunder of the German troops. They were singing loudly. They marched beneath the windows of Mario Fiorentini's apartment, facing the impassable tunnel.

Bentivegna looked to Calamandrei, who was poised at Via Boccaccio, ready to signal. The chorus of voices grew loud. He lit his pipe.

Suddenly the *portiere* of the Palazzo Tittoni stepped out on the street, just in front of the rubbish cart.

"Hey!" Bentivegna snapped. "The Germans are coming. We're going to attack them. You'd better get out of here!" [7]

The *portiere* withdrew. Now he saw another man. It was the driver of the truck parked nearby. He was standing at the vehicle making a minor repair. Bentivegna chased him with a look in his eye the man seemed to comprehend. He disappeared.[8]

The Germans were at the bottom of Via Rasella. Three abreast, 156 men in battle dress, with an escort of armored vehicles, they turned and began to climb the narrow street.

There were ninety marching steps to Via Boccaccio, where Calamandrei stood. Bentivegna stared at the commander. In Via Boccaccio, near the steps that led to Via Giardini, three *gappisti* also watched for Calamandrei's signal. They were to break out for the second stage of the attack. Behind them, Pasquale Balsamo was at the top of the steps. He too looked toward the tall, thin figure with the cap, ready to move near his cover position at the tunnel. At the bottom of Via Rasella, Carlo Salinari, in full view of the moving column, prepared to lead his men in the rearguard assault. At the top of the street, Carla crossed from the gates of Palazzo Barberini, taking shelter from the blast behind the southwest corner of Quattro Fontane. She could hear and feel "the pounding heels, a cadence resounded on the pavement . . ." *

The entire neighborhood was shaking now, as the troops moved like a roaring piston to fill the gaping street. Bentivegna would always remember the singing and the beating sound, the "Boom. Boom. Boom." [9]

The afternoon shadow had crossed Via Rasella and lay at the walls of the shops and houses on the south side of the street. The head of the column passed the photo shop at number 132 on one side and the barber's at number 56 on the other. At number 140 the street widens in Via Boccaccio and narrows again somewhat farther on. When the column reached this point, Calamandrei, walking across the street, raised his cap.[10]

At the Palazzo Tittoni, Bentivegna put his pipe to the fuse. It ignited at once. He placed his own cap on top of the rubbish cart to indicate everything was in order. Crossing before the eyes of the first ranks of the Bozen Regiment, 11th Company, he walked briskly to Quattro Fontane.

The fuse expended itself. The hissing sound was lost under the German song and the clamor of heels against the stone. In less than fifty seconds now, it would detonate the giant

* From an untitled and unpublished poem by Carla Capponi. It was written some weeks after the attack, during a period of hiding after an escape from the Germans. It records her impressions of the moments before the explosion in Via Rasella. Here is an excerpt: "The sun heavy with cruel light/ rays embedded in the red haze of spring/ Men passed like shadows on the lines of ashes and asphalt/ faces that do not cling to memory/ . . . Long pain marked the minutes/ quivering like struck blades of steel about to fall upon us/ we who were closed in the narrow street/ our hearts compressed in our breast/ There remained an insufficiency of being needing fixed contours/ a gesture, not a mountain of words/ Under the pounding heels/ a cadence resounded on the pavement/ echoing in the heart (Only the brain left the vow intact)/ At a nod from Franco it was understood/ that the moment of judgment had arrived/ Eyes upon us at every corner/ watching, waiting/ and it passed, swept away with fear/ the timidity of youth/ of our twenty years." (Copy of Italian original given by Carla Capponi to author, Aug. 20, 1965.)

bomb of TNT and iron and steel—and the machinery of death which would not run down for the next thirty hours.

The time was 3:45.

XV

As THE last seconds burned away, Carla Capponi stood at the corner, near the entrance to 158 Via Quattro Fontane. She saw a bus coming down from Via XX Settembre and, in the opposite direction, Spampanato's men, who had persisted all this time in observing her. Bentivegna was hurrying toward her.

Next door, in number 159 Quattro Fontane, two brothers, Umberto and Angelo Pignotti, who made and sold leather and canvas handbags, were in their little shop. They were chatting with a friend who had come by, a clerk from the Banca d'Italia.[1] At the low end of Via Rasella, a foreign journalist, a woman named M. de Wyss rounded the corner. She was headed for the photographer in number 132, who developed her films.[2] On Via Nazionale, about 1,200 feet south of Via Rasella, Obersturmbannfuehrer Kappler was riding in a car returning to his office in Via Tasso.[3] In an apartment at number 7 Via XX Settembre, Vincenzo Florio, a wealthy Sicilian, who a few hours earlier had been released from Via Tasso, was celebrating the occasion with his brother and nephew.[4] Farther up the street, in number 28, Enrico Biagioli, the last known survivor of the 1867 abortive insurrection of papal Rome, led by Garibaldi, lay dying in his bed, slipping rapidly away.[5] In a building in Via Rasella, a fifteen-year-old boy was visiting with his friend and they were doing their homework.[6] In the barber shop at number 56 a man was being shaved.[7] On the balcony of the Ministry of Corporations in Via Veneto, where Consul Möllhausen and his press officer were taking a breath of air, the last of the applause from the hall was fading and Pizzirani was rushing up to them.

"Did you see?" Pizzirani cried excitedly. "What a success! We should have held the meeting at the Adriano. It would have been grandiose!" [8]

At that moment the bomb in Via Rasella went off.[9]

It was a tremendous explosion. It rocked the entire block and could be heard throughout the center of Rome. The rigid shaft of German troops snapped like a breaking walking stick. Two dozen men were blown apart. They fell in puddles of blood. The rubbish cart and the steel case inside it disappeared. Shrapnel whistled through the street. It pinged on German helmets and sliced and chopped through human flesh. Dying and wounded men fell to the ground. They lay groaning among parts of arms and legs, in many cases their own. They were immediately drenched in a rain of slivers and sheets of glass. Hunks of concrete were chopped from as high as thirty feet out of the façades of the buildings across the street from Palazzo Tittoni. An armored truck that had been escorting the column was demolished. A hole of about thirty cubic feet was blown out of a stone wall. Water began to gush from it, washing down the graded street, mixing dust with steel and blood.[10]

A powerful concussion of air burst up Via Rasella. It knocked everything in its path to the pavement. The passing bus was lifted from the street and hurled against the gates of the Palazzo Barberini. The three children playing in the garden were bowled down. Carla and Bentivegna, who had just rounded the corner, were jolted by the hot wind. As she passed him the raincoat, Carla could see people fleeing the stricken bus and scattering in every direction. The children got up and ran. Spampanato's men began to chase Carla. She reached into her purse and drew out her gun. Before she could fire a shot they turned around and ran off with everyone else.[11]

The instant they heard the explosion, the three partisans in Via Boccaccio stepped into Via Rasella. They tossed the four mortar shells and made their escape precisely as planned, disappearing beyond the tunnel. One of the noisy shells failed to detonate. But before the sound of the bomb in the rubbish cart had faded, the three other mortars exploded in rapid succession. The result was four shattering blasts.

On the corner of Via Due Macelli and Via del Tritone, Giorgio Amendola, who had seen the column of troops go by, was joined by Sergio Fenoaltea of the Action Party.

"What happened?" asked Fenoaltea, shaken by the explosions. "Do you think it was the partisans?"

"That's possible," Amendola replied with a canny air the other man understood.[12] If there was a note of passion in his voice, Fenoaltea knew why. Amendola's father, the leader of the early liberal opposition to Mussolini, had tried to fight fascism in Parliament. He died of a beating at the hands of the Duce's *squadristi*. They walked off now to meet De Gasperi, who at the moment was wondering about the disturbance outside the Propaganda Fide.

Vincenzo Florio, the Sicilian who had been released from Via Tasso, heard the explosions and ran out into the terrace. He could see a dense cloud of smoke rising over the entire quarter. In Via Rasella, the street was full of cries of agony and fear. The men at the rear of the German column tried to escape but were trapped by the partisans led by Salinari.

The foreign correspondent de Wyss, who was near Salinari when the bombs burst, heard screams and yells. Then wild machine-gun fire from the Germans spun her around and she ran off seeking safety. Out of the corner of her eye, she saw Germans grabbing civilians. When she reached Piazza di Spagna she stopped. A boy of about twelve, who had been thrown to the ground by the blast of air, stood near her panting for breath. He told de Wyss that he had already been seized by the Germans, but had dashed under the arms of a soldier and run away.[13]

The German survivors at the head of the column fled at once into Via Quattro Fontane. Some of them regrouped in front of the Barberini movie theater, firing wildly in the direction from which they ran. One of the Germans continued on to the Ministry of Corporations. Möllhausen, Buffarini-Guidi, and other Nazi and Fascist officials had gathered at the entrance of the building. They were trying to determine just what was going on. The German soldier raced up to them. In a breathless, choking voice, he explained that he and his comrades had been attacked in Via Rasella.[14]

Suddenly, someone opened fire from the middle of Via Veneto, directly in front of the Ministry. The shots were aimed at an open window of a hotel across the street. Other Germans and Italians began shooting at the window, although none of their fire was returned. This fact soon became clear, at least to Buffarini-Guidi, who ran out into the street and ordered the men to stop. The guns quieted. But over the coughing sounds of starting cars and motorcycles, shots could still be heard coming from Via Rasella.[15]

Now a convoy of Germans and Italians set out for the narrow street, while troops and police were sealing off the entire district.

In Via Rasella, on the southeast corner of Via Boccaccio, where there was a post of the Public Security police, a small group of partisans had engaged some of the Germans in an exchange of pistol fire. They were suddenly joined by some civilians who had weapons and Public Security agents, who took up their arms on the side of the partisans.[16]

When Salinari's men ran out of ammunition, they withdrew. But the shooting continued. The Germans mistakenly assumed they were also being attacked from the apartment buildings. They turned their machine-gun fire on the windows, especially above the tiny shops on the northwest corner of Via Boccaccio. The bullet holes in the concrete have never been filled.

By this time, Amendola and Fenoaltea had entered Propaganda Fide. De Gasperi immediately asked them what was going on outside.

Amendola said it was probably "one of those partisan actions."

"Certainly it must have been one of *yours*," De Gasperi replied. "Don't you Communists ever get tired?" Then the future Christian Democrat prime minister, who would one day decorate the partisans in Via Rasella as patriots, cast political differences aside for a moment. He was smiling and friendly and he repeated an old saying to Amendola: "*Che una ne pensate e mille ne fate*"—"If one of you thinks of it, a thousand of you do it." [17]

It was now some moments before 3:50, less than five minutes since the bomb had exploded. Both GAP detachments, the four squads of partisans, had made their escape without incident. German casualties amounted to nearly 60 per cent of the column: 26 men were already dead; 60 wounded—16 of them mortally.

Carla and Bentivegna ran toward her mother's house in Piazza Foro Traiano. They crossed Via Nazionale an instant after the Germans had cordoned off the streets behind them. But a German in an SS car saw them running and he cried out: "There they are!"

Another man in the car, an Italian, said, "No, no, don't be silly. I know him very well. He's a relative of mine—a dimwit who's always chasing girls." [18]

The Italian was a cousin of Bentivegna's who worked for the SS. They were allowed to pass.

XVI

THE FIRST of the Nazi-Fascist leadership to arrive in Via Rasella was Questore Pietro Caruso. He had been at the celebration in the Ministry of Corporations. He drove over escorted by a Fascist soldier. He reached the street in less than a minute, and he saw some of the German survivors gathering up the remains of the SS column and placing bodies and parts next to each other on the Via Rasella sidewalk at the northeast corner; the row was about fifty feet long. "Others," he said later, "were shooting frantically against the windows of the buildings" farther down the street.[1] They aimed at open windows, curtains moving in the breeze, and empty shadows. Caruso was immobilized. He did not know what to do.

General Mälzer arrived on the scene. He was still drunk. The appalling spectacle of death and ruin that met his eyes made him at once both maudlin and livid with rage. His face flushed and he began to rave. He ordered his men to immediately round up every man, woman, and child who lived in Via Rasella. At the sight of Caruso, he demanded the presence of the Italian Police, and the Questore hurried back to Via Veneto to carry out the order.[2]

Colonel Dollmann reached Via Rasella alone. He was horrified. "Everywhere there were large puddles of blood," he would recall. "The air was full of groans and cries, and shots still rang out . . ."[3]

Mälzer came up to Dollmann. He was "waving like a madman, crying in a voice choked with tears."[4] He explained what had happened.

"Revenge!" he shrieked, "revenge for my poor *Kameraden!*" He said he was going to blow up the entire block of houses in Via Rasella.

Such a thing, Dollmann replied, would be "out of the question."

The general shouted at him, "Perhaps you want to help the murderers?" [5]

By this time the German soldiers in Via Rasella had been joined by paratroopers of the Storm Division, men of the Rome or Death Battalion, and the PAI police.* They were dragging everyone from the houses in Via Rasella. Doors, locked or unlocked, were opened with a burst of machine-gun fire. They went from shop to shop, cellar to cellar, and apartment to apartment, kicking and shoving the civilians into the street. They prodded them with the butts of their rifles and drove them to the gates of Palazzo Barberini. There the people were separated—the men from the women and children—and lined along the gates. They were ordered to place their hands behind the back of their heads.[6]

The arbitrary, senseless shooting continued. Mälzer paced up and down the street. He gesticulated insanely and barked irrational commands. Seeing an elderly man who was unable to keep his arms raised, Mälzer walked up to him and began to slap his face. He shouted that he would shoot everyone on the spot.[7] Among the prisoners were Donna Bice Tittoni, the two Pignotti brothers and their friend from the Banca d'Italia, the man who was being shaved in the barbershop, and the boy who was doing his homework—dragged from his friend's home while he sobbed for someone to notify his mother. About 200 persons in all were now lined up against the gates; some of them had merely been passing by.

Via Rasella, aside from the rubble of flesh, concrete, and glass, was now littered with plaster, pieces of furniture,

* *Polizia Africa Italiana.* Rome abounded in Italian police organizations and parapolice, some of which, such as Koch's squad, were virtually self-authorized. Among them were Caruso's regular police, the Republican National Guard, the Public Security Police, the Finance Guard, the Provincial Police, the Italian legion of the SS, the state police, which included OVRA (the secret police) and the PAI, and the Fascist Militia.

broken doors, and smashed dishes. Water flowed rapidly in the gutters and in the irregular cracks between the cobblestones, cascading into the tiny sewer at the bottom of the street.

Rumors began to circulate that another attack was taking place near La Rinascente department store, near Piazza Colonna. Caruso was dispatched with party leader Pizzirani to investigate. The Questore had just returned from Via Veneto, and on the way his soldier-escort had been killed by a stray German bullet.[8]

Consul Möllhausen and Minister Buffarini-Guidi drove up together, turning into Via Rasella. At this point the uncontrolled shooting was particularly violent. Möllhausen was stunned by what was going on. He saw the civilians being pulled out of the houses and beaten in the streets. Many were trembling and he noted a look of astonishment on their faces.

Mälzer, he saw, "was in the condition of a man who has lost all control of himself and was also under the influence of alcohol." [9]

The general came up to him and a loud argument broke out between the two Germans which could be seen and heard throughout Via Rasella.[10]

"Here, here, are the beautiful results of your politics!" the Stadtkommandant raved, indicating the Via Rasella. "Here is what happens when they send us diplomats! But now all that will change!"

Möllhausen, junior in both rank and age to Mälzer, was at first bewildered by the outburst. He looked back at him dumfoundedly.

"I am going to blow up the entire block of houses!" Mälzer continued. "I have already given the necessary orders. I'm going to blow the whole thing up. I swear it. And I want to see who's going to be able to stop me!"

He was not bluffing. Möllhausen saw German trucks of the engineers. They had arrived in Via Rasella a few moments before. Cases of explosives were being unloaded. The youthful Nazi diplomat, who would later be reproached by his superior, Ambassador Rahn, as being "inept and imprudent" in this affair, reminded the general that women and children might still be inside the houses.

"None of that is important to me," Mälzer replied. "Here, the houses go up in the air—even if tomorrow the diplomats get me fired!"

Dollmann tried to intervene. Möllhausen had lost his composure. Dollmann pleaded with him to leave, saying he would try to placate Mälzer's anger.

"*Herr General*," said Möllhausen. "I ask you not to do it. Try to calm yourself. This is a mattter not only of your own good name, but of Germany's. Don't forget, now we are the ones that have been attacked and we are therefore at a psychological advantage . . ."

"My soldiers," Mälzer cried, tears streaming from his eyes. "My poor soldiers! I'm going to blow up the whole neighborhood, with whoever is in the houses. And you, Möllhausen, with your face of a Byzantine Christ, I'm going to throw you in jail at once."

The argument continued more heatedly, as the 200 persons with their hands held over their heads looked on in amazement and fear. Scores of German and Italian soldiers also watched. They were as surprised as everyone else. Finally Mälzer called to one of his officers and ordered him to contact Kesselring, the commander in chief of the German armed forces in Italy.

"Telephone the Field Marshal at once," he cried. "Explain the situation. Tell him that I ask for full powers and tell him, too, that the *Herr* Consul takes exception to my orders."

"One moment," Möllhausen shouted to the officer, "since you are using my name, tell the Field Marshal why I take exception."

"I remind you once more," Mälzer shrieked at Möllhausen

now, "this is my business and I am the commandant here. Furthermore, no one asked you to come here!" With that, he nodded correctly and gave a half salute. He turned around and walked away, leaving Möllhausen standing alone in the middle of Via Rasella.[11]

Möllhausen burned with the anger he was trying to hide. He worried about what might result from this public clash with the highest authority in Rome. He decided to go to the Embassy to try to reach Kesselring before Mälzer did. With Press Attaché Borch, who Möllhausen said was "petrified," they drove off in the direction of Villa Wolkonsky.

They had not gone more than a few hundred feet when they saw Kappler's car coming from the opposite way. Möllhausen motioned for him to stop. On the corner of Via Quattro Fontane and Via XX Settembre the two officials spoke briefly to one another.

Kappler had heard the explosions in Via Rasella on his return to Gestapo headquarters from the luncheon with Mälzer. He had not thought anything of it at first. The moment he had arrived at his office in Via Tasso, three telephone calls came in urgently requesting his presence at the scene of the attack. Nevertheless he did not as yet attach any particular importance to what he had been informed had taken place. Now, at the sight of Möllhausen, he was struck by the fact that the Consul was "extraordinarily excited." [12]

"That crazy Mälzer wants to blow up all the houses here," Möllhausen said. "He needs to be stopped at any cost!" [13]

Kappler could think of nothing to say in agreement or otherwise and they parted. His driver parked the SD car in Via Quattro Fontane and Kappler began to walk down the hill to Via Rasella. He was now approached by Dollmann, who asked him to calm Mälzer.

"That madman wants to blow up the whole district," Dollmann said.[14] Kappler remained unmoved. He had always thought of Dollmann as given to hysteria.

The general was standing somewhat behind Dollmann on the corner of Via Rasella, Kappler observed that Mälzer was flushed with excitement and covered with sweat.

"You see, Kappler?" Mälzer said. He pointed to the row of dead bodies lined at the corner. "You see what they have done to my boys? Now I am going to blow all these houses sky high with dynamite!" [15]

When he turned the corner into Via Rasella, Kappler was presented with what he later described as a "terrible picture." [16] The presence of the Gestapo officer, however, with his pale, inscrutable face, added a measure of stability to the situation. He spoke calmly and easily with the distraught general. After a few moments he asked if he might be permitted to take charge. Mälzer agreed and Kappler immediately ordered his own officers into action. They had also arrived at the scene by now. Major Durante Domizlaff, Chief of the 3rd SD detachment, and Captain Hans Clemens organized the search of the houses in Via Rasella, beginning with an investigation of the roofs. Their efforts would prove fruitless except for the discovery of a red flag, which Clemens considered incriminating. Kappler directed another of his officers, Captain Kurt Schutz, to interrogate the survivors of the SS column. Others were dispatched to collect bomb fragments from the street, and they soon recovered the mortar shell that had not exploded. Its fuse had caught fire, but had not burned entirely. The casualties were counted and the wounded men were, after a long delay, taken to the hospitals.

Kappler urged Mälzer to return to his headquarters. He protested at first, but finally agreed and was helped into his car. Before Mälzer departed, Kappler asked him what he thought should be done with the civilians who were still lined up along the gates of Palazzo Barberini.

The "King of Rome," whom Dollmann used to call General Boom-Boom-Boom, swept his hand like a brush across his view of the row of men, women, and children. "They are all to be shot," he replied.[17]

The time was 4:15 P.M. EIAR—Radio Rome—had just come on the air, opening its schedule of daily broadcasts with a children's program.

XVII

WHEN CARLA and Bentivegna arrived at her mother's apartment on the fifth floor of a building in Piazza Foro Traiano, Bentivegna collapsed and fainted. He blanched and his breathing was barely perceptible. Carla thought his heart had stopped. Her mother gave him some medicine through an eyedropper. In a few moments he revived, attributing his seizure to nervous exhaustion.

He removed the street cleaner's uniform and they tried to destroy it. Unable to rip the heavy fabric, they threw it into the kitchen stove, but it would not catch fire. Finally they bundled the uniform in a small package and went down to the street again to get rid of it. Carla wanted throw it in the Tiber, but Bentivegna thought that too risky. They hid it in a dark corner near the church of Saint Peter in Chains and it was never seen again.

The *gappisti* had planned to rendezvous in the park at Piazza Vittorio. But now, with the curfew coming on, it was too late for Carla and Bentivegna to spend much more time in the streets. They decided not to go.* They had ar-

* As a result of the Germans' delay, very few of the partisans went to Piazza Vittorio. GAP commander Salinari, who did go, found no one there. He returned home, worrying if everyone had escaped. He had seen the group in Via Boccaccio get away safely, but not Carla, Bentivegna, or Franco Calamandrei. Calamandrei, after he had heard the explosion, lingered in the neighborhood for about half an hour. He then turned back, walked toward the tunnel, and casually glanced up Via Rasella as he passed. He could see the Germans running back and forth at the top of the hill and soldiers still firing against the buildings. He then went to Piazza Vittorio, where he too saw no one.

ranged to pass the night at the home of a friend of Carla's mother, a Jewish woman named Pontecorvo Pertici. She lived at number 7 Via Antonio Gallonio in what was then a new district around Piazza Bologna at the eastern limits of the city. It was dangerous, perhaps reckless, to hide in the home of a Jew which might be discovered and raided at any moment, day or night. Nevertheless they set out to cross the city now, unsure of anything that lay beyond this day—certain only of what had been done in Via Rasella.[1]

XVIII

CONSUL MÖLLHAUSEN arrived at the Embassy at about 4:15 P.M. He was still very irritated. He opened the door to his office and went straight across the lengthy room to the telephone. There was a chair in his path and he kicked it violently, sending it smashing against the front of his desk.

He called Kesselring. OBSW Headquarters was at Monte Soratte, a lone sugarloaf hill just north of Rome. The Field Marshal was out. He was visiting the front. He could not be reached and would not return until evening. Möllhausen asked to speak to General Siegfried Westphal, Kesselring's chief of staff, but he was engaged in a conference. The Consul finally was connected with Colonel Dietrich Baelitz, chief of operations. He explained what had taken place in Via Rasella. Baelitz agreed that until he could speak with Westphal, he would reply negatively to any request by Mälzer for full powers, including permission to carry out the threat to blow up the houses in the district.[1]

Baelitz then reported the incident to *Oberkommando der Wehrmacht* (OKW)—the Fuehrer's general headquarters deep in an East Prussian fir forest. Baelitz stood by, holding for a reply.[2]

The news was immediately taken to Hitler. It was the Fuehrer's rest hour. He was in the *Wolfsschanze*, his concrete "wolf's lair," from where he fought his world war. For the Fuehrer, who would soon celebrate his fifty-fifth and penultimate birthday, it had been a relatively peaceful day. At luncheon that afternoon he had been moved to reminisce about frivolities of the distant past and the pleasures of the German countryside, especially the Rhineland.[3]

He had told members of his staff who had dined with him some hours before:

> One of my greatest delights has always been to picnic quietly somewhere on the roadside; it was not always easy, for our column of cars would often be pursued by a crowd of motorists eager to see their Fuehrer off duty, and we had to employ all sorts of ruses to shake off these friendly and well-meaning pursuers sometimes; for instance, I would drive up a side turning, leaving the column to continue along the road. . . . In this way we managed occasionally to snatch a few hours of peace and tranquility. On one occasion, I remember, a family out gathering mushrooms came suddenly on our picnic party. In a few moments these kindly folk had alerted the neighboring village, and the whole population was surging toward us, filling the air with their shouts of "*Heil!*" [4]

At 4:30 P.M. OKW was back on the telephone. A staff officer at the *Wolfsschanze* conveyed to Colonel Baelitz the Fuehrer's reaction to the news of the attack in Rome. "He is roaring," said OKW. "He wants to blow up an entire quarter of the city, including everyone who lives there, and a very high proportion of Italians is to be shot. For every German police officer killed, they should shoot thirty to fifty Italians." [5]

XIX

THE NEWS of the Via Rasella attack was spreading fast. By word of mouth it had already crossed and recrossed the city, and now, before 5 P.M., it had penetrated the clay-colored walls of the Vatican. A British officer, Major Sam Derry, who was confined inside the Vatican and was living under the protection the Holy See had been given by the Germans, received information "within an hour of the big bang in Via Rasella." * Derry was operating an underground aid service for escaped Allied war prisoners hiding in Rome. He feared a new wave of German roundups and dispatched his messengers throughout the city to warn the men under his care.[1]

By telegraph and telephone the news traveled beyond Rome. The Chief of the Province of Rome, Edoardo Salerno, sent a coded telegram to Mussolini in Gargnano:

> SS detachment was today struck by explosive devices believed to have been launched from window of building adjacent Palazzo Tittoni. About thirty soldiers were killed and others injured. Public Security agents and officials rushed promptly to the scene assisted German police isolating and rounding up men living in the zone. I immediately accompanied to the site Interior Minister [Buffarini-Guidi], who intervened with other Italian and German authorities.[2]

Centers of the Fascist Government and German military and diplomatic missions in the northern Italian towns by Lake Garda received reports, too. The Germans, in turn, called

* The news was "somewhat garbled," the Briton later wrote, "but even allowing for exaggeration, I could see that this time our Communist associates had achieved more than usual . . . even an Allied Bomber, while perhaps doing more widescale damage could scarcely have expected to write off a larger number of German troops in a single blow." (S. Derry, *The Rome Escape Line*, New York: Norton, 1960, p. 173.)

Berlin. Very soon the information reached the Prinz Albrecht Strasse, headquarters of the SS, and then Reichsfuehrer Heinrich Himmler himself.

In Via Rasella by 5 P.M. the houses were still being searched and the aimless shooting continued. Herbert Kappler, however, had completed his investigation, at least to the extent that he felt necessary at the time.* [3] He was ready to report his findings. Some Germans, impressed by the precision of the attack, were saying that it must have been organized by "the English." † But Kappler had already ruled out that theory, principally because of, he said, the "primitive" detonator of the unexploded, Italian-made mortar shell.[4]

The 200 civilians, whom Mälzer had ordered shot, were still standing with their hands high, lined up against the gates of Palazzo Barberini. Some of them were crying; others had a dazed look of incredulity in their eyes. About half were women and children. Kappler and Dollmann now had them regrouped in front of the Hotel d'Italia across the street. They were then turned over temporarily to the Italian authorities. The Fascist police marched them straight up Via Quattro Fontane to the barracks in the Viminale, the block-shaped compound of the Ministry of Interior.

In the meantime, Dollmann and Kappler separated and

* Later Kappler sought to justify why he had not investigated further. The bomb fragments and other clues, he said, were wrapped in a handkerchief and placed by one of his men in an SD car. That car, according to Kappler, was stolen from Via Rasella—"probably by a bold partisan"—and the evidence was never recovered. True or not, as will be seen, there would soon be little reason to continue the investigation. (*See* note 3 as above.)

† The general consensus of the rumors that circulated in the city was recorded that evening by Roman journalist Carlo Trabucco, a friend of Bonomi's and the CLN Christian Democrats. He wrote in his diary: "No one knows who set off the bomb or bombs. It is said they were Communists; others speak of deserting Austrian soldiers. In any case, it remains an accomplished fact on a significant day, and thus all the more meaningful. The radio up to now has not mentioned it, nor have the newspapers said anything." (C. Trabucco, *La prigionia di Roma,* Rome: S.E.L.I., 1945, p. 190.)

drove away to the same destination. They sped up the swerving incline of Via Veneto to the Corso d'Italia headquarters of the German commandant of the city.

In Kappler's car, Captain Schutz, who had questioned the survivors of the column, reported to his chief. The men of the 11th Company had little to say, he told Kappler. They knew only that a bomb had exploded almost at the midpoint of the formation while they were climbing to the top of Via Rasella. Some of the men had said this was followed by smaller explosions. Not one of the Germans who was still in a condition to speak had noted anything suspicious in advance of the attack.[5]

It was a little past five o'clock when Dollmann walked into the Stadtkommandant's command post. To the tall SS man, it seemed "the confusion was brimming; everyone had come up with his own program for expiation and rumors of new attacks were rampant." [6]

Mälzer was on and off the telephone. He had sobered somewhat. Like Consul Möllhausen, he too was fearful of the consequences of their loud encounter in Via Rasella, which later became known in Nazi circles in Italy as an "unprecedented scandal." [7] The general called Colonel Dollmann to his side. He asked him to go to the Embassy, giving him a free hand to try to reconcile the matter. Dollmann said he would do his best and departed. Mälzer thought highly of Himmler's man in Rome. Dollmann was among the general's closest and most trusted advisers. On the other hand, Dollmann, the man of *Kultur* who had taken his doctorate in the politics of the Counter Reformation *magna cum laude*, regarded Mälzer, in his own words, as an "idiot clown." [8] He laughed among his colleagues at Mälzer's pretentiousness, his coarseness, his insufferable stupidity, and his drunkenness. Now Dollmann had his own motives for wanting to see Möllhausen: The "King of Rome" had to be stopped.

Having dispatched Dollmann as his emissary, Mälzer received Kappler. In the presence of some of his officers, he listened to Kappler's report between continual telephone interruptions.

The *Attentat* in Via Rasella, Kappler said, was, in his opinion, the work of Italians belonging to the anti-Fascist parties. "It was carried out principally by an explosive contrivance launched from an undetermined height and by bombs probably thrown by persons from the roofs of various houses." [9] He reported that the number of German dead had risen now to twenty-eight.

Mälzer was called again to the telephone. Kappler stood by patiently, listening as the general spoke. He could not help overhearing that Mälzer was talking with someone of equal or even higher rank. What they were discussing was made clear to him too by Mälzer's frequent use of the word "*Repressalie*"–"reprisal." [10]

The receiver still at his ear, Mälzer suddenly nodded to Kappler. He passed him the telephone and said that General Mackensen wanted to speak with him.

Eberhard von Mackensen was the aging son of the illustrious Field Marshal August von Mackensen. He was Mälzer's direct superior and commander of the Fourteenth Army. Second only to Kesselring in the military sector, Mackensen headed the operations at the Anzio front–a war zone which included Rome. He was a white-haired, rigid Prussian who affected a monocle. He was proud of his family name and disdainful of the low-bred Nazis, including Adolf Hitler.

Mackensen had already been informed of Hitler's reaction to the Via Rasella attack. He had been telephoned by Colonel Baelitz, who was unable to reach Kesselring. He thought that the Fuehrer's demands were excessive. Now Mackensen asked Kappler for further details and for an opinion on how reprisal measures could be carried out.[11]

Kappler replied that he and the head of the SD in Italy, General Harster, had once discussed such an eventuality and had agreed at the time as to how to handle the matter should a reprisal be called for. They would execute, he said, persons already sentenced to death or life imprisonment, as well as those not yet tried by a court but who were expected to receive the death penalty.[12]

In that case, said Mackensen, "execute *Todeskandidaten* [candidates for death], that is, persons condemned to death, condemned to life imprisonment, and detainees who have not yet been judged but are guilty of crimes punishable on pain of death." [13]

He set the ratio of the number to be shot at ten Italians for every German killed in Via Rasella. If there were not enough prisoners in this category, he said, it would be all right to shoot as many as there were and to later falsely publicize that the full amount had been executed.[14]

With that, the telephone conversation ended. As Kappler and Mälzer understood it, the matter was still in the discussion stage. The order for the executions would have to be officially confirmed. Mälzer told Kappler to draw up a list in the meantime of the 280 persons—ten times the number of dead Germans—to be shot.[15]

Kappler began his work immediately. From Mälzer's office, he telephoned the Italian police to help him.[16] He was aware that in Via Tasso and in the German wing of the old Roman prison Regina Coeli there would not be enough *Todeskandidaten*. He would need some of the prisoners held by the Fascists, too. He tried to reach Pietro Caruso at Police Headquarters, but the Questore was out. Caruso had been investigating the disturbance in Piazza Colonna. Finding only a single Fascist who had hurled a hand grenade against a building, he had continued on to Public Security Headquarters to notify other police units of the Via Rasella attack.[17]

Kappler left word that he would very shortly come by in person. The German, who detested the Italian police, let it be known that Caruso had better be there when he arrived.[18]

XX

KESSELRING'S CHIEF of staff, Siegfried Westphal, the youngest general in the German Army, stepped out of the conference room at OBSW headquarters on Monte Soratte. It was about 5:15 P.M. He was immediately briefed by Colonel Baelitz on the attack in Via Rasella, Möllhausen's fight with Mälzer, and Hitler's wild demand to blow up a part of Rome and kill more than a thousand Italians.

Both men agreed that this would be unreasonable, although they believed that the Italians had to be punished. Rome had to be discouraged from such actions against the Germans. A message had to be conveyed to the people, Westphal later said, "in order to scare them . . ." [1]

Westphal was not averse to calling OKW and voicing his objections. Only a little more than two weeks earlier, on March 6, he had been to see the Fuehrer and had found him "perceptive and understanding." [2] At Berchtesgaden, in the mountaintop retreat *Berghof*, he had sat with Hitler for three hours, patiently explaining why, despite reinforcements, it was impossible to throw the enemy at Anzio back into the sea.*

Now he was prepared to counsel against hasty decisions. Westphal telephoned Rastenberg headquarters. He was put through to the office of the Chief of Operations, General Alfred Jodl.

"Hitler," said the voice of an officer on the other end of the line, "is still very excited and he feels that this sort of thing can only happen at the Southwest Front." [3]

* The reason was, Westphal said to Hitler, that "after almost five years of war the troops were physically exhausted . . . it was therefore very rare that one succeeded in delivering a sustained attack." (S. Westphal, *Heer in Fesseln*, Bonn: Athenaeum, 1952, pp. 246–247.)

With the Fuehrer so adamant, nothing could be done now, at least not until Kesselring's return. The Field Marshal was due back at Monte Soratte in an hour or two. Westphal and Baelitz, calling the various German command posts in and around Rome, began to piece together a full report to be ready when Kesselring arrived.

XXI

STANDARTENFUEHRER DOLLMANN reached the Embassy in Villa Wolkonsky a little after 5:30 P.M. He found Möllhausen struggling with the erratic telephone service to the north. He was trying to get through to Ambassador Rahn at Lake Garda, but he finally gave up and sent a telegram instead. Möllhausen had already called Berlin, reporting to the Foreign Office in the Wilhelmstrasse.[1]

Dollmann explained that he had come in behalf of Mälzer. The Consul a few minutes before had received a conciliatory call on the same subject from General Westphal. Westphal had said that while Möllhausen had overstepped his authority, he was morally correct in opposing Mälzer.[2] Now Möllhausen was pleased to see that what he called an "angel of peace" had been sent by Mälzer. Dollmann's mission was at once successful.[3]

The two Germans, who were the highest political representatives of National Socialism in Rome, turned next to the subject of the coming reprisal. To Dollmann at least, a reprisal seemed certain, considering what he had seen and heard at Mälzer's headquarters. It was an act that had to be avoided, he felt.[4]

He and Möllhausen would later conclude that the attack in Via Rasella had been a ploy to provoke the Germans into striking—the fiercer, the better—against the people of Rome in order to intensify the hatred for the occupiers and to increase the popularity of the Resistance.[6] That the unexpected reprisal reaction would in fact destroy the partisans' original objective did not apparently enter into their deliberations, although others would perceive this quite readily.

To foil this presumed trick on the part of the Roman Resistance, according to Dollmann, "we felt it useful to discuss immediately the opportunities of handling the case with maximum prudence—above all from the political point of view." [6]

By 6 P.M. they reached agreement that they would wait until receiving word from their respective superiors, Ambassador Rahn and General Karl Wolff of the Higher SS and Polizeifuehrer of all police forces in Italy. In the meantime, they would keep each other informed of any new developments.[7]

Dollmann left the Embassy. Outside, as the late afternoon sun sank beyond the Tiber, he decided that there was something further he could do. If there was one man in Rome who could stop the reprisal or at least stay the hand of the militarists until the political men had a chance to intervene, he felt that that man was the Pope. And Dollmann, who enjoyed excellent relations with the Holy See, knew precisely how to get a message to Pius without delay.

He got into his car and drove west, toward the Vatican.[8]

XXII

THE LONG orange rays of fading daylight still lingered on the top story of the corner building at number 2 Via Principe Amedeo. They deepened the yellowish color of the stone.

At 6 P.M. the door to the cell in Pensione d'Oltremare occupied by Lieutenant Maurizio Giglio and eight other prisoners was flung open. An equal number of Koch's men entered the room in a violent rush. They had been aroused by the news of the attack in Via Rasella and the death of their German *Camerati.* Now they began to kick and punch some of the men in Giglio's cell, although the lieutenant was left undisturbed. In a few minutes their fury was spent. They withdrew from the room, having covered the beaten men with spittle and insults.[1]

The American who was planning Giglio's rescue with a bold and open attack on the pensione sat in the twilight of the early evening. Major Tompkins was on the terrace of the apartment in Parioli. From his view above the cypress trees of Villa Borghese, he watched the graceful, migrant swallows returning to Rome with the onset of spring. The man who had procured and shared the apartment with Tompkins, an Italian ex-pilot in hiding whose name was Lele, came hurrying in from the street. He had learned of the attack in Via Rasella and now reported what news he had to the OSS spy.[2]

The entire district was in turmoil, he said after sketching what little was known about the actual assault. The Germans and Fascists, it was being said, had killed and wounded some 200 civilians. They had gone from house to house beating people and then arresting all the men in the quarter.[3]

Tompkins' first reaction was that the partisan strike had been pointless. There was no reason, he felt, to kill "nondescript" German police. "Why," he thought, "hadn't whoever was responsible for the attack risked his courage against Via Tasso or picked off Kappler and his gang of butchers?" [4] He and Lele wondered what the Germans would do now. It would not be good for the underground, Tompkins concluded. "What saddened us even more was to contemplate the beauty and precision of the attack, the organization of which appeared to have been damned-near perfect!" [5]

XXIII

THE 7 P.M. curfew was closing in, and there was a nervous busyness in the streets of Rome. People hurried behind the closing *portone* of their or someone else's home—the latter being illegal. To be caught outside after curfew, as will be seen, could mean death.

Before retiring from the streets, Romans could buy the afternoon newspapers, which had come out by now. None of them, however, including *Giornale d'Italia* and the Vatican's *l'Osservatore Romano*—both of which bore the date of the following day—even mentioned the Via Rasella. Neither Barzini's Stefani news agency nor the radio had said anything. At seven o'clock German language lessons went on the air, and the next regularly scheduled newscast was not until eight.

Giornale d'Italia carried a full account of the morning's Fascist ceremonies, under the headline "The Roman Celebration of the Historic Date." There was no late world news, other than that which had already been reported in *Il Messaggero*. The editorial was titled "Who Wanted This War?" And the latest from the financial section was that German-occupied Milan was floating a one-billion-lire, forty-year loan at 4 per cent interest beginning from 1945; in the Roman stock market, Italgas was up one and a half lira and Fiat was unchanged at fifteen lire a share.[1]

L'Osservatore Romano gave prominence to an emotional account of the funeral services conducted for the unfortunate chauffeur killed in an Allied bombing.[2] The Vatican newspaper also announced the appointment of Professor-Doctor Riccardo Galeazzi-Lisi, Pope Pius' personal physician, as director of Vatican City's health services.* [3]

* Galeazzi-Lisi became *persona non grata* at the Vatican following Pius' death in 1958. The doctor published some indiscreet articles immediately after the Pope died. (*Cf.* C. Pallenberg, *Inside the Vatican*, New York: Hawthorne, 1960, p. 39.)

A small ad on the same page in *Osservatore* read: "Metabolic diseases (liver, arthritis). New method (really) for radical treatment. Professor Cremonese, Via Icilio 22 . . ." [4]

XXIV

AMONG THE Romans hurrying to get off the streets before the curfew hour was an old man with a white goatee, the head of the CLN, Ivanoe Bonomi. He had been in the home of Monsignor Pietro Barbieri, which was annexed to the offices of the *Enciclopedia Cattolica Italiana* in 14 Via Cernaia. Monsignor Barbieri was the Vatican's liaison with the CLN.

Earlier that afternoon, Bonomi had met in the prelate's apartment with the right wing of the Resistance. De Gasperi had come to the meeting after having been visited by Fenoaltea and Amendola. He told Bonomi that the Action Party's proposal to exclude the monarchy until free elections could be held was unacceptable to the Christian Democrats.[1] The Liberal representative said that his party would quit the Resistance committee.[2] The Democratic Laborite was hesitant and favored further talks.[3] If the Via Rasella attack came up at this meeting, it has not been recorded.

"I am very irritated," Bonomi noted before leaving the Monsignor, "and I do not see any way to patch up with new concessions a disagreement that can crop up again at any moment." [4] When Sergio Fenoaltea of the Actionists arrived, Bonomi announced that "the Presidency is in crisis." [5]

By this hour, returning to his hiding place in the extraterritorial church of San Giovanni in Laterano, the aged anti-Fascist had made his decision. He would resign.

XXV

PIETRO CARUSO arrived at Police Headquarters at about seven o'clock. Kappler and his men were waiting. The Questore had been notified earlier that Kappler had called and was coming to see him. But he had been delayed at the Public Security office, and Caruso could plainly see that Kappler was furious that he was late.[1]

The German said that on orders of the Commandant he needed some people who were to be shot. He had a number of his own prisoners, but the Italian police would have to contribute. He asked for about eighty men.[2] Moreover, Kappler said, he needed the full list of persons arrested in Via Rasella. He wanted to go through the names, checking with Italian police records for possible suspects.[3]

Caruso said that he thought the figure eighty seemed high and asked if Kappler would accept less.

The German said no.[4]

Caruso did not care to press the issue. Only a few weeks earlier the Germans had asked him to deliver a supply of bicycles and when he failed to produce the required number, two Nazi officers came to see him. They said that if the equipment were not handed over by five o'clock that afternoon there would be trouble. A man of scarce intelligence, Caruso did, however, understand the seriousness of Kappler's impatient demand. The Allies had already warned the Italian Fascists of the consequences of criminal acts.[5] The Questore, who had begun to accumulate gold ingots, diamonds, and British banknotes to finance the inevitable flight from dying fascism, sought now to protect himself from ending in the dock of a war-crimes court. He thought he could hide behind the image of what he believed was the authority of the Fascist state.

"For now," he said to Kappler, "let's make it fifty." [6]

He added that in any case he needed permission from the Ministry of Interior. To obtain it, he would go to Minister Buffarini-Guidi, who both men knew happened to be in Rome, staying at the Excelsior.

Kappler, anxious to return to his office in Via Tasso, did not protest for the moment. He left some of his officers behind, however, to go through the list of the Via Rasella detainees.[7]

With Kappler departed, Caruso ordered his police to return during the night to Via Rasella and search the houses once again for suspects. He also sent out an alarm to arrest Romans who had police records that might indicate complicity.[8] He did not know precisely what these actions might yield, but he wanted to establish a documentary record of his activities. With this, he could show the Germans that he, too, was concerned about the men who were serving and dying in a foreign land for the Third Reich. The same documentation, he hoped, would legalize his own deeds and shift the responsibility to his superiors for whatever crimes he would be called upon to commit.[9]

XXVI

FIELD MARSHAL Albert Konrad Kesselring returned from the front at 7 P.M. That afternoon he had made a major decision which would affect the people of Rome and the course of the war.

Kesselring, who had passed thirty-five of his fifty-nine years in the German Army, had long ago grown accustomed to taking actions that altered the lives of whole nations. An artillery captain in World War I, he rose rapidly to the rank of general when Hitler came to power. With Göring he helped build the Luftwaffe. He had been a commander in the air war against Britain and he had dispatched the bombers to Rotterdam. These were among the first indiscriminate, massive air attacks on civilian populations.*

Supreme Commander of the German armed forces in Italy, Kesselring would pursue his military career until the last moment of the war. When the Fuehrer, betrayed by almost all of his generals, finally named Kesselring head of the entire Western Front, he sent his armies to battle even after Hitler's suicide and the surrender of virtually every other German military formation. He was, as he titled his postwar memoirs, *Soldat bis zum letzten Tag*–a soldier to the last day.

This March 23, he had inspected the troops of Mackensen's Fourteenth Army. Plans had been drafted earlier for a new offensive at Anzio. If he could not drive the enemy into the sea, as Hitler wished, he could certainly hold Rome for many more months, perhaps half a year. General Mackensen had advised that a new offensive would fail.[1] At Anzio this day, Kesselring had evaluated the quality of his 65,000 combat troops. Only the 3rd Panzer Grenadier Division had been

* In the case of Rotterdam, May, 1940, the Germans declared that the city had to surrender at once or be wiped out. The Dutch yielded, but during the negotiations the Luftwaffe destroyed the city anyway. Kesselring later defended the air attacks as militarily necessary. (W. Shirer, *The Rise and Fall of the Third Reich*, New York: Simon and Schuster, 1960, pp. 722–723.) Three years later, when the Germans were marching into Rome and meeting resistance from civilians and Italian soldiers, Kesselring repeated this blackmail. He threatened to send 700 airplanes to bombard Rome into submission if his surrender ultimatum were not met by the next day. The Italian Army capitulated and Rome fortunately escaped the fate of Rotterdam. (C. Delzell, *op. cit.*, p. 274.)

Eight years after Germany had been defeated, Kesselring indicated that he regretted not using his bombers more often against civilians–at least Italian civilians. Discussing the war in Italy, he said that bombing "would naturally have been the most effective means." But he abstained from this out of consideration for civilian populations. If experience had given him a new concern for defenseless people, it was neutralized by their ingratitude. Kesselring concluded, "Events have taught me that this consideration is rewarded with very little thanks. In the future such scruples will have to go by the board . . ." (A. Kesselring, *A Soldier's Record*, New York: Morrow, 1954, p. 276. This is the English translation of Kesselring's memoirs, *Soldat bis zum letzten Tag*, Bonn, 1953.)

rated first-class fighters. Now, having returned to his headquarters at Monte Soratte, Kesselring decided to postpone the counterattack against the British and Americans scheduled for March 29.[2] This secret decision meant—as only Kesselring could know at this moment—the imminent loss of Rome.*

If ever there was a time when there was no need to punish the Romans, it was now.

Soon the Field Marshal and his armies would leave the Eternal City and, eventually, Italy too. But his name, Kesselring, would stay behind forever, in ignominy.†

His chief of staff, General Westphal, now reported to him about the Via Rasella.[3] It was the general consensus among the Germans from here to Rastenberg, Westphal informed him, that the Romans had to be punished. The Fuehrer, he continued, was calling for a reprisal judged here to be too large. Kesselring was told that in his absence Mackensen had

* On Apr. 10 the plan was abandoned entirely. While the Allies were building up for their own offensive, planned for early May, Kesselring now slowly began to reduce his strength at Anzio. On May 11 the Allies launched their drive to break through Kesselring's weakened lines, and three weeks later Rome fell, as the Germans regrouped farther north. (Historical Division, Department of the Army, *Anzio Beachhead*, Washington: Government Printing Office, 1947, pp. 105–106.)

† In northern Italy, where Kesselring's armies were finally defeated on Apr. 25, 1945, there is a testament to the memory of the Nazi Field Marshal. Engraved on a large marble slab, it stands in the city of Cuneo. Its author was the late Professor Piero Calamandrei, rector of the University of Florence and founder of the political and cultural journal *Il Ponte*. It reads:

"You will have, Comrade Kesselring, the monument you demanded of us Italians. But we will decide of what stone it will be built. Not of the scorched rocks from the defenseless villages you outraged and destroyed. Not of the earth from the cemeteries where our young brothers lie in peace. Not with the inviolate snow of the mountains, where for two winters they challenged you. Not with the spring of these valleys that watched you flee. But only with tortured silence, which is harder than any boulder. Only with the rock of this vow, sworn by free men, who willingly gather, in dignity rather than in hatred, who decided to redeem the shame and the terror of your world: On these roads, if you will ever return, you will find us once again in our places, with the same pledge, in life and in death, a people close to one another, around the monument that is called, now and forever, Resistance."

provisionally set the ratio of Italians to be shot at ten to one, which was lower than the Fuehrer's demand. Mackensen had assigned Kappler to select persons for the reprisal among prisoners "worthy of death." This was where the matter stood, the chief of staff concluded.

Kesselring restrained his reaction. He rarely verbalized his thoughts. After some deliberation, he telephoned OKW and spoke directly to Jodl.[4]

The Field Marshal, as he said later, agreed with Jodl that he had to "achieve a deterrent effect." [5] But he sided with Mackensen with regard to the extent of the reprisal, especially since there were not nearly enough *Todeskandidaten* for executions on the scale the Fuehrer seemed to favor.[6]

Jodl asked if any of the partisans who had carried out the attack in Via Rasella had been captured. The answer was no.[7] The conversation dragged on and OKW finally deferred to the men in the field.

Kesselring believed that he had just engaged in "an honest effort to exercise humanity." [8] He now issued the following order to the Commander of the Fourteenth Army: "Kill ten Italians for every German. Carry out immediately." [9]

XXVII

THE EMBRACING arms of Saint Peter's Square seemed to widen, as the car belonging to SS Standartenfuehrer Dollmann moved along the Via della Conciliazione approach to Vatican City.

To the right of the beautiful piazza, beneath the windows of the Pope's apartment, Dollmann stopped the car and got out at the monastery of the Order of the Salvatorians. He raised the iron ring and let it fall on the forbidding door. The sound echoed through the cloisters. In a few moments a monk responded to his call. Dollmann was known to him; there was no need for either man to speak. The Salvatorian ushered the SS man across a barren expanse of stone floor. They climbed a single flight of stairs to the simple office of the Abbot General. Dollmann and the head of the religious order greeted one another as friends.[1] They spoke German.

The Abbot General was a white-haired man with strong, sharply defined features. He stood before an illuminated map of the world sparsely dotted in red where the rare Salvatorian missions existed. Beside the map was a color print of a mountain village in Germany. The Abbot General's name was Pankratius Pfeiffer. He had been a peasant boy raised in the Bavarian Alps. But now that he was sixty, his religious life had brought him to a principal role in the historic setting of occupied Rome.

Pfeiffer was known in both the Vatican and the Rome installations of the Wehrmacht and the SS as Padre Pancrazio. He was the Pope's personal liaison between the Holy See and the German occupiers.[2] The padre, through contacts dating back many years, had developed an excellent rapport with the Germans who were now in Rome.*

In the hard months since September, Padre Pancrazio had often received Dollmann at the monastery. Many times they had sat through the night in negotiations. These had resulted in the release of men held by the SS or even secret papal audiences for high Nazi officials.[3] Padre Pancrazio, in turn, was a frequent visitor to the headquarters of the Stadtkommandant and to Kappler's Gestapo prison in Via Tasso.† [4]

* Monsignor Alberto Giovannetti, a Vatican diplomat who wrote the semi-official history of the activities of the Holy See during the occupation period, records Pfeiffer's mission, referring specifically to his "good relations with Field Marshal Kesselring and General Mälzer." According to Giovannetti, "the good padre, sent by Pius XII, achieved many successes with his interventions during the occupation of Rome," at the German offices. (A. Giovannetti, *Roma città aperta,* Milan: Ancora, 1962, p. 256.)

† It was Padre Pancrazio who rushed to the German commandant of the city on the day of the roundup of the Jews of Rome with the historic mes-

Dollmann began now to speak of the Via Rasella. Padre Pancrazio had apparently already been informed of the attack, but he had not yet learned through his other Nazi sources of the reaction. Dollmann said that there would be a reprisal. He did not know at this time to what extent the military men would go. Certainly, however, it would be a bloodbath of sizable proportions. Dollmann then asked Padre Pancrazio to pass this information at once to the Pope. Pius, he believed, could "thwart or delay" the Germans who were crying for vengeance.[5]

Padre Pancrazio agreed to contact the Vatican immediately.[6]

Such a catastrophe, it would seem, could not be permitted to happen in the Holy City. As Bishop of Rome, the Pope was in the city of his own diocese; the Romans, in the language of the Church, were his children. If the reprisal could at least be delayed, the intervention of Dollmann, Möllhausen, perhaps Ambassador Rahn, and certainly the German Ambassador to the Holy See, Weizsäcker, might prevent this St. Bartholomew's night—if only by the simple passage of time in which the German wrath could exhaust itself in a relatively innocuous vacuum.

In the past hour or so, Dollmann went on to say, he had conceived in broad terms his own plan to punish the Romans. The people of the city could not, of course, go unpenalized. His plan was to be carried out on a political level, which would gain a propaganda victory for the Germans. He outlined this program to Padre Pancrazio.[7]

---

sage of Bishop Hudal, calling for "an immediate suspension of the arrests." Hudal, rector of the German Catholic Church in Rome, said that "otherwise I feel the Pope will be forced to take an open position against these actions, which will undoubtedly serve the enemies of Germany as a weapon against us Germans." In this case both Pfeiffer and Hudal had not first consulted the Pope. When Pius learned of what they had done, he did not support their initiative and did not protest the arrests, saying, in fact, nothing at all. (The text of Hudal's letter and the German telegrams to Berlin reporting the Vatican's reaction is in Friedländer, *op. cit.*, pp. 185–186. *Cf.* also R. Hochhuth, *The Deputy—Sidelights on History*, New York: Grove, 1964, pp. 326–327.)

He would, Dollmann said, have the families of the victims of Via Rasella flown immediately to Rome. A solemn funeral procession would be organized and the cortege would cross the city at noon on March 25. The widows and orphans would be at the side of the fallen men. There would be speeches by the clergy. All the bells of the 400 churches of Rome would ring. Special editions of the newspapers, with large photographs of the victims, would be distributed free.

At the stroke of noon, Dollmann continued, Field Marshal Kesselring would go on the radio. He would say that the Romans would have to pay for the financial support of the fatherless families. "This would be the last act of German clemency," Dollmann would have Kesselring declare. "In the future, every citizen, man or woman, will have the destiny of Rome in his own hands, capable of saving it by actively contributing to the timely exposure of assassins, for example, by denouncing them. Otherwise, in the event of other incidents, the entire responsibility will fall on Rome and its population." [8]

"Excellent!" said Padre Pancrazio when Dollmann completed his exposition. "I am certain that the Vatican will be very enthusiastic. And I will go at once to inform them." [9]

Before departing, they agreed to contact one another the following day, when Dollmann would have word from his superior, General Karl Wolff, and Padre Pancrazio from his, Pope Pius XII.[10]

XXVIII

IN THE *Hausgefängnis* in 145 Via Tasso, the prisoners of the Gestapo were ending their day abruptly. It was 8 P.M., the hour they were closed into the cells that had once been the rooms of a middle-class apartment house. For most of them this night of March 23 would pass quietly. The shrieks and the sobs of men and women, the sound of leather being lashed against a naked back would not be heard tonight. A few persons would be taken from their cells and interrogated, but with relative calm and only briefly.[1] This was unusual. It would not be unnoticed.

In cell number 13, on the third floor of the five-story building, Don Pietro Pappagallo sat quietly on his cot. An uneasiness had come over him that he could not explain.[2] Even now there was something in the air that would be sensed by many men in the hours that lay ahead.

Don Pietro, fifty-five, was a native of a town near the Adriatic called Terlizzi. He had been ordained in the Roman Catholic Church thirty years before, and he had come to Rome in the early 1930s. He served as a cardinal's secretary and, until his arrest seven weeks ago, had been a functionary of the Basilica Liberius at Santa Maria Maggiore–Saint Mary Major–the Romanesque church on the Esquiline hill which is the depository of a fragment of the manger of Jesus Christ. Don Pietro was also the chaplain of the sisters in the Bambin Gesù convent.

On his green card in the SD prisoners' registry on the first floor, the charges against him were scrawled in a certain hand: "Communist activities." [3] He was an expansive man with a thunderous, confident voice and a mind too artless for the clandestine life. Partisans, political suspects, and people without identity documents had come to his furnished room in Via Urbana. With false papers or hiding places, he had found them ways to survive.[4] A Communist student once said of Don Pietro: "If he were the friend of the King of the Universe, we would pray to Him." [5] In January a woman who called herself a *contessa* came to Don Pietro and said she needed help. He helped her and she betrayed him for a reward from Obersturmbannfuehrer Herbert Kappler.[6]

Now, almost every day, the nuns of the Bambin Gesù

would send Don Pietro a package of food or fresh linens. Everyone knew he was a "*buon' uomo*," they said, and the Pope, *Papa* Pacelli, would most surely have him freed.[7] This night, a fellow prisoner in his cell would remember, Don Pietro would sleep hard.[8]

In another cell in this squat modern building which until only recently had served as the cultural section of the German Embassy, a young man who was a soldier in the German Army thought more of food than of sleep. His name was Joseph Raider.[9] He was an Austrian who had deserted the Wehrmacht near Anzio and, with the help of a wealthy Italian family, had acquired forged documents. A former interpreter, he was able to assume an Italian identity. He tried to make his way to Rome, but was arrested in the countryside by a German patrol and taken to Via Tasso. There, despite his papers, he was charged with being an American spy in disguise and was beaten repeatedly when he denied it. The daily food ration of a piece of sour bread and some watery soup[10] had been cut in half for Raider. At the hands of the Gestapo, he had had the hairs of his moustache pulled out one by one. But he had not been interrogated for two days, and now he dared to believe this night that they wanted nothing further from him.

XXIX

By eight o'clock Obersturmbannfuehrer Kappler had returned to his headquarters in the south wing of the Via Tasso building. By using the heavily guarded entrance at number 155, he did not have to look at the ugly prison behind the façade of yellow marble. He had climbed the few steps of the entrance hall, passed the almost-life-size portrait of the

Fuehrer in uniform, and was now in his office. The room was the same shape and size as one of the larger cells on the prison side of the building. Unlike his prisoners, however, Kappler could look out on the pleasant *giardino alla francese* —a private garden for the men of the SS, with myrtle groves, tall cypresses around a pond, and a marble fountain. The men and women crowded into the cells could look only at the freshly laid pink bricks that sealed the windows to the outside.

Kappler was at work on the list ordered by General Mälzer. At a few minutes past 8 P.M., he received a telephone call that disturbed him somewhat.[1] It came from an officer named Major Böhm who was attached to the office of operations at Mälzer's command in Corso d'Italia. Böhm said he had just received an official order that "within twenty-four hours ten Italians for every German killed in today's attack are to be shot."[2]

Kappler, who was unaware of the conversations between Kesselring's headquarters and OKW in Rastenberg, was surprised that the executions were to be carried out in so short a time period. To him this seemed at variance with his interpretation of his telephone talk with Mackensen, the Commander of the Fourteenth Army.[3] He asked Böhm for the source of this order and was informed that it had been received not from Mackensen but from Kesselring.* [4]

Kappler then telephoned OBSW at Monte Soratte. He spoke to the officer on duty. He told him about Böhm's call and asked for a confirmation. The order was confirmed. To Kappler's question as to whether it had originated at OBSW,

* Kappler's situation is a good example of what Crankshaw calls "confusion as a fine art." The overlapping of authority and ill-defined powers were features of the Third Reich that were as calculated as involuntary. The Germans, says Crankshaw, "brought to a high pitch the art of evading responsibility by losing all sense of it in total confusion." (Crankshaw, *op. cit.*, p. 45.) This "art" would continue to be practiced in the following hours in Rome.

the duty officer replied: "No, it came from much higher up." [5]

To Kappler, that meant OKW or the Fuehrer himself.[6] At this point he began to regard with the highest importance his assignment to select the names of 280 persons "worthy of death." On going through his prisoner files, he very quickly reached the conclusion that even with Caruso's contribution, he would still not have enough people for his list. He had several ideas about how he might solve this problem, but it seemed necessary to him to report first to his immediate superior in the north. He put in a call to the headquarters in Verona of General Wilhelm Harster, *Befehlshaber der Sicherheitsdienst*—head of the SD in Italy. At 9 P.M. the call was put through. The conversation lasted three-quarters of an hour.[7]

Kappler began with a summary of what had happened in Via Rasella and what he had learned on the basis of his investigation. He then repeated the order he had received, as well as his earlier agreement with Mackensen to select *Todeskandidaten*. He complained that of the 290 prisoners under his jurisdiction not very many had actually been condemned to death or had been tried and sentenced to prison terms. Furthermore, said Kappler, fifty-seven of his detainees were under arrest only because they were Jews and they were awaiting deportation.[8]

Harster, a thickset, forty-year-old Bavarian, had already earned the reputation of being a very efficient hard worker. Until recently he had been head of the Nazi security police in Holland responsible for rounding up the Dutch Jews. One day, as a result of his work in the Netherlands, Major General Wilhelm Harster would be charged in a court of law with "the responsibility for the death of Anne Frank." [9]

Now he discussed with Kappler the various possibilities of completing the list. About the persons arrested in Via Rasella, Kappler reported that only a very few had been in possession of evidence—such as a red flag and Communist propaganda leaflets—that might merit conviction by a German military tribunal. It was soon clear that if Kappler were to limit himself merely to *Todeskandidaten* it would be impossible for him to complete his assignment. According to Kappler, his superior at this point solved the dilemma, saying, "What do you want to do? If you can't reach the right figure, take as many Jews as you need. The important thing is to complete the list." [10]

Following his long talk with Harster, Kappler called in his men and put them to work at his side. He telephoned the presiding justice of the German Military Tribunal in Rome and asked for authorization to include in his list the persons condemned to death by the Tribunal, as well as those awaiting trial. He also asked the German judge's permission to take persons tried on charges that might have brought the death penalty but due to attenuating circumstances had been limited to only a prison term.[11]

The president of the Tribunal, now passing judgment in this city that 2,000 years before had given Western civilization many of its concepts of law and justice, immediately authorized the inclusion on the death list of the first two categories.[12] He could not, he said, take responsibility for turning over the prisoners in the third group. He told Kappler that this authority would have to come from the Chief Justice, who was attached to Kesselring's command. Kappler made the request. Permission was granted.[13]

Kappler now left the Via Tasso. He crossed the quiet, blacked-out city to the Viminale barracks, where the people arrested in Via Rasella were being held. The list of their names had come to his desk and he wanted to check its accuracy personally. From the preliminary investigation made by his men, it seemed to him that some of those arrested were potential *Todeskandidaten*.[14]

XXX

In the Villa Orsoline, at the site in the north of Italy called X, Benito Mussolini, celebrating twenty-five years of fascism, was unexpectedly faced with a choice between two political evils.

He had received Chief Salerno's telegram from Rome reporting the attack in Via Rasella. A subsequent message told of the order for the German reprisal.[1] Now, in the waning hours of this Fascist holiday, the decision either to stop it or not had been thrust into the hands of the Duce: the man who Hitler had only recently declared was Italy's "greatest son . . . since the fall of the ancient world." [2]

For the Duce, to protest would mean to defy the will of the German ally, the guardian of his weakened regime. To be a spectator at the slaughter of his countrymen by a foreign power on Italian soil would mean that he could never again pretend to be anything more than a *fantoccio*—a puppet—dangling on the German strings.

For the moment he did nothing. According to his private secretary, Giovanni Dolfin, he was "awaiting more details" from Minister Buffarini-Guidi.[3]

The Germans are furious, Mussolini told his secretary that evening. The angriest of them all, he said, is Karl Wolff.[4]

General Karl Wolff held absolute police power in occupied Italy. He would soon be heard from in Rome.

XXXI

At 9:40 p.m., in the Pensione d'Oltremare, Lieutenant Giglio was taken out and beaten by Koch and his men for the fifth time since his arrest.[1] Twenty minutes later he stumbled back into his cell, escorted by Walter Di Franco. His face was cut and distorted. He fell on his cot and nervously wiped away the blood with a corner of the bedsheet. Di Franco suddenly began to punch Giglio repeatedly in the jaw. The young lieutenant, too weak to resist, murmured faintly. In his delirium he called for the help of his mother. Di Franco leaned over the cot and raised Giglio to a standing position. He straightened his sagging victim and with the full weight of his body, kicked Giglio in the testicles.[2]

"*Mamma, Mamma mia*," he cried, "they've killed me!"[3]

Di Franco once again pulled him upright. He drove his foot between Giglio's kidney and base of his spine. Giglio sank to the floor. The blood drained from his pulpy face. His orderly, Giovanni Scottu, helped him onto the cot and he dabbed his lips and brow with something wet. Di Franco and a guard began now to kick Scottu and they threw a bucket of water into his face. They then dragged him off to the interrogation room. He returned to the cell at 11 P.M. Giglio, it seemed to Scottu, was hovering between life and death.[4]

XXXII

At via Tasso, Herbert Kappler had returned from the Viminale barracks with ten more names for his list. Among them were the two brothers Umberto and Angelo Pignotti, who ran the handbag shop in Via Quattro Fontane, and their friend the clerk from the Banca d'Italia. As for those Kappler did not include, he had told them they would soon be released.

In this last hour of March 23, 1944, Kappler knew he would have to spend the rest of the night at work in his office. The number of German dead had risen from twenty-eight to thirty-two. "In order to keep to the proportion,"

Kappler later recounted, "320 men 'worthy of death' were needed. . . . The moment arrived when it occurred to me that even if I had all the Jews in the cells of Via Tasso killed, I would not have reached the necessary number." [1]

He decided, however, to deal with this problem in the morning, after he had gone as far as he could with the files he had before him.

That night, Consul Möllhausen went to Via Tasso. He had learned that Kappler had been ordered to draw up the list for the reprisal. He found his colleague leaning over his desk, immersed in his work. The two Germans were alone in the stillness of Kappler's office.[2]

"I do not have to tell you," said Möllhausen, "how removed I am from any thought of aiding or favoring the enemy. We are at war and I do not forget it. But what you are about to do goes beyond war and the Fatherland . . ."

"All those who will be selected," Kappler replied, "will be, or already have been, sentenced to death. Or else they are guilty to the extent of being *Todeskandidaten* . . ." [3]

"Listen, Kappler, if I were in your place my conscience would tremble. I do not know how I would act. But I certainly would feel myself at a decisive turn in my life. Kappler, remember that one day you, too, will be called to account before the tribunal of God." [4]

"Möllhausen, I can only promise you I will do what I am able to do. And this is what it is: For every name that I write, I will think three times." [5]

XXXIII

Near midnight, GAP commander Salinari sat by the radio in his apartment, listening for news.[1] On the BBC program from

London there was a report that Italian Army units had attacked German troops in Yugoslavia.[2] At 11:45 a program of Neapolitan songs had begun on Radio Rome, which would end its broadcast day at twelve o'clock. About the Via Rasella, nothing had been said—nor would be.

In another part of the city, in the Via Antonio Gallonio home of the Jewish woman who was hiding two *partigiani*, Carla Capponi was also at the radio. She wondered why it had been silent about the eventful day.[3] Rosario Bentivegna was playing chess with the woman's fourteen-year-old boy. It was his way of pretending for a while that these were other times.[4]

In Via Rasella, with its buildings gun-scarred, sacked, and emptied of nearly all their residents, the street was quieter, more peaceful than it had ever been. Caruso's men had come and gone in the night. They had stripped the homes almost bare.

Before the day ended, a man cut this date into the wall of his cell in Via Tasso. He was a general in the Italian Air Force. He had fought the German entry into Rome and had joined the armed Resistance when the city was occupied. Tonight, he was in solitary confinement.

For Sabato Martelli Castaldi, in the long and narrow cell number 3, this had been his sixty-sixth day in Kappler's prison.[5] On the forty-seventh he had written a message to his wife which had been smuggled out and brought to her. He had set down on a scrap of paper:

> I think about the night they gave me twenty-four lashes on the soles of my feet . . . I did not give them the satisfaction of a single cry, except on the twenty-fourth I responded with a "raspberry" that left those three scoundrels looking like three authentic idiots. (That raspberry on the twenty-fourth blow was an epic! It shook the Via Tasso

and the flogger's whip dropped from his hands. What laughter! Nevertheless it cost me a delayed outburst of punches.) What is worst here is the lack of air. I eat very little, otherwise I would be ill and I would lose the clarity of mind and spirit which is needed here at every moment.[6]

Martelli Castaldi, age forty-seven, added March 23 to a ladder of lines chiseled somehow into the plaster wall. He had marked his calendar for the last time.[7]

XXXIV

In the meantime, an urgent message had arrived at Kappler's office. It came from Fasano on Lake Garda, headquarters of the Higher SS and Polizeifuehrer for Italy.

Kappler, the telegram stated, was to abstain from any action until the arrival of General Karl Wolff. He was flying to Rome the following day. Dollmann was to be told to meet him at the Viterbo airport at 3 P.M. on the 24th and to arrange an immediate meeting with Field Marshal Kesselring at Monte Soratte.[1]

In the late afternoon, tall, blond, strikingly handsome Karl Frederick Wolff had held a long telephone conversation with Reichsfuehrer Himmler. They had discussed the Via Rasella incident. Wolff had formerly served as Himmler's chief of staff and later as his liaison with Hitler. Exactly one year earlier Wolff had personally arranged the delivery of 300,000 Jews to the gas chambers.[2] Now he would fly south to take charge of the hostile situation in Rome.

He would carry with him a decision reached that afternoon between Himmler and himself—the deportation of virtually the entire adult male population of Rome.[3]

PART THREE

The Massacre in the Caves of Ardeatine

March 24, 1944

"Death is ugly for whoever fears it."

—Scratched into the wall of solitary-confinement cell number 3 in the Via Tasso Gestapo prison[1]

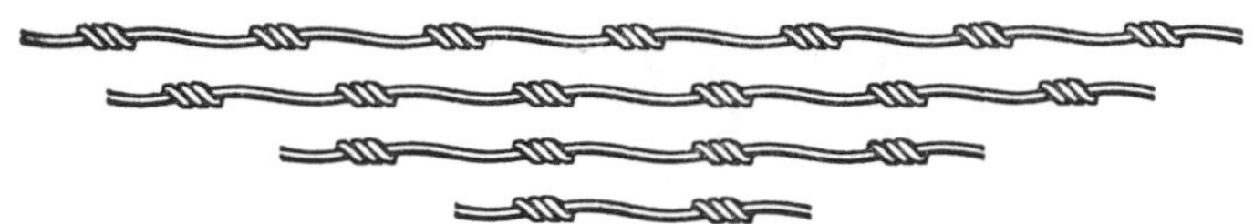

I

In the solitude of his office in Via Tasso, Herbert Kappler worked through the night. The silence of the first hours of the new day was broken only by an occasional sound of the war at the beachhead and the scratching of his pen.

The message from General Wolff, at least for the moment, had changed nothing. Unless there were further word from OKW, Wolff's message could not countermand the Fuehrer's order, under which Kappler was busily engaged. A copy of the telegram had been dispatched to Dollmann and now, as far as Kappler was concerned, it was temporarily put out of mind.[1] Whatever Wolff was planning, only time would reveal.

The SD chief was encountering great difficulty in compiling the list of the 320. As for those already condemned to death or prison sentences, he did not feel it necessary to "think three times" before including them. "I trusted myself to the responsibility of the judges," Kappler later said.[2]

But in the category of persons who had actually been convicted and had received the death penalty, Kappler had only three men.[3]

They were, of course, innocent of any crime and guilty only of fighting for the liberation of Rome from the men who were about to destroy them. They were Manlio Bordoni, of the Action Party; Carlo Lucchetti, a partisan of the *Bandiera Rossa;* and Gioacchino Gesmundo, a Communist professor-turned-saboteur, who was arrested and condemned by the

German Tribunal for having been found in possession of two sacks of four-pointed nails.* [4]

In the second category—persons who had been tried and sentenced to prison—Kappler could find only sixteen names.[5] Though their terms ranged from but one to fifteen years, he considered them now "worthy of death." He included all in the list. Among them were an architect, two brothers in their thirties, a student, a carpenter, and an opera singer.

Nor was there any need to think more than once about the fifty-seven Jews. "It was better," it seemed to Kappler, "to place Jews on the list rather than Italians, whose guilt was more difficult to demonstrate." [6]

A recount revealed that at this point there were actually sixty-five Jews available to Kappler.† He included all. Among them were five members of the Di Consiglio family—two teen-age brothers, their grandfather, and their father and his brother; Attilio and his fifteen-year-old son Michele Di Veroli; Pacifico and his son Angelo Sonnino—in all, multiple members of thirteen families.

Added to the ten names he had collected among the Via Rasella detainees, Kappler now had ninety-four candidates for death.

He began to pore over the files of men awaiting trial under his jurisdiction and under the Feldgericht's. He made his selections, added the names to his list, and then specified the crimes: *Jude*, or *Spionage*, or *Kommunismus*.

Among them were Aldo Finzi, the former Fascist Undersecretary of Interior who once had given a bouquet of flowers to Donna Rachele; General Sabato Martelli Castaldi, who had jeered his torturers in Via Tasso; Joseph Raider, the deserter from the German Army; and Don Pietro Pappagallo,

* Strewn on the roads, these were highly effective in blocking the German supply lines to Cassino and Anzio.

† There were several Jews arrested for reasons other than their religion, such as partisan activity and anti-Fascist political crimes. They were dealt with by Kappler under other categories.

chaplain of the sisters of Bambin Gesù. The priest's crime, as Kappler later put it, was his being "an active associate of a group of Communist terrorists."[7]

The time was about 2 A.M. On the prison side of the Via Tasso an old and distinguished Italian lawyer lay awake on a square mat in cell number 7. He was trying to decipher the scramble of sounds he heard outside his cell.[8] His name was Placido Martini, a native of Latium. He had always been an anti-Fascist. After September 8 he had founded the liberal movement *Unione della Democrazia Italiana* and helped organize partisan bands to fight the Germans in the Castelli Romani. He had been captured in January; the sixty-four-year-old *avvocato* at Via Tasso had been the victim of one hundred lashes on the soles of his feet.[9]

This night he was unable to sleep. A few minutes before, he had heard the Gestapo guards open cell number 8 and take one of the men out for interrogation. He had recognized the voice of General Dardano Fenulli, a fellow anti-Fascist who had fought the Germans at the pyramid and had joined the monarchist *Fronte Militare Clandestino della Resistenza* (FMCR). The guards had taken some other men, too, but Martini had not been able to determine who they were. Now, scarcely five minutes later, they were all returned to their cells. The old *avvocato* wondered. What did it all mean?

Kappler added General Fenulli's name to the list, as well as *Avvocato* Martini's. He also included the names of other FMCR men. He had been holding them since their arrest following the Anzio invasion. At that time, Kappler, in a highly successful series of raids, had virtually crushed the monarchist Resistance Front and the intelligence service, *Centro X*. He had captured their leaders, including the bold organizer Colonel Giuseppe Cordero Lanza di Montezemolo. Kappler considered Montezemolo one of his most dangerous prisoners. He kept the colonel in isolation in cell number 1, a sealed, totally dark room which had been a modern tiled kitchen. Montezemolo had been tortured repeatedly. The last time a doctor had seen him he was running a very high fever.[10] He too was placed on the list.

With the inclusion of names from these categories, Kappler by 3 A.M. had reached a figure of 269 *Todeskandidaten*—fifty-one short of the total needed. He had run out of candidates. Of the prisoners in his care, there was but a single name remaining whom he considered worthy of death. It was Paolo Petrucci, the Allied espionage agent who under the name of Pietro Paolucci had been acquitted two days earlier by the *Feldgericht* and absolved of all charges. Kappler added his name anyway. Now he could go no further. The balance of fifty persons would have to come from the Italian police.

Continuing to reexamine his list of 270 names, the Gestapo colonel decided to wait until daybreak before contacting the Fascists. If the Fuehrer's order to kill ten for one "within twenty-four hours" had to be interpreted literally, there would still be ample time for him to complete his part, supplying the *Todeskandidaten.*

He did not know what would happen then, but the inevitable climax seemed to him assured by the momentum that had already been generated. Kappler later remembered: "At a certain moment during the night, I said, 'By now the wheels are turning by themselves . . .' "[11] They could be stopped only by the unexpected and the improbable.

II

THE SUN rose in Rome on March 24, 1944, at approximately 6 A.M. It was Friday, another beautiful morning. The curfew was lifting and, occupied or not, the city began to stir, springing gloriously alive. The stone and memory of twenty-seven centuries were beyond the grasp of the German hand. They would survive this tragic day.

In cell number 13 of the Via Tasso *Hausgefängnis*, Don Pietro Pappagallo awoke at dawn from a restless sleep. He was disturbed. He prayed and he meditated much longer than he usually did.[1] At seven o'clock the guards threw open the doors of the cells. They shouted the imperious "*Aufstehen!*" The prisoners, one by one, went to the toilet. Each man and woman was allowed about two minutes and, upon request only, was given two or three sheets of six-by-eight-inch cut newspaper. Immediately afterward they were returned to their cells. There they scrubbed the floors and made the beds. Then they waited for the day's single ration of food to be brought in metal cans from the kitchens of Regina Coeli.

In one of the prison cells, ten Jews, all of whom were men, were getting acquainted with this routine. They had been arrested that morning and brought directly to Via Tasso.[2]

The sun was not yet high enough to stream through the windows of Kappler's office at the south end of the building. But it was time now to pursue the Fascist police. Unable to speak directly with Questore Caruso at this hour, he reached by telephone the commissar of the Public Security office, Raffaele Alianello.

Kappler said that he had been up all night and had managed to compile a list of 270 "guilty individuals."[3]

This, he said, had required a "maximum effort"[4] since he had needed the cooperation of the *Feldgericht*, which permitted him to include persons he normally would have no right to take. Since he had succeeded in this, the Italians would now have to give him only fifty persons, instead of the eighty he had originally asked for. If possible, they should be political criminals.

Kappler concluded that he was expecting Alianello to handle this matter with the greatest urgency. He told the commissar to get in touch with deputy chief of the state police, Cerruti, in order that Caruso be directed as to what had to be done.

Alianello lost little time in carrying out Kappler's request. In a while the Obersturmbannfuehrer received a call from Cerruti. Cerruti said that Questore Caruso would come to Kappler's office early that morning. They would then be able to reach an agreement about the time and place for the delivery of fifty men.[5]

Kappler then telephoned Pietro Koch in the Pensione d'Oltremare. He told him to draw up a list of as many names as he could from among the men he held in his own prison and to come to his office for a meeting with Caruso. Koch agreed.[6]

III

PIETRO CARUSO drove to the Excelsior in Via Veneto at about eight o'clock. The S-shaped street, which lay outside the commercial center, was still in early-morning silence. In the lobby of the great hotel, the sounds had not yet risen above a whisper.

Caruso asked for Minister of Interior Buffarini-Guidi. The clerk rang the suite and was informed that *sua eccelenza* was still asleep. Caruso insisted on seeing him and finally was shown into Buffarini's room. Awakened, he was still in bed, propped in a sitting position against some pillows.[1]

The Questore reported to Buffarini that Kappler had asked him to deliver a number of men to be shot in reprisal for the attack in Via Rasella. First he had asked for eighty, said Caruso, now he wanted fifty.

"I defer to you, your excellency," Caruso said.[2] He hoped that Buffarini would take charge of the matter and deal directly with Kappler.

The Minister of Interior could have done much more than that. He was influential with General Wolff and, further, could have dealt directly with his personal friend, Reichsfuehrer Himmler himself. He could have asked Mussolini to speak to Hitler. Apparently, however, Buffarini had already telephoned the Duce, who the night before had been "awaiting more details" from his minister.

It would seem that having discussed the matter, the Duce had reached his decision before retiring some hours previously.

Now, Buffarini-Guidi replied to Caruso, "What can *I* do?" he asked. "You must give them to him. Otherwise who knows what will happen. Yes, yes, give them to him." [3]

Caruso felt relieved. He regarded this as an order.[4]

Having returned to Police Headquarters, Caruso received a telephone call from Kappler.[5] The German reminded him that he was expecting the delivery of political prisoners and that he was to come to his office this morning.

"Koch will give me his list, and you will complete it," Kappler said, speaking in Italian.

"I don't have as many men in my prison as you need," Caruso replied, referring to the request that they be persons held for political crimes.

Kappler said, "Then give us some Jews." [6]

Caruso now called one of his aides in the *Ufficio di Polizia* and explained the situation. He told him to prepare a preliminary list. He then went to Via Tasso.

When he arrived, at 9:45, Caruso was brought into Kappler's office immediately. Pietro Koch was already there. Koch's list was complete, although it was far less than fifty. Kappler told the two Fascists to work out the details between themselves, but he needed the full list of fifty no later than 1 P.M.[7] He would inform them as to where and when the men were to be physically handed over to the Germans. At this moment Kappler had no notion how and by whom the executions would be carried out. His only concern was, as ordered, to produce the 320 men who, in his judgment, deserved to die.

Caruso and Koch departed. Together they went to Police Headquarters to undertake the same task at which Kappler had spent the entire night. The Italians would, however, face difficulties unencountered by the German. In any case, at least one name, selected by Koch, was already included: Lieutenant Maurizio Giglio.

IV

IN AN austere little room of the Saint John in Lateran basilica, seat of Pope Pius' bishopric, the head of the Roman Resistance wrote his letter of resignation.[1]

When he had returned to San Giovanni last night, Ivanoe Bonomi had found Socialist Pietro Nenni in hiding there, too. To Nenni's surprise, he told him of his intention to quit. It was not, he said, an unconsidered decision, but one that had long been studied. He was not responsive to Nenni's pleas that he change his mind. Now the old politician had verbally informed all of the delegates to the CLN. There remained this morning only the historical task of putting his resignation on paper.

As a group of young seminarians convened in the papal cathedral, Bonomi recorded the reasons for his self-dismissal. The "extremist interpretations" by the Socialists and the Actionists of previous CLN resolutions to assume full powers and exclude the monarchy could "naturally not be shared by those parties who had in October accepted a formula which represented the last concession to contrary opinion, and who therefore did not intend to go any further."[2] In view of the war situation, it was the duty of all Italians to delay these questions, and now that the Communists apparently supported the other left-wing parties, Bonomi could not go on.

Bonomi's consciousness of the gravity of his resignation emerged from the solemn tone of his words. His act would formalize the end to anti-Fascist unity and dissipate the active fight against the enemy. To the extent that it would isolate the left and weaken the armed Resistance, with its goal of popular insurrection, Bonomi's decision to defend the monarchy was supported by elements of the right and by the Church. But the parties of the left could have only themselves to blame if they permitted themselves to be detached from the strong anti-Fascist sentiment of the people to be set adrift on a flimsy raft of technical issues. Their intransigence could be justified only if they intended to stand alone, attempting to rally public opinion to their side, defy the Allies, and, if need be, fight for a Socialist Italy. This none of the left-wing parties was prepared to do.

"I believe that the country must come before party," Bonomi said in concluding his letter to CLN delegates. "This is the disagreement and the substance of why, in resigning as President of the Committee, I give you the freedom of going your way and take to myself the freedom to serve my country according to the dictates of my conscience." [3]

V

AT NOON Kappler went to the Corso d'Italia headquarters of General Mälzer. The Stadtkommandant had summoned him earlier that morning for a conference at his office.[1]

Lest there be any confusion, Mälzer began by telling Kappler that the order had definitely come from Hitler. At this point Major Hellmuth Dobbrick, commander of the 3rd

Bozen Battalion, entered the room. Since it had been his formation that had been destroyed in Via Rasella, he also had been sent for by the general.

Kappler informed them now that with the addition of fifty names from Questore Caruso, the list would be complete by one o'clock this afternoon. He then reported in detail on how he had compiled the list, what criteria he had used, and how he had solved the many problems that had arisen in the past fifteen hours or so.

General Mälzer, following Kappler's oral report, turned to Dobbrick. He said that it was now up to him, as *Kommandeur* of the 3rd Battalion, to avenge his men. Dobbrick, and the troops of the Bozen Battalion, were thus ordered to execute the 320 men on Kappler's list. It had to be done immediately.

Major Dobbrick refused.[2]

He adduced a long list of disconnected and transparent arguments, the least plausible of which appeared to be that his men were untrained in the use of weapons and that they were superstitious. It was clear to Mälzer and Kappler that the major had no interest in revenge and, presumably, little faith in the legality of the Fuehrer's order. Two days later, Dobbrick's insubordination would be reported to General Wolff in an official complaint by Kappler.* [3] But there was no time for that now. An executioner had to be found.

Mälzer now telephoned headquarters of the Fourteenth Army and spoke with Mackensen's chief of staff, Colonel Wolfgang Hauser. He requested that a detachment of soldiers be made available at once to carry out the executions.

Colonel Hauser, who would soon be promoted to general, refused.[4]

His reason was more tenable than Dobbrick's and he spoke with the assurance of knowing he would not be challenged.

* No formal action was taken against Dobbrick. He continued to head the 3rd Bozen Battalion, which later withdrew to northern Italy, where the antipartisan operations continued.

He said, "It was the police who were struck, it is the police who must make the expiation." [5]

When Mälzer hung up, he repeated what Hauser had said. He now looked at the Gestapo officer. "It's up to you, Kappler," he said.[6]

Kappler hesitated. He finally agreed and said he would turn the assignment over to his men.

No, Mälzer replied. As the commandant of the SD in Rome, he said, it was Kappler's duty to set an example. This was an order.[7]

For Kappler this order was not without a touch of irony. When he had wanted to kill—five times since the outbreak of the war he had asked to be shipped to the front as a soldier—the orders had been otherwise. Now, if he sought one, there seemed to be no way out. Until this moment, despite his years of police work in the Gestapo, he had never by his own hands killed anyone. But he could think of neither reason nor argument why he should not execute 320 human beings.

VI

WHEN KAPPLER returned to his office in Via Tasso, he called an immediate meeting of the twelve officers in his command. He told them that "within a few hours 320 persons would have to killed." [1]

All men under him who were of German nationality, he said, officers, noncommissioned officers, and soldiers, had to participate in the executions. The officers had to set an example, he continued. They must be the first to shoot. Anyone who refused would be brought up on charges before the Tribunal of the SS.

"Everyone," Kappler later recalled, "was in agreement with me that for the maintenance of discipline it was indispensable that the commandants take part in the operation at least once, as a kind of 'symbolic necessity.' "[2]

They began now to discuss the matter, seeking to determine the most effective and economical way to bring the massacre to its conclusion in the shortest possible time.

Speed was essential for two reasons: The Fuehrer's order had designated that the killings had to be completed in twenty-four hours; seventeen hours had already been spent. More important was the fear that if the people of Rome were to learn that a massacre was being committed in their streets, no one could gauge the intensity of their reaction. The partisans might mobilize a lightning attack. The entire city might explode. For reasons of security the killings had to be kept secret until they were complete.[3]

The first problem was the number of men under Kappler's command who would be available for the executions. Including himself, there were at this date 74 men of German nationality attached to the SD in Rome—Kappler, his 12 officers, 60 NCOs, and one soldier.

Since this was "much less than the number who had to be shot," Kappler would remember, "I calculated the number of minutes necessary for the killing of each of the 320. I had the arms and ammunition computed. I figured the total amount of time I had. I divided my men into small platoons, which would function alternately. I ordered that each man shoot only one shot. I specified that the bullet enter the victim's brain from the cerebellum, in order that there be no wasted firing and that death be effected instantaneously." [4]

To further conserve time and ammunition, every shot was to be fired "at the closest possible range," from low to high, if possible.[5] However, Kappler said, the barrel of the gun was not be placed in actual contact with the neck of the victim. To do otherwise would slow down the process, since the condemned man would have to present his head to the executioner in a fixed position.

Kappler assigned Captain Kurt Schutz to command the operations and Captain Erich Priebke to take charge of being certain that everyone on the list was actually executed.

The question now arose as to the site of the killings. Executions were usually carried out at Forte Bravetta, a medieval military compound on Via Aurelia, the westward road to the sea. But according to Kappler, this could not be used "because Italian custom required that every victim be tied to a chair and we did not have the time for all these formalities." [6] In outdoor shootings of this type, it would not be easy to remove so many bodies. To construct a burial ground, given these circumstances, seemed to Kappler out of the question. In discussing this crucial point, Kappler was struck by the idea of using a cavern or a grotto.

"I thought of creating a kind of large, natural death chamber," he said later.[7]

One of his officers, Captain Köhler, said he knew of such a place not very far from Via Tasso, about two miles south. It was a network of tunnels in Via Ardeatina, among the Christian catacombs. Its existence had become known to the Germans only recently. An Italian Army regiment, which after September 8 had gone over to the Resistance, had hidden its vehicles in the caves. But an informer had reported this to the occupiers.[8]

Kappler told Captain Köhler to go at once to the site with some engineers. He was to investigate the feasibility of using these caves with a view, said Kappler, toward having them "transformed into a sepulchral chamber by closing the entrances." [9]

Before the meeting ended, Kappler made a further decision not to provide religious assistance to the condemned men, most of whom were Catholics. "I did not have a chaplain come along because I knew that condemned men usually stall for time in speaking with a priest. And I could not afford more than one minute for each man." [10]

The meeting was adjourned. Kappler instructed Schutz to attend to the details while they waited for Köhler to return from his inspection in Via Ardeatina. He then went down to the street level of the Via Tasso building. He noted that the time was 1 P.M. He walked into the mess hall.[11]

Kappler was too busy and nervous to eat. He gathered his NCOs, who were having their lunch. He went over with them what had been decided at the meeting with his officers and informed them that they would have to "participate in the action." [12] He spoke calmly but was nevertheless very keenly aware of the macabreness of what had to be done and the effect such an assignment might have on his men. He addressed some words of encouragement to them, and in his mind he wondered how he might lighten their burden at the time of the actual executions. But as yet he said nothing of that.

Suddenly Captain Schutz appeared in the mess hall. He had important news. As a result of yesterday's attack in Via Rasella, he informed his chief, another German of the 11th Company had died a few minutes ago. The death toll had climbed to thirty-three.[13]

Kappler thought a moment. "I asked myself how I could increase the list." [14] Then he remembered that a few hours earlier Schutz had told him about the ten Jews who had been arrested and brought into Via Tasso that morning. He felt it his duty to adhere to the ratio set by the Fuehrer's order. He told Schutz to include the ten Jews on the list.[15]

In the meantime Captain Köhler returned from the caves and was now in the mess hall waiting to report to Kappler. After the Obersturmbannfuehrer had dispatched Schutz once again, Köhler declared that "the officer of the engineers who went to the place feels it is technically simple to seal off the entrance to the caves." [16]

Kappler was pleased. He sent for his chauffeur, an Italian

named Massimo Parris. He decided to go with Köhler to see with his own eyes where the executions—now to number 330—would take place.

VII

MESS ON the prison side of the Via Tasso—for which there was no fixed hour—was portioned out this day a little past 1 P.M. The *minestraccia* consisted of cabbage cores and rotten potatoes served in the water they had been boiled in. Two little rolls made from rancid dough were also included in the daily ration.

Some of the prisoners had noticed that while the food was being distributed the guards had appeared more subdued than usual. One of the men being held on the third floor noted that they had "the air of people who were frightened and even the Hauptscharfuehrer [warrant officer] on duty was not screaming obsessively, as he normally did. He went from cell to cell with a funereal manner about him." [1]

In cell number 7, Luigi Garrone, a fifty-eight-year-old journalist accused of espionage, remarked about this strange atmosphere to his fellow inmates. After seeing the warrant officer, he was convinced something must have happened.

"That's nothing new," one of the prisoners remarked to Garrone. "He's quiet because he has a hangover. Whenever he drinks too much, he gets that way." [2]

Now that the meal had been served, there was nothing to do except wait until sometime after five o'clock, when they would be allowed to make their second and final of the daily visits to the toilet.

In cell number 7, where the old lawyer *Avvocato* Martini was held, some of the men were sleeping and some paced nervously from one wall to another. This cell was known among the prisoners as "*La Settima*"—"The Seventh." It had a certain notoriety because of its approximation to a room on the other side of the building where SS men received their women and sometimes organized orgies. In *La Settima* one could hear the sounds of these bacchanalia, as well as the cries that came from the room where prisoners were tortured. One night a man in this cell counted the cracks of 162 lashes of the whip. Then he covered his ears.

Now, at some minutes past one o'clock, *Avvocato* Martini was seated on his mat, his head buried in his lap. Suddenly he looked up and turned to the journalist Garrone. "I wish I knew what happened last night," he said. "They took General Fenulli out of cell number 8 and some others from other cells. It seems they were interrogated but it lasted only about five minutes."

Garrone did not know what to say, but another man, whose name was Carlo Camisotti, replied, "Maybe they just needed a few details about something or other." [3]

Camisotti, a forty-one-year-old laborer, was recovering from wounds he had received in an interrogation a few nights earlier. His body, from his neck to his thighs, was striped with about forty welts an inch and a half in width. Without revealing the names of his comrades, he had confessed to partisan activities. Now, he was expecting to be transferred, as was customary, to Regina Coeli, where conditions were less stringent, to be formally charged and eventually tried.

A few silent minutes went by. Then the men in *La Settima* became aware of a great deal of movement in the corridor. The door was opened and one of Kappler's men from the registry office stood on the threshold.

"Shamishotti!" he cried, pronouncing the name incorrectly.

The partisan thought he was going to be sent to Regina Coeli. He arose and began to collect his things, including a piece of bread that he had left in the mess tray. The guard stopped him. "*Los, los!*" he shouted, grabbing the Italian by the arm and shoving him outside.[4]

"Martini!" the SD man now called. The lawyer, confused and suspicious, followed the German's command.[5]

"Chiricozzi!"

Aldo Chiricozzi was sleeping. He was eighteen years old and had worked as a clerk. He had already been interrogated and he too was looking forward to being transferred to Regina Coeli, where the food was better and one was allowed to smoke, write a letter, and read a book. He leaped to his feet, full of enthusiasm, and went out with the others into the hall.[6]

The door to *La Settima* was closed now and locked. Those who remained could still hear names being called in other cells on the floor.

"Fenulli! *Los, los!* . . . Bernardini! *Los, los, los!* . . . Don't take anything. We'll take care of your belongings . . ."[7]

On other floors of the *Hausgefängnis* the same scene was being enacted. In cell number 13, Don Pietro Pappagallo was called by a guard. He had spent the entire morning in prayer. At one o'clock he had not touched his food, and only at the insistence of his cellmates did he manage a few bites. When he heard his name, he turned solemnly to his comrades and to each of them he said, "*Addio.*" To one of the men in 13 it seemed that Don Pietro sensed this was the end.[8]

In the hall, the priest stood beside Joseph Raider. The Austrian deserter had been taken from another cell on the fourth floor. They exchanged a few words and Don Pietro blessed the young man, which provoked the laughter of two German guards.[9]

One of Kappler's NCOs, named Krausnitzer, came by. He was carrying lengths of rope, each about fifteen inches long and a half inch in diameter. He tied the prisoners' hands behind their backs. The dorsal side of the wrists were linked together, which made the bond more constricting. Now the men were led downstairs to the street.

In cell number 7 one of the remaining prisoners had his eye against the peephole. He watched the men who had been called prepare to leave. Suddenly, he turned to his comrades. There was a look of alarm in his eyes. "They sure are taking a lot of them!" he said.[10]

VIII

AT A few minutes before 2 P.M. Kappler was ready to depart for his inspection of the caves in Via Ardeatina. He went out on the street in front of the Gestapo headquarters with Captain Köhler. At the north end of the building he saw Captain Schutz, who was directing the prisoners coming out of the entrance at number 145. There were several vehicles parked at the curb—unmarked, canvas-covered trucks which were used by the Germans for deliveries of meat. These would not be adequate. They would have to use other trucks, too, which were similar in capacity but were painted with the emblem of the Red Cross.[1]

Kappler noted that the prisoners' hands were tied behind their backs. He went up to Schutz and asked him why he had done that.

It was to prevent any escape attempts, said the captain.

Had the victims been told of their fate? Kappler wanted to know.

Schutz replied that at first he was going to tell them, but then he decided against it. He was afraid, he said, that as they drove through Rome toward the caves the prisoners would cry out that they were being taken away to be shot. This might bring on spontaneous attacks against the trucks by the people, he said.[2]

Kappler agreed. "Our escort was insufficient," he would recall.[3] It would be unable to deal with any attack by the population to liberate the prisoners from the trucks.

Kappler and Köhler drove off to the caves now, while the prisoners were still filing out of the building—most of them wondering what this highly irregular activity was all about.

Moving south from Via Tasso, Kappler's car passed through the Roman wall at the gate of Porta San Sebastiano, where the Appian Way begins. About 2,000 feet down the ancient route there is a fork in the road. Here the Apostle Peter is said to have stood before a vision of Jesus Christ and asked, "*Domine, quo vadis?*" A little church marks the sacred place. To the left the Appian Way continues on between the cypresses and the asphodels to the Adriatic and the outposts of Imperial Rome. Kappler's driver was instructed to go to the right, along Via Ardeatina, another Imperial road, twenty-four Roman miles from the old port town of Ardea.

Another 2,000 feet sloping southward on the downgrade, the Ardeatine caves lay just off the right side of the road. Kappler turned into the gravel-covered clearing before the entrances. Situated between the catacombs of Saint Calixtus and Saint Domitilla, the network of tunnels had forty years earlier been excavated from the side of a twenty-foot elevation of land. It was known then as the "*arenario ardeatino*" —"Ardeatine sand pits."

A sandy, volcanic dust called *pozzolana,* had been mined from the caves. This was used in making concrete. It provided the building material for most of the new districts of Rome built by the Fascist regime in the 1930s, including parts of Parioli and the area around Piazza Bologna. Now the caves were exhausted and abandoned.[4]

Unknown to Kappler the site had already been marked by violent death. Three miners had been killed by cave-ins in digging the tunnels, in one of which a wooden cross still stood in a pile of sand. In another tunnel, which would not be seen by the Gestapo officer, the corpse of a man who had been dead for some time lay within a heavy overcoat, almost fully skeletonized. No one would ever know how it got there.[5]

There were three entrances to the caves. Once inside, Kappler was immediately engulfed in darkness and an intensely permeating dampness. A torch had to be lighted. The labyrinth was comprised of passageways about 150 to 300 feet long, 10 feet wide, and approximately 15 feet in height. They intersected one another.[6]

With Captain Köhler, Kappler said later, "I inspected the corridors, choosing the points best adapted for the operations." [7]

There was little difficulty in selecting the execution sites. They would be at the end of tunnel A (see diagram).[8] The prisoners, according to the regimen stipulated by Kappler, would be led into the caves through entrance B and proceed along tunnel B to transverse tunnel C, which was about 100 feet from the principal ingress. At the intersection of tunnels A and C, they would be slaughtered.

Meanwhile, at Via Tasso, Captain Schutz, who had been entrusted by Kappler to direct the shootings, gathered the Germans. He explained the methods to be used. Anyone, he said, who could not bring himself to participate in the execution—officer or not—would be placed at the side of the victims and he, too, would be shot.[9] Now everyone was ready to go.

Precisely at 2 P.M. the first truckload of Italians departed for the Ardeatine caves. They were escorted by their executioners.

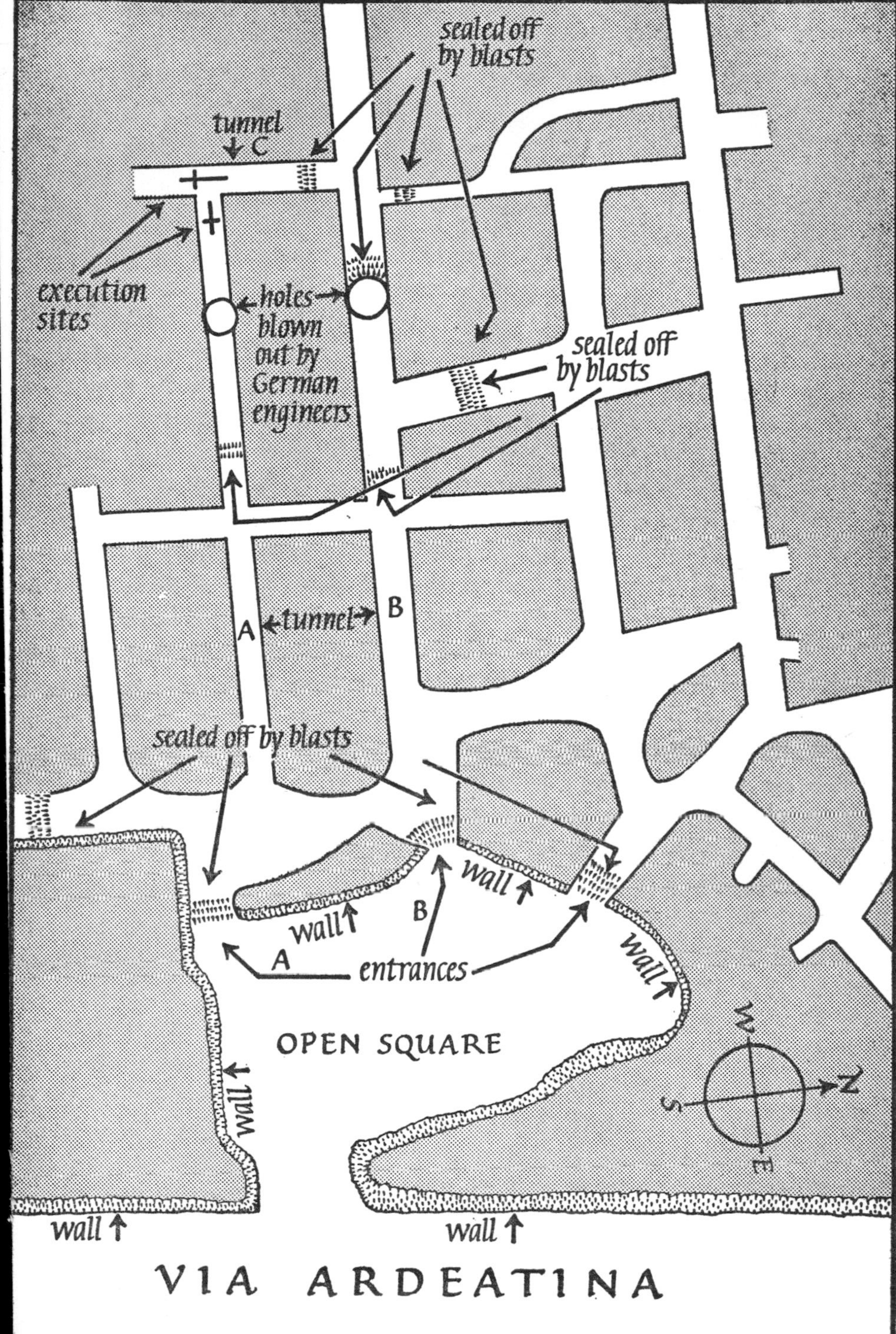

sealed off
by blasts
tunnel
C
execution
sites
holes
blown
out by
German
engineers
sealed off
by blasts
A
tunnel
B
sealed off by blasts
wall
wall
B
A
entrances
wall
OPEN SQUARE
wall
W
N
S
E
wall
wall
VIA ARDEATINA

IX

AT 2 P.M. the Third Wing of Regina Coeli—the German-controlled section of the prison—was outwardly peaceful. The daily meal had been served and generally this was a period for relaxation; the afternoon cleaning chores would not begin until four o'clock. This day, however, the prisoners were whispering nervously to one another. Through peepholes and gratings, with signs and with gestures, they were communicating what had been learned about the attack in Via Rasella.[1]

Suddenly, on the street floor of the old, cavernous prison the iron doors clanged open. Echoing clacks from heavy German boots penetrated every cell. The prisoners fell silent. The regular guards went from cell to cell locking the square peepholes, while the inmates strained to comprehend the meaning of the barking commands being issued by the intruders. On the third floor a captured partisan of the Action Party, Andrea De Gasperis, rushed to the cell door as soon as the guard had passed. He and his comrades had managed sometime before to break the peephole. With the aid of a tiny mirror he was able now to watch what was going on in the corridors of the Third Wing.[2]

German guards were moving from cell to cell. They carried a long, typewritten list. They shouted names and harsh orders. One of the Germans now approached De Gasperis' cell. The prisoners knew him as the cruelest and most arrogant of the guards. They had named him The Dog. Opening the door, he ordered one of the men, Filippo Rocchi, to get out. Rocchi had not been involved in partisan activity or politics. A thirty-five-year-old shopkeeper, he had been arrested by mistake and had been told he would soon be released.

"Rocchi embraced us," De Gasperis later recalled, "then

he asked the guard if he were being taken to Germany. The best he could say in reply, that cursed dog, was to emit three or four guttural '*Raus!*' and he gripped him by the arm and dragged him out of the cell."

De Gasperis rushed back to the peephole. He saw many of his friends being led away. He called to one of them, a young man of twenty-three named Epinemio Liberi, who had fought with the Latium partisans. He replied with a nod and a German pushed him forward. Then Liberi turned to De Gasperis and said, "*Addio*, Andrea, it's all over."

As the row of condemned men passed by De Gasperis' window, he suddenly saw two of his closest associates, Spartaco Pula, a twenty-four-year-old housepainter and Domenico Ricci, thirty-one, a clerk. They had fought the Germans in the partisan bands of the Action Party. Pula's brother, Italo, also had been called from Kappler's list. They had been told they were being taken to Germany to work. One of them said to De Gasperis as he passed, "Don't worry, we'll escape during the trip." [3]

In the women's lavatory on the first floor of the Third Wing, a Roman lawyer, *Avvocatessa* Eleanora Lavagnino, had just finished rinsing her mess tray—a privilege given only to female prisoners.[4] Coming out of the washroom, she crossed the first-floor bridge to return to her cell. She looked down and noted a group of about twenty prisoners huddled together. She paused for a moment and saw some six or eight unfamiliar German faces. Working in pairs, they held a long list and were pushing others from the cells toward the group gathering downstairs. The Germans seemed to her to be in a great hurry, but since the prisoners did not have their belongings with them she concluded that they could not be leaving, although everyone, including she, had been expecting a mass departure at any moment for forced-labor service in Germany.

The *avvocatessa* continued on, walking slowly, confused by the rush of activity. In one of the cells of the women's section she saw a physician, Luigi Pierantoni, who, captured forty days before, for partisan activity, had organized an infirmary service in the Third Wing. Accompanied now by a German hospital orderly and a regular guard, the thirty-eight-year-old doctor was preparing a syringe for an injection he was about to give one of the women prisoners.

Just as she reached the door of the open cell, she heard and saw two Germans calling Pierantoni's name from their list. When he responded, she later recounted, "they did not even let him complete his work. They took him by the arm and pushed him along with the usual '*los, los*' . . . I drew back so as to let Pierantoni pass and I tried to exchange a few words with him, but that was not possible. All I could do was offer a questioning nod, and he replied with a shrug, which to me meant that he had no idea of what was happening. As for me, I was pushed toward my cell, with the cry, '*Komme, komme, los, los!*' "[5]

Andrea De Gasperis, at the broken peephole on the third floor, saw the German guards coming to his cell once again. It was opened now for a second time. They called the name of a Jewish peddler, Giacomo Di Porto. Di Porto had been arrested with his entire family, all of whom were in the Third Wing—his wife, his two-year-old son, five-year-old daughter, and two other children.

According to De Gasperis, his hands were still bruised from the torture he had suffered at the Via Tasso. "He turned to us. There was a lost look in his eyes. Totally defeated, he asked us, 'Are they going to shoot me? But why?' "

Di Porto went out. He took a few steps and leaned against the iron bars. The cell door was closed and De Gasperis went back to the peephole. He could see Di Porto, who was motionless. "The warrant officer came up to him, slapped him twice in the face, and dragged him to the stairs. With a shove, he threw Di Porto down the steps. The cry of pain from the falling man was merged with the bestial wails of the murderous warrant officer. Disheartened, I drew away from the peephole . . ." [6]

X

IN THE Pensione d'Oltremare, Walter Di Franco came into the cell occupied by Lieutenant Giglio and eight other men. The time was 2:15.

Everyone was to be turned over to the SS, Di Franco announced. Anyone who wished to could send a last letter to his family.

Men began to cry. Giglio, who could barely stand, went among them and tried to encourage his fellow prisoners, most of whom were businessmen who had scant association with partisan or other political activity.

Helped by his orderly, Scottu, Giglio staggered to the toilet. He could urinate only blood. Di Franco saw them and attacked the two men, knocking both of them to the ground. A woman, who worked in the pensione as a maid, brought Giglio a glass of milk. When the lieutenant drank it, he passed out. A guard threw water in his face and he regained consciousness, but he was unable to stand.

He was carried out of his cell by Koch's men, thrown into a truck and brought to Regina Coeli.[1]

XI

IN THE Vatican by this hour a decision had been reached by Pope Pius XII not to intervene, to remain silent during the massacre, and to react to it with great caution.

Despite Padre Pancrazio's earlier enthusiasm, his representations at the Vatican at the behest of Standartenfuehrer Dollmann had, it would seem, been received with little favor.

An inquiry about the impending executions was apparently made by the Vatican in diplomatic channels through the German Ambassador to the Holy See.[1]

Following this, Weizsäcker telephoned Kesselring several times. They discussed the reprisal, but the substance of their conversations is not known.[2] The German reply, however, has been recorded by the Vatican itself. Referring to the Via Rasella incident, according to Monsignor Alberto Giovannetti, a high prelate in the Vatican State Secretariat, "The Germans linked this 'terrorist' action to the fate of the open city. They threatened to reexamine their attitude."[3]

The negotiations between the Vatican and the German occupiers were in danger of being broken off. From the point of view of the Vatican, the partisan attack could not have come at a more critical moment. The Pope's plan for an orderly exchange of military power in Rome between the Nazis and the Allies with the exclusion of the anti-Fascist Romans had suddenly been thrown into serious jeopardy. Until this moment, indications from both belligerent parties had appeared to the Vatican as offering great promise of success. Now the unprecedented attack in Via Rasella seemed to foreshadow a new wave of stepped-up partisan activity and even an all-out insurrection. This could spoil everything for the Pope and open the pandora's box of uncertainties which so many had labored so hard to keep under lock and key.

The Pope openly expressed his outrage about the attack in Via Rasella.[4] Padre Pancrazio, Pius' liaison with the occupiers, was, it appears, instructed by the Holy See not to go to the German offices that day.

His absence would not go unnoticed, at least at Gestapo headquarters. "I had accepted many interventions," Kappler later declared. "The Vatican had entrusted a prelate for some missions at all German offices. But Padre Pancrazio was not to be seen that day." [5]

Pius' schedule on March 24 was unusually heavy. He had meetings with cardinals of the Holy Office and the Congregation of Rites. There was an audience with a special envoy from Finland. The Pontiff also visited the Apostolic Vatican Palace to attend the Quinta Predica Quadragesimale, ceremonies held in connection with the Lenten period.[6] There was time nevertheless to give the first formal recognition from any quarter to the tragic events that were quietly unfolding during these hours, to the knowledge of a very limited few.

Someone in the Vatican had by the early afternoon already drafted in the vague language that was characteristic of Pope Pius himself a highly authoritative statement. This would appear on page 1 of *l'Osservatore Romano* in the edition that in a few hours would come out on the streets of Rome.*

Under the title "*Carità Civile*"—"Civil Compassion"—it read:

> We recall that on other occasions we have addressed ourselves to the grave times through which the country is passing. Now in these anxious hours we turn specifically to Rome.
>
> Our appeal is made directly to the conscience of the population, who have so admirably demonstrated their spirit of sacrifice and profound sense of dignity. Do not with violent urges shatter this attitude, which is so worthy of the virtues of our people. Every ill-considered act would

* These infrequent pronouncements, which contrary to *Osservatore*'s usual style were printed in italics and unsigned, appear to have originated from Pius himself. He attached a great deal of importance to the Vatican newspaper, which was founded by his grandfather Marcantonio Pacelli. Pius, who frequently read the galleys before the paper went to press, would often telephone his corrections, criticisms, and precise instructions to *Osservatore*'s editor, Count Giuseppe dalla Torre. (*Cf.* Pallenberg, *op. cit.*, pp. 19–20.)

have no other result than to end by injuring many innocent people, already too tried by anguish and privation.

All those upon whom it is incumbent to maintain public order have the task of assuring that it is not disturbed by any attitude whatsoever that can be, of itself, a reason for reactions which would give rise to an indefinable series of painful conflicts; those who can and know how to effectively influence the minds of the citizenry—above all the clergy—have the high mission of persuasion, pacification, and giving comfort. . . .[7]

Such were the Pope's ministrations on the day of the Ardeatine massacre.

XII

IN A meat truck moving south to Via Ardeatina, Don Pietro prayed in a voice that could scarcely be heard. There were tears flowing from his eyes. Joseph Raider still stood beside the priest. The prisoners exchanged silent glances with one another. Through a small opening in the canvas, Raider could make out the features of the Appian Way. No one could know where the Germans were taking him. To the south of Rome lay only the battlefronts. Raider overheard a guard whisper to another, "They're going to be made into manure . . ."[1]

Captain Schutz had already arrived at the entrance to the Ardeatine caves with some of his fellow officers.

They were to form the first platoons, in order that they could return to Via Tasso and permit other Germans to leave their posts for their turn as executioners.

All access roads to the caves had been blocked by the SD. On the elevated land above the excavation, German troops had been stationed to patrol the area and prevent any civilians from approaching the execution grounds. Unseen by the Germans, however, a forty-five-year-old hogkeeper named Nicola D'Annabile would observe the entire operations in front of the tunnel entrances. He was standing above the catacombs of Saint Domitilla, about 250 feet from the Ardeatine caves.[2]

Schutz rebriefed the men he would command. Using a German soldier as a model, he ordered him to get to his knees. Schutz indicated the point at the base of the neck at which to fire the 9mm. Maschine Pistole.[3] This was an automatic, German-made pistol that operated on the same principle as a machine gun: it continued to fire its ammunition as long as there was continuous pressure on the trigger. Once again Schutz reminded them that if anyone refused to shoot he would die at the side of the Italians.

The truck carrying Don Pietro Pappagallo and his fellow prisoners turned off the road. In the clearing before the Ardeatine caves the driver made a sweeping U-turn and backed up his vehicle with the rear of the closed truck facing the entrance to the tunnels. The back doors opened and the prisoners were ordered by the SD guards to get down in twos. Their hands, already tied behind their backs, were linked to one another in small groups. Don Pietro's right was joined with Joseph Raider's left.[4]

Raider noted that another group of prisoners from Via Tasso had arrived before his. He recognized some of them. They were standing at the mouth of the tunnels and some were already inside. He and Don Pietro lingered somewhat behind the others, who had descended from the truck and gathered in a semicircle.

By now no one could doubt what awaited them inside the tunnels. A desperate murmur welled among them. In their eyes they bore a look of utter hopelessness.[5]

Raider saw *Avvocato* Martini, the lawyer who had been in

cell number 7. Standing near him also were General Simone Simoni, a World War I hero who had fought the Germans on September 8, and Colonel Montezemolo, the head of the monarchist military Resistance front. The aristocratic colonel was wearing a blue, English-made sweater.[6] His face was swollen and there was an enormous bruise under his right eye.[7]

The semicircle of doomed men began to grow. Somehow it massed around Don Pietro. The lamentful murmur among them became louder. Suddenly someone turned to Don Pietro and in a voice that was shaking and urgent, he cried to the priest, "Father, bless us!" [8]

Don Pietro, who was a robust and powerful man, ripped and twisted himself free of the bonds around his wrists. He raised his arms and prayed aloud, imparting to all the last rites.

In the confusion, Joseph Raider, who had been tied to the priest, found himself free. At one of the entrances to the caves, he saw, there was a pile of earth that had been accumulated as a result of some previous digging works. The mound had hardened and it formed a low earthen wall. Behind it, there was a grassy opening and the uneven terrain led to the top of the elevation above the caves. Seeing this, the Austrian was overcome with anxiety. It seemed to offer the last and only possibility of escape from what now had become revealed as certain death. For a moment he was indecisive.

When Don Pietro completed the benediction, the men rushed around him and the Gestapo guards immediately moved in to break up the distraction. Raider, in the midst of this disorder, decided to attempt to flee. Unseen, he leaped to the top of the wall of earth and scaled the slope to the field above the excavations. Then he dropped to the ground and rolled in the grass, out of sight of the guards below.[9]

"I lay there for a few seconds without moving," he said later. "Then I decided to disappear from the place. There was nothing I could do to help those poor devils. When I got up to run, I was taken by surprise by an SS guard . . ." [10]

The two German soldiers–Raider and his captor–recognized each other. Raider was known to the guard not from the Via Tasso prison, but from the period when he had served in the Wehrmacht as an interpreter. The guard knew Raider as a deserter–the fact that he had managed to conceal under the cover of an Italian identity. He was surprised at first to find Raider in this situation, but he began to realize what had probably happened. Two other guards came up to them now.

Raider's captor turned to them and said, "Here, *meine Herren*, I present you with a deserter who has deceived us with a foreign name." [11]

The guards were delighted with the discovery.

"Now," one of them said, "we will see who you really are. If you are Italian you will be shot. If you are German your life will be spared." [12]

The young Austrian confessed. "I was loaded into a truck and brought back to Via Tasso. On the road back I became aware of the broken rope that all this time had dangled from my left hand. I thought of Don Pietro. I closed my eyes and recited the Lord's Prayer . . ." [13]

Meanwhile, inside the Ardeatine caves, the executions had not yet begun. The Germans were awaiting the first arrivals from Regina Coeli.

XIII

At 3 P.M. General Karl Wolff, accompanied by his adjutant, Sturmbannfuehrer Eugen Wenner, landed at Viterbo airport, fifty miles north of Rome on Via Cassia. Standartenfuehrer Dollmann was there to meet them.

Dollmann had arranged a meeting between Wolff and Field Marshal Kesselring. The three SS officers got into a car and proceeded to Monte Soratte, a distance of about twenty-two miles. None of them was aware of what was about to take place in the Ardeatine caves.[1]

Wolff, as Dollmann recalled, "was very nervous and irritated. As we went toward Monte Soratte, he asked me to tell him all the details of the Via Rasella episode. He declared he would not take any measures until he had spoken with Kesselring. However, he added that he had already received orders directly from Himmler on resolving the situation in Rome."[2]

The car moved southward along the back road that passes through Monte Cimini on the east bank of Lake Vico. Dollmann, who had spent the past hours refining his political program to score a propaganda victory at the expense of the Via Rasella partisans, now began to unfold his plan to the Polizeifuehrer.

As they neared the goat-country town of Caprarola, a series of shots suddenly rang out from the bush. The bullets were aimed at the SS car, whose route from Viterbo to Monte Soratte was heavily traveled by Nazi officials. Dollmann's driver roared away and they escaped the outburst unharmed.

"You see!" Wolff cried when the danger had passed. "You and your humanitarian programs. You see! Himmler is right. We have to set an example here."[3]

XIV

AT 3 P.M. the sentry on duty at the entrance to Regina Coeli, Michele Usai, allowed a German meat truck to pass. Usai saw twelve Germans get down from the truck and enter the prison. Each of them was carrying a length of rope.[1]

On the second tier inside the prison, *Avvocatessa* Lavagnino had returned to her cell. The peepholes in the women's section had not been locked. Like everyone else, she was trying to determine exactly what was taking place this strange afternoon. Observing the activity of the Germans, the lawyer saw clearly that the lists had not been drawn up by the prison registry, since the guards had to return to the same cell two or three times in order to get the men on their list. She later recounted:

> Thus, at cell number 288, which was directly across from me, there were two pickups for four prisoners. In number 286, the cell door was opened three times and four trips were made to take away five prisoners. Young and old, tried and still to be tried, sentenced and acquitted. There was no order to it! . . . Among those selected were . . . a restaurant owner arrested five days earlier for having served food to Jews; on the floor above there was a seventeen-year-old boy arrested on the street for violating the curfew.[2]

Downstairs on the main floor, the group continued to grow. The Jews and the non-Jews were divided. The latter group was positioned between the central stairway and the entrance gates; the former, between the stairway and the rear windows. What kind of departure could this be? The prisoners were not permitted to bring their personal belongings or their food parcels. Some were being pushed along the catwalks while they were still buttoning their pants and tidying their hair with the palms of their hands.[3]

The Germans came now to cell number 278. Inside there were four men who had been crippled fighting for Mussolini. Among them was a twenty-seven-year-old jurist named

Alberto Fantacone. Maimed and put out of action three months after Italy's entry into the war on the side of the Germans, he had become an anti-Fascist and then a partisan in the Resistance. At Via Tasso, where he had been tortured, he had managed to get a message to his wife before being sent to Regina Coeli. "I am here," he wrote, "not for having committed grave crimes, but for having believed in something that represents an ideal . . . I do not despair because above and beyond all things, I have complete faith in God." [4] Now the four crippled men were taken to the group downstairs.

In cell number 297, Signora Genserico Fontana was ushered out to the second-floor bridge. She was permitted to nod good-bye to her twenty-six-year-old husband, who was among the men gathered below.[5]

Some weeks ago, before her own arrest, she and her friend Signora Romeo Rodriguez had paid a prison guard 100,000 lire. He had asked for the money and whatever gold they could give, to obtain the release of their husbands.[6] Both men had been lieutenants in the Carabinieri. This was the one Italian police organization considered untrustworthy by the Germans because of its loyalty to the King and the high degree of antifascism among the men.* Instead of gaining freedom for their husbands, both women had been arrested themselves. Signora Rodriguez had already said good-bye to her husband that day. Taken from his cell, he had passed hers and said, "Don't worry, they're taking us to work." [7] He was twenty-five years old.

Now, from the catwalk, Signora Fontana waved farewell.

She was then led back to her cell, having been reassured by the guards that the men were being taken away for labor service. The roundups continued.

* The Roman Carabinieri was broken up as an organization by the German occupiers. Some 1,500 were captured and deported to the north; 7,500 went into hiding, many to fight in the Resistance. Eleven Carabinieri were executed in the Ardeatine caves.

At 3:15 P.M., sentry Michele Usai watched the first group of prisoners depart. Their hands were tied behind their backs. They were loaded into the truck.

One prisoner said, "But what do they want to kill us for?"[8]

He was struck by a German guard. The truck departed, moving south along the left bank of the Tiber.

XV

DEEP INSIDE the Ardeatine caves, a German lighted a torch. A medic carried a flashlight in his hand. Captain Erich Priebke held a copy of Kappler's list. Captain Schutz was ready. The executions were about to begin.

Kappler again made a brief speech to his men, reminding them that their orders had come from the Fuehrer and that they, as officers in the Gestapo, had to set an example. "At that moment," Kappler would recall, "I was very upset."[1]

The first platoon of five Germans then went to the mouth of the caves. In the clearing outside, the prisoners stood in the crisp air of the spring afternoon. Many of them had not been outdoors since last December. The sun lay almost level with the elevation into which the tunnels had been dug. It glistened on the grass above but left the entrance to the Ardeatine in cool shadow. Some of the men were singing.[2]

The first platoon chose five of the waiting prisoners, each German selecting the man he would kill.[3] They told the five Italians to come with them. Tied to one another, they were led to the rear of the center tunnel. Along the walls, soldiers held torches to light the way. At the second intersection the platoon and its victims turned left and halted. Captain Priebke demanded their names.

Only last Saturday night, in the company of a beautiful

Italian actress, Priebke had been at a gay party in Parioli, in an apartment in Via Ruggero Fauro. At the same party, by a strange set of coincidences, Priebke had met OSS undercover agent Peter Tompkins.[4] The American had been introduced as a wealthy Fascist of a well-known family. Tompkins had just been informed of Lieutenant Giglio's capture. He had been uneasy in the presence of the Gestapo officer, who had stared at him suspiciously at various moments during the evening. Both men had been drinking heavily. The next day Tompkins wondered if he had in any way revealed his true identity. A confidant told the American, "When you get full of gin . . . you might as well have a sign on your back: USA! Luckily our friend Erich wanted to make that girl so badly and was too busy grabbing at her breasts—I don't think he noticed very much." [5]

Now Erich Priebke scratched the first five names from his list. Soon he would cancel out Lieutenant Giglio.

The five prisoners taken by the first platoon were forced to their knees and ordered to turn their heads to the wall. There was no resistance. The executioners took their place at the backs of their victims. A German soldier with a torch came up behind the men who would fire.

The flickering light was poor. Major Domizlaff, who was in the first platoon, said later that "one scarcely saw the target against which one had to shoot." [6] Captain Schutz stood off to the side. He would give the command to fire.

The five men waited for death. Among the first to die was Domenico Ricci, the thirty-one-year-old clerk who only an hour ago had passed the broken peephole of Andrea De Gasperis' cell.[7] Ricci was the father of five children. In his pocket was a scrap of paper. In clear block letters Ricci, a Catholic, had written, "My dear God, we pray that You may protect the Jews from the barbarous persecutions. 1 Paternoster, 10 Ave Marias, 1 Gloria Patri." [8]

"Ready!" Schutz cried. "Aim! Fire!" [9]

On a hill above the Ardeatine caves the hogkeeper Nicola D'Annabile, who had secretly been watching the activity in the clearing below him, heard the shots. He noted the time: 3:30 P.M.[10]

The German medic flashed his light on the fallen men. He pronounced them dead.

Kappler decided that he would set his example in the second platoon. "I went to a nearby truck," he later admitted, "and I took a victim with me, whose name was crossed out by Priebke from his copy of the list. Four other officers did the same. We led the victims to the same place and, in the same way, a little behind the first five, they were shot." [11]

Ten men were dead.

Kappler returned to his office. If he were to keep to the letter of the Fuehrer's order, he was already seriously behind schedule. The executions had to be completed by 8 P.M.—twenty-four hours from the time the order had been issued from OBSW. His main preoccupation at the moment was Caruso. The Questore had not yet turned in his list, which had been due more than two hours ago.

At Via Tasso, Kappler sent more of his men to take their turn in the execution squads. He then telephoned Caruso. The Questore said that he and Koch were still working on the list. The German demanded that the fifty prisoners on Caruso's list be ready to leave Regina Coeli at once. He said they were to be turned over to one of his officers, Obersturmfuehrer (Lt.) Tunnat. There could be no delays.[12]

Kappler then told Lieutenant Tunnat to go immediately to Regina Coeli. To increase the pressure on the Fascist officials, he ordered Tunnat not to wait beyond 4:30 P.M.[13] He then called Commissar Alianello of the Public Security office and dispatched him to Caruso to help speed up the process.[14] He appointed Alianello, with whom he had often worked closely, to expedite the actual delivery of the prisoners into German hands. Alianello was to personally take Caruso's list and rush it to the prison registry.

During this flurry of office work, Kappler received a telephone call from a Gestapo officer at the Ardeatine caves. One of his junior officers, Kappler was told, was refusing to shoot. Kappler said not to take any action against the man. He himself would return to the caves and handle the matter.[15]

Inside the tunnels the insubordinate first lieutenant was taken aside and the executions continued. The officers were ordered to participate a second time. Discipline was becoming sloppy. Some platoons were killing the Italians one by one. Some victims resisted. They had to be beaten down with gun butts. One man, a twenty-six-year-old seaman named Antonio Pisino, did not have to be shot. He was killed by a blow from a blunt object that smashed his skull.[16]

Bodies were strewn about without order. By now they formed a ghastly mosaic about seventy-five feet long.[17] It was clear that unless they were stacked, the patchwork of dead men would soon extend out to the open road. But piling the corpses would be too laborious a task and would take too much time.

When Kappler arrived at the caves, he spoke with the mutinous officer, SS Obersturmfuehrer Wetjen. He had been overheard to say of Kappler, "He gives the orders, but he doesn't have to carry them out." [18]

Kappler was kind. "I did not reproach him; I made him realize that his act would influence the discipline of the men." [19]

He asked Wetjen why he had refused to shoot. The younger German replied that he felt "a revulsion." [20] Kappler explained all the reasons why he had to carry out his orders "like a good soldier."

"You're right," said Wetjen. "But it's not that easy."

"Would you feel better if I were at your side when you fired?" Kappler asked.

Wetjen agreed. "I put my arm around his waist," Kappler remembered, "and we went together into the caves."[21] For the second time, Kappler took part in an execution platoon. Wetjen and his chief, standing side by side, each killed his man.

To Kappler many of his men appeared downcast and beaten, and the majority of prisoners were yet to be executed. He had anticipated that this might happen. Ordering a temporary halt to the executions, he told his men to take a long break.

"Everyone was spiritually depressed," Kappler said later.[22] He opened some Cognac he had brought with him from Via Tasso and the bottle was passed among the men "to restimulate them."[23] Kappler advised them to get drunk.

During this rest period, the men who had already been killed were piled on the backs of the first five.

XVI

AT REGINA Coeli the roundups in the Third Wing had been completed. The two groups of prisoners—Jews and non-Jews—were being prepared for their departure. It was past four o'clock.

They were ordered to line up in threes, and a man from the SD began to call the names. The first count fell short of the required number. Some guards were dispatched to the third tier of cells and they returned with another group of prisoners. On the second count there was one prisoner too many. The first man in sight was grabbed and ordered back to his cell.[1]

On the Jewish side, the men were moving among each other, trying to stand close to friends or family so that they might be together in the event of a long journey. They now were ordered to line up. There were twenty-two rows of three. An unevenness in the ranks brought a command from the Gestapo man to straighten up and face right. One of the Jews, seventy-four-year-old Mosè Di Consiglio, turned left instead of right. He was the eldest of the six members of the Di Consiglio family who had been taken from their cells. He was in poor health. His confusion between right and left drew a few smiles from his friends. Suddenly, however, the Gestapo man came up to the hoary old Roman merchant and slapped him twice.[2]

When the first roll call had been completed, the German who was sending them to slaughter shouted, "Anyone among you who can do heavy labor, such as digging and the like, raise your hand."

The men looked at one another questioningly. Then, slowly, fearfully, some hands went up, as others began to whisper among themselves.

"Well?" asked the Gestapo man, who was dressed in civilian clothes. "How many of you are willing to work?"

There was more whispering among the Jewish prisoners, more movement. Suddenly all hands were in the air.

"Well then," said the German, "everyone wants to work. That's fine! I will read your names again. If any of you are not called, step out of the line."[3]

The list was read: "Anticoli, Lazzaro . . . Coen, Saverio . . . Di Consiglio, Mosè . . . Di Porto, Giacomo . . . Limentani, Davide . . . Piperno, Claudio . . ."—scores of names . . . shopkeepers, merchants, peddlers. Almost all of them had been born in Rome. They lived in the little cobbly streets behind the synagogue on Lungotevere de' Cenci and sold their wares from pushcarts in Via Arenula and Campo de' Fiori. For 2,000 years the Jews had lived there. Only they and the popes remained from the last days of Imperial Rome. In the tiny Jewish quarter on the right bank of the Tiber, their ancestors had watched the Emperor Augustus dedicate the Theater of Marcellus. Their children played in its ruins —at least until the Germans came and children hunted the cats of Rome for food instead.

Until the mass roundup of October 16, the Jews of Rome believed themselves immune to crimes they heard were being committed by the Nazis against the Jews of other countries. "These things don't happen in Italy," it was being said.[4]

When the roll had been called, one of the group had not been named. Apparently he had been taken from his cell in the disorderly rush. He was Franco Di Consiglio. His father, his grandfather, his two brothers, and his uncle had all been called. The Di Consiglios had been arrested on March 22, the day after Franco's seventeenth birthday. Franco, like his brothers Marco, nineteen, and Santoro, eighteen, was learning the butcher's trade. Inexplicably, he had not been selected by Kappler, who had, however, listed the other five Di Consiglios.

Now, following the roll caller's instructions, Franco took one step out of the line. He too wanted to work. The German asked his name. He checked it against his copy of the list. Unable to find Franco Di Consiglio, the German added the young man to the others.[5] Now six Di Consiglios would go to the abattoir in the Ardeatine caves.

Avvocatessa Lavagnino could see the Jewish group clearly from her cell on the second tier. "When left to themselves," she recounted, "the Jews regrouped and spoke animatedly, but softly. Someone exchanged nods with the women on the first floor. Others wrote hurriedly on scraps of paper and gave them to prisoners in nearby cells on the street floor. We threw cigarettes, matches, and bread to them. At this point, the peepholes were closed and all we could do was try to listen."[6]

Obscured from the eyes of the prisoners who would remain behind, the doomed men were stripped of their coats. Now their hands were tied, dorsal to dorsal, behind their back. Marching in threes, they were led outside.[7]

In the women's section, Signora Lavagnino heard "the shuffling of feet moving away in columns. They did not, however, go out the usual way, through the main entrance, but went through the courtyard gate. I got up on my cot and from there I climbed to the bars. They were marching just undeı me, too close to the wall for me to see them . . ." [8]

From the barred window in the men's lavatory, prisoner Carmello De Stefanis could see almost the entire courtyard.[9] De Stefanis, who was suffering from injuries after being tortured in Via Tasso, had been granted permission to go to the lavatory, and now he was able to watch the men being taken away.

A nineteen-year-old partisan who had fought in the Castelli Romani, he had just seen his four cellmates taken away, leaving him the only remaining occupant.

There were three meat wagons in the courtyard. The prisoners, De Stefanis saw, were lined up once again and ordered into the trucks.

Suddenly a woman who had been standing outside the prison broke through the German guard and ran up to one of the men. She was the wife of Alfredo Mosca, a fifty-three-year-old electrician who had been arrested for anti-Fascist activities. Hoping to find a way of visiting her imprisoned husband, she had come earlier to Regina Coeli, only to see scores of men being taken away.

"Alfredo!" she cried, heedless of the threats by the police. "Alfredo, *mio!*"

Mosca, bound at the wrists like all the others, struggled free from the restraints of a guard and said his last good-bye. The woman was finally turned away and the departure continued.[10]

Some of the prisoners, because their hands were tied, were unable to mount the platform at the rear of the trucks. They fell to the ground. From his vantage point at the window of the prison lavatory, De Stefanis saw the Germans lift the fallen men and "swing them into the truck like sacks." [11]

Loaded with some 200 victims, covered by an armed escort, the German vans drove away. It was dusk.

XVII

WHEN LIEUTENANT Tunnat, accompanied by an interpreter, Sondefuehrer Wilhelm Koffler, arrived at the Italian section of Regina Coeli, Caruso's list of fifty names had still not been delivered. Tunnat demanded to speak to the Questore. Reached by telephone at Police Headquarters, Caruso, who was typing the list himself, said it would soon be ready. He agreed to telephone some of the names to the prison registry so that the men could be rounded up in the meantime.[1]

Tunnat then went to see the director of Regina Coeli, Donato Carretta. The German said he intended to move the prisoners no later than 4:30 P.M. Carretta, who had not been informed of the transfer, telephoned the registry and then Caruso for confirmation. The registry, which had received only a few of the names by telephone, said it would be impossible to have the men ready by 4:30. Tunnat worked himself into a rage and called Commissar Alianello. If the list were not here immediately, the lieutenant shouted into the telephone, he would take the prison personnel instead.[2]

By 4:30, however, Alianello had not yet arrived. Tunnat decided not to wait any longer. A truck was backed into position and the Germans began taking prisoners at random, grabbing the first men in sight. Among them were ten men who had been arrested on nonpolitical charges. They had at that moment been standing in the registry, collecting their belongings. The charges against them had been dismissed. They were to be released.[3] The guards protested vehemently.

Tunnat drove off with about thirty men and said he would return for the rest.

Commissar Alianello arrived some minutes later. He had the list in hand. While he was being told by Carretta that the Germans had already taken a number of the men, including some not on the list, Caruso called to see if everything was in order. The Questore wanted to speak with the prison director, but Alianello got on the wire and explained what had happened.

"How could they?" Caruso asked.

"They just took them away," said the commissar.[4]

There was little that could be done now, they felt. It was decided, apparently between Caruso and Alianello, to substitute the names of the men who had been taken indiscriminately for an equal number of those who had been selected by Caruso. The choice of who would live and who would die was left to Alianello and Carretta.

Carretta checked with the registry and learned that eleven unlisted men had been taken. There would be eleven substitutions.

"I did not know who to cancel," Alianello said later, "because I didn't know any of them." [5]

They looked at the list. It appeared almost innocuous. Signed by Questore Caruso, it simply said: "The Chief Guard at Regina Coeli prison will deliver to Lieutenant Tunnat of the German Police, which has made the request, the below named detainees who are restricted to this prison and are at the disposition of this Police Headquarters." [6]

This was followed by two columns of twenty-five names and the date: Rome, March 24, 1944–XXII (the twenty-second year of fascism).

While the remaining prisoners were being gathered for the last departure to the Ardeatine caves, the question of who among them would be spared hung momentarily in the balance. The men who would give the answer were of opposite breeds. The commissar was a dedicated police officer who had long served the Fascists and later the Nazi occupiers. Prison director, Donato Carretta, a fifty-year-old bureaucrat, was, on the other hand, secretly opposed to the Fascist regime. Despite his timid, almost frightened appearance, he had taken many risks in behalf of the men the Fascists arrested. He permitted an underground aid service to operate in the Italian-controlled part of Regina Coeli. Carretta had helped some men escape, including, only a few weeks earlier, the anti-Fascist leader Socialist Giuseppe Saragat.*[7]

Caruso's list contained some of the most active members of the Resistance, especially in the Action Party. They were not listed alphabetically, but apparently in the order of how "guilty" they were considered by the Fascists. The first six names were Actionists. One of them, Pilo Albertelli, thirty-six, a renowned writer, intellectual, and professor of philosophy, was already almost dead. He had organized the military command of the Action Party and had been arrested by Koch. At the Pensione d'Oltremare, Albertelli had been tortured to within the last breath of his life. But he had not informed on his comrades.

"You adopt your weapons and methods," he had said. "I use the only one I have: Silence." [8]

When Caruso had learned that Albertelli would not talk, he said to Koch's men, "Go get his wife and bring her here. Torture her in front of him." [9]

But the partisan professor would escape that agony in the Ardeatine caves. Albertelli, until March 20, had been in the same cell with Lieutenant Giglio. Giglio was number 31 on Caruso's list.

Alianello chose eight names to be excluded from the list. His selection was made on the basis of his belief that some men were less incriminated than others. ". . . at the bottom

* Saragat is presently the President of Italy. The tragic fate of Donato Carretta is described on page 229.

of the list," he later said, "there were the names of eight Jews."[10] He told Carretta that these must have been added to reach the total of fifty.

They were struck, as well as a non-Jew also considered less guilty than the others by Alianello. Carretta eliminated the name of one man because he was in the prison hospital and was too weak to be moved, even to his death. The name of the eleventh man had to be crossed out by Carretta because he could not be found inside the prison.[11]

The others had to wait for Lieutenant Tunnat to return and get them. Two of them were father and son Umberto and Bruno Bucci. Umberto, the father, had already confided to a fellow prisoner who would remain that "if we are to be shot, take down the crucifix from our cell and give it to our family. Tell them not to cry, but to seek comfort in Christ as we in our suffering have done." [12]

Months later, he and his son would be found by their exhumers locked in a final, eternal embrace among the dead in the Ardeatine caves.[13]

XVIII

In via Ruggero Fauro, a narrow but modern street that runs through Parioli, Major Peter Tompkins had returned to the flat where he had met SS Hauptsturmfuehrer Erich Priebke. A late afternoon party had been arranged with the women who had been there with Captain Priebke. According to Tompkins, he and Italian agent Franco Malfatti wanted to test whether it was safe to reoccupy the apartment, which was useful for their activities.[1]

Tompkins was as yet unaware that Lieutenant Giglio was on his way to his death. Although Koch's prison in Via Principe Amedeo was under surveillance by Franco Malfatti's men, they had inexplicably failed to see Giglio carried bodily from the Pensione d'Oltremare and thrown into a waiting meat truck.

Hopelessly uninformed, still dreaming of engineering Giglio's escape, the American lit a fire. The only wood he could find was from pieces of furniture and a washboard. "The girls arrived," he would recall, "and we sat around the fire consuming tea and cakes and brandy. Soon I began to forget the realities of the world outside and enjoy the company of the girls, especially the one called L., with whom I had been to fetch Captain Priebke . . ." [2]

Apparently the apartment was safe. But he would soon have to leave in order to be back at his own flat before the seven o'clock curfew. There, the OSS team would reshuffle its futile and unsatisfactory plans for the attack on the Oltremare.

XIX

STANDARTENFUEHRER DOLLMANN and General Wolff arrived at Monte Soratte some time after 5 P.M. In Kesselring's outer office they learned from an adjutant of "the measures for the expiation" of the Via Rasella attack, which were taking place in the Ardeatine caves.

Wolff, according to Dollmann, "got red in the face and burst into the Field Marshal's office." [1]

He was told by Kesselring about the orders that had been received from Hitler and which were being executed by Kappler.

"Wolff replied that beyond punishing those responsible for the Via Rasella, Himmler was inflexible in his demand that all Communists or suspected Communist elements had to be radically eliminated from Rome." [2]

Himmler had given orders, Wolff said to the Field Marshal, to organize a "forced exodus from the capital." [3] As soon as possible, the Polizeifuehrer continued, the entire male population from the most dangerous neighborhoods were to be rounded up. This was the best way of smashing the partisan movement.* It meant that everyone between the ages of fifteen and sixty, heads of families included, had to be shipped to the north.

Kesselring was reserved. This was a matter of evacuating about one million men. He was not, he said, in a position to give a definitive reply at this moment. It would require about three divisions of his Fourteenth Army to carry out an orderly evacuation. He had to examine the possibilities of detaching so large a number of troops from the Anzio war zone.

While Kesselring was considering the means of inflicting this new catastrophe on the Romans, Wolff said he would move ahead on the details of the plan. He called for an urgent conference to be held that night. He wanted to consult with Kappler, the Commander of the Fourteenth Army, Mackensen, and other Nazi officials in Rome.[4]

Dollmann took to the telephone and summoned his colleagues to the conference. It would be held at the Excelsior, following the hastily arranged dinner to be given in honor of their unexpected but nonetheless distinguished guest.[5]

XX

IN THE flickering light of the black tunnels of Ardeatine, as night and curfew fell quietly on all of Rome, the massacre continued.

* At a Hitler-Mussolini conference four weeks later Wolff would express his confidence in this measure. The Resistance is breaking up, he would report; "in the valleys infested by the partisans good results had been achieved by deporting the entire male population." (Translation of German minutes of meeting of Apr. 22, 1944, morning session, in US State Department Bulletin, Oct. 20, 1946, quoted in Deakin, *op. cit.*, p. 684.)

By this hour it had degenerated to an incredibly heinous orgy of slaughter which no longer had either coherence or comprehension. All of Kappler's plans to systematize the executions into some workable order had gone awry.

Under the pressure of having to gain time, the Germans had discovered a way to solve the space problem of the accumulating corpses. They forced their victims, while still alive, to climb to the top of those already dead. There, on the flesh of their slain comrades, their fathers, or their children, they kneeled and presented the napes of their necks. They fell, layer after layer, in a pile.[1] The murderers had to scale the carnal heap themselves to be in the correct firing position.[2]

Laced with Cognac, the Germans had become hideously sloppy in their work. As many as four bullets were being fired into the skull of a single victim.[3] Human heads were literally being blown from their bodies. They were splattered on the tunnel ceiling. When the bodies were exhumed, thirty-nine were found decapitated.[4]

Spent shells and whole, unused cartridge clips fell among the cadavers. Some of the Germans aimed badly. Their bullets did not pass through the brain, but only through the face, ripping away eyes and noses in a drizzle of human blood. Or else the bullets did only little damage, emerging from the frontal side of the neck without having struck any vital body organ. Some victims therefore did not die instantly. They lay, unconscious from the explosive concussion, dying on the death heap.[5]

The pile by now had risen to a height of about sixty inches. Having taken the shape of a pyramid, it had become impractical, and a second accumulation had been started alongside and at right angles to the first, in an intersecting tunnel. Together they would occupy an area of 160 square feet.[6]

Some Italians died crying "*Viva l'Italia!*"[7] One German soldier—only one—could not go through with his part in the massacre. His name was Sondefuehrer Günther Amon. He would later recall that he went into the tunnels with his execution platoon, "but when they raised the torch and I saw the dead men, I fainted . . . I was horrified by the spectacle. One of my comrades took my place and fired for me." [8]

For the greatest part, however, every human sensibility had become numb, if not irrevocably destroyed. As terrible as it seems, by all evidence most of the victims cooperated with their slayers and went passively to their deaths.

Before the seven o'clock curfew a few people who lived or worked in the sparsely settled area of the catacombs were becoming aware of what was taking place in their midst. A young engaged couple, out strolling in the warm early evening, heard the repeated crackling of the muffled shots. When they approached the barricaded Via Ardeatina, they were warned by some of their neighbors not to go farther. "The Germans are in there," they were told.[9]

Some of the guides from the catacombs of Saint Calixtus, which lie between the Appian Way and Via Ardeatina, tried to learn what was going on. They were turned away at gun point by the Germans. A youth from a nearby *osteria* sneaked alongside one of the German trucks and stole a rifle. He was caught, put up against a wall, and threatened with immediate execution. A Silesian monk named Szenik, who was one of the German guides at the catacombs, intervened and saved the young man.[10]

A Roman priest, returning from the *campagna*, was stopped as he tried to enter the city along Via Ardeatina. He heard from the entrance to the caves the voices of some of the prisoners singing the Garibaldian hymn "*Si scopron le tombe.*" The priest knew at once that it was the wail of tragedy. He prayed: "*In manu tua, Domine . . .*" [11]

When Lieutenant Tunnat and Sondefuehrer Koffler returned to the caves with the final truckload of victims, night had fallen. As the vehicle swung around in the clearing, only three other prisoners remained to be executed. "Kappler spoke to them calmly," according to Koffler, "then they were led into the caves and some shots were heard." [12]

Now the last group came down from the back of the truck and moved forward into the tunnels from which they would never, even in death, emerge.

The time was 8 P.M. When the final bullet had passed through the skull of the last man to die, the German engineers immediately began to seal the caves. Several carts of explosives were wheeled in, and the two intersecting tunnels that contained the dead men were mined. Unused material, including gelatine tubes, were tossed onto the heaps of cadavers.[13] The access tunnels were also mined. During the hour, two powerful explosions were heard by the monks in the nearby catacombs.[14] The engineers withdrew. They would return the following day to complete the sealing operations.

Inside the tomb, the two mounds of bodies were covered with a blanket of powdery volcanic dust.[15] The blast had shaken the sandy substance loose from the tunnel ceilings. Bound at the wrists, their knees still flexed in eternal supplication, they lay upon each other, bearing witness to the German crime. Their lives, which had been evaluated as being worth one-tenth of a German's, had in truth been devalued even further. The executioners had murdered not 330 men but—as Hauptsturmfuehrer Priebke would soon report to Obersturmbannfuehrer Kappler—335. To Kappler's question as to how this could have happened, one of his men would reply, "It was an error, but since they were already there . . ." [16]

Three hundred and thirty-five human beings. Three of them would remain forever unknown. Nine others would be found by their exhumers in such poor condition that scientists and family would be unable to match their names to their bodies. Of the 323 who would be identified, the following statistics would be compiled (they would be kept and modified when necessary by the father of one of the victims):[17]

Ages, 14 to 75. Catholics, 253; Jews, 70. Occupations: Accountants, 3; actors, 2; administrators, businessmen, and industrialists, 7; architects, engineers, and surveyors, 5; Armed Forces: Air Force, 3; Army, 18; Carabinieri, 11; Navy, 6; artists, designers, and painters, 5; banker, 1; butchers, 5; carpenters and cabinetmakers, 11; civil servants, 4; clerks, commercial assistants, and secretaries, 40; chauffeurs and drivers, 7; construction workers, 2; electricians, 5; film technicians, 2; insurance man, 1; landowners and peasants, 10; lawyers, 11; mechanics, 13; merchants and shopkeepers, 42; musician, 1; peddlers, 16; pharmacists and physicians, 4; police officer (Public Security agent), 1; political scientist, 1; postal-telegraph personnel, 4; priest, 1; printers and typographers, 2; professors, 5; servants and waiters, 2; shoemakers, 5; store clerks, 7; students, 9; telephone company personnel, 2; trainmen and railway personnel, 3; and workers in various trades, 28.[18]

Not all were Italians. There were one Belgian, one Frenchman, three Germans, one Hungarian, one Libyan, three Russians, and one Turk.

At least one of the 335 was at this hour not yet dead. The bullet had passed through the muscles and blood vessels of his neck without damaging his head. He would lift himself from the pile and struggle to a corner, where he would die alone.[19]

One man either had not been tied or had broken out of the ropes, perhaps after he was presumed to be dead. Clutched in his free fist, his countrymen would one day find, was a handful of peanuts.

In the pockets of many of the dead were last messages to their families, their friends, and to the world. But every word that had been written in ink would be washed from the paper in the drippings of decaying human flesh. Only a few penciled notes would survive.[20]

One man had written to his parents: "If it must be that we never see each other again, remember that you had a son who willingly gave his life for his country, staring his executioners in the eyes!"[21]

In the pocket of eighteen-year-old Orlando Orlandi Posti there was a scrap of paper with some lines and numbers. It was an unfinished pencil game of "Naval Battle." The youth, taken by the Gestapo while visiting with his mother, had left his last words in a letter smuggled out of Via Tasso:

> God will soon put an end to the human suffering through which the whole world is passing. He will make it so that everyone can return to his home and thus peace will return to every family and all will be restored to normal.[22]

In the meantime Kappler had returned to his headquarters. There was a message from Dollmann for him to attend the conference with General Wolff at the Excelsior. He had to leave at once. On his way out he stopped at the Via Tasso mess hall, where the men who had killed the 335 were having a belated dinner. He told them to pass the night getting drunk again. Drink Cognac, he said. This, the Obersturmbannfuehrer told them, was the best way to erase the impressions of the hours before. It was an order.[23]

Every evening, for the next ten days, the executioners would drink themselves into a stupor.[24]

XXI

Rome and the world were unaware of this latest Nazi *Blutbad*. The evening newspaper *Giornale d'Italia* had nothing to say as yet of even the attack in Via Rasella, which was common knowledge throughout the city although no news medium had mentioned it.

The biggest story of the day continued to be the eulogistic accounts of the Fascist anniversary celebration not only in Rome, but throughout all of occupied Italy. Another front-page story was headed, "The Pope Enjoys Good Health." Based on an exclusive interview with the Pope's personal physician, Dr. Galeazzi-Lisi, it was an official Vatican denial of foreign press reports that Pius was ill. The new head of Vatican City health services had told a Fascist journalist that morning that the Pope was in excellent condition and that he maintained a full daily work schedule. He suffered only from anguish, the doctor was reported to have said, brought on by the war, "with its repercussions in privation, sorrow, and the destruction of irreplaceable artistic and religious monuments . . ."[1]

The only indication in the Fascist press of a German reaction to the Via Rasella was an unexplained announcement by the food administration. Beginning the following day, Saturday, March 25, the daily bread ration would be cut from 150 grams per person to 100—about the weight of a single roll which was made from a spongy substance from elm trees, dried chickpeas, mulberry leaves, corn flour, and a small amount of rye.[2]

In *l'Osservatore Romano*, the Vatican statement drafted earlier in the day was read now by some as foreboding a punishment more severe than the cutback in food rations.

To an American woman hiding from the Germans in a Roman convent, this message from the Church seemed ominous. She wrote in her diary: *

* Her diary would later be published under the pseudonym Jane Scrivener. A friend of a former US Ambassador to Spain and others in diplomatic circles, she has apparently not publicly revealed her true name. (*See* J. Scrivener, *Inside Rome with the Germans*, New York: Macmillan, 1945.)

This evening the *Osservatore Romano* appealed to all Romans to refrain from acts of violence in this most serious period of the war; acts, it says, which would only provoke severe reprisals giving rise to an infinite series of painful episodes. It concludes by begging the clergy and all those who can influence the people to persuade them to be strong, patient and self-controlled for their own sakes and for that of the city.

The writer of this short appeal (published on the front page in italics) must already know something of the consequences of yesterday's occurrence in Via Rasella. Perhaps we shall know tomorrow.[3]

XXII

ANOTHER AMERICAN in Rome, Major Peter Tompkins, who had returned from the party in Via Ruggero Fauro, heard a rumor at this hour of a German threat to shoot 300 hostages because of the Via Rasella attack. The source of the rumor was a Swiss woman who was caring for the apartment which had been procured for the OSS man. Tompkins disregarded this information, which in fact was untrue since the Germans had made no such threat, choosing for reasons of security to present the people of Rome with a *fait accompli.* In any event, Tompkins and his Italian associates did not alter their plans to raid the Pensione d'Oltremare; neither did they relate the rumored unprecedented threat to what the enemy's reaction might be to their attack. Tompkins and his men believed that the Germans would pay no heed to an assault on the Koch band.[1]

In a somewhat pathetic and ironic manner, the American spy continued to plot with Socialist partisan Franco Malfatti the liberation of Lieutenant Giglio.

"From Sensi, the good Swiss nurse," according to Tompkins, "we obtained, along with the latest rumor, a small roast beef, which we washed down with a bottle of good red wine while heatedly discussing the most effective way to get Cervo out of the hands of the brigands who were holding him prisoner." [2]

Though they had not seen Giglio carried away from the Oltremare, Malfatti's men had succeeded in the past twenty-four hours in learning important details about the building in Via Principe Amedeo. One of the men, Tompkins was told, had discovered that the apartment below the pensione was empty. Though they had earlier agreed not to attack unless there were less than fifteen armed guards in the prison, they now felt in a position to make the decision to break into the vacant apartment and with a charge of dynamite collapse the floor above. "In the confusion," Tompkins later recounted, "we would overcome the guards and free the prisoners. This would have given a tremendous boost to the low morale of the Resistance." [3]

The raid was set for the following day.

In the *cantina* hideout in Via Marco Aurelio the partisans of the Via Rasella reassembled and began working again.[4] No one had been hurt; they had not been identified. The attack appeared to be a complete success. They discussed the rumors that were running wildly through the city. "It was being said," according to Carla Capponi, "that the Germans were enraged; that the German command was exasperated by the repeated partisan attacks." [5] But in the absence of any hard news, the partisans, like all of Rome, could only wait and get on with the war. A messenger arrived at the *cantina* with the latest orders from the military commanders. They held a meeting. Everything seemed normal.

"The whole city speaks of the Via Rasella . . ." the Roman diarist Carlo Trabucco recorded that evening.[6] Foreign journalist de Wyss noted in her diary: "The Via Rasella is on everybody's lips." [7]

In the Via Tasso prison, the men who remained in cell number 7 asked a guard about the prisoners who had been taken away. "You should be happy," they were told in a whisper, "you are much better off than those poor fellows." [8]

The Third Wing of Regina Coeli had been draped for hours in thick, dismal silence. Somehow everyone knew the unspoken truth. Men and women—comrades and loved ones of those who had been sent away—looked at one another in hushed pain, unwilling to be the first to express the common fear. Suddenly the harsh stillness was cut with a piercing, mournful wail. It echoed through the corridors, against the bars of steel, and in every cell: "*Assassini! Tutti li hanno ammazzati! Tutti!*"—"Murderers! They killed them all! Everyone!" [9]

XXIII

SOME MINUTES before the conference at the Hotel Excelsior, Standartenfuehrer Dollmann telephoned Padre Pancrazio. Despite their agreement of twenty-four hours ago, neither man had contacted the other. Neither had been able to enlist his superior to their cause.

Now Dollmann informed Padre Pancrazio that there was no longer any purpose to their previous meeting. It was too late to do anything about impeding the reprisal. The Pope's representative had nothing to say beyond expressing his regrets that their efforts had been unsuccessful. With this the brief conversation ended.[1]

Dollmann entered the lobby of the Excelsior with General Wolff. They found Kappler there, waiting for them. Kappler, who had not slept in thirty-six hours, looked to Dollmann like a "true executioner." His eyes were "flaming in their deep, livid sockets."[2] The three Nazi officers went immediately to Wolff's suite in the hotel.

Once inside the rooms, Kappler burst forward in his best barracks voice and reported to Wolff. "General, sir," he exclaimed, "the orders to carry out reprisals were executed today . . ." This had been done by his own men, he said, "liquidating by shooting 335 persons."[3]

Wolff asked for further details, beginning with a full explanation of how the attack in Via Rasella could have taken place. Kappler reviewed the events of the past two days, including the particulars of the massacre.

The Polizeifuehrer replied that 335 executions were not enough. The people of Rome, he said, did not "merit favored treatment."[4]

At this point Consul Möllhausen and Press Attaché Borch entered the room. Dollmann went up to them and whispered, "Things are going very badly."[5]

The first order of business was the drafting of the communiqué to be released to the Fascist press by the Stadtkommandant's office, announcing the massacre.[6] It had to have the greatest possible impact on the Romans.

Two points had to be resolved before the communiqué could be issued. The first was a legal issue.

Kappler, aside from executing five persons too many, had apparently overstepped his authority in ordering another ten men to be shot when he learned of the death of the thirty-third German soldier. Not one of his colleagues or superiors wanted to share this responsibility with him. The Fuehrer's order, as interpreted by the Nazis in Rome, had become operative at the point when General Mälzer charged Kappler with carrying out the executions. At that hour Kappler had been ordered to shoot 320 men—everyone on his list and Caruso's supplementary list. No one had authorized him to kill an extra ten prisoners—and certainly not five others at random, for which there was no juridical basis.[7]

If someone, someday, had to pay for this error, everyone this night in Rome was in tacit agreement that it should be Kappler alone. Although in the short range it was in the Germans' best interest to announce the higher figure, strict secrecy was maintained regarding Kappler's double mistake. Kappler himself would perpetuate the secret as long as possible.

The second point was of a political nature. It evoked a lively discussion. The communiqué sought to place the blame for the reprisal on the Roman Resistance in order to turn the people's hatred of the Germans to hatred of the partisans. The occupiers, however, had no clue that might indicate which group of partisans had launched the Via Rasella attack. Doubtless, it must have come from the left wing of the underground. But to accuse one sector of the Resistance might rally the people around the other. Aware of conflicts in the CLN and the opposition of the monarchists to the activities of the left-wing parties, the Germans decided to accuse everyone. The formula they adopted could not have been more workable. They attributed the Via Rasella operations to *comunisti-badogliani*—the Communists and the King-Badoglio grouping, the monarchists.

Nothing could be more calculated to set the the right against the left. If the monarchists denied having anything to do with theVia Rasella incident they would fall squarely into the Germans' trap. The Resistance movement would shatter beyond all repair. For the *badogliani* to stand at the side of the Communists, however, would be to share responsibility and whatever wrath the Germans could arouse.

In any event it certainly would increase the already extreme friction among the anti-Fascists.*

* The author of the devastating phrase "*comunisti-badogliani,*" which would come under repeated scrutiny by Italian political analysts, has remained anonymous. Dollmann maintains that it came from OKW and that efforts by Borch to delete the "stupid phrase" were blocked by Himmler. If so, this would again attest to the lack of political acumen on the part of the Nazis in Rome who were responsible for the political sphere of the occupation. (*Cf.* E. Dollmann, *Roma nazista,* Milan: Longanesi, 1949, p. 249.)

With the wording of the communiqué approved, it was dispatched for translation into Italian and cleared for release the following morning.

General Wolff turned next to the principal item on his agenda. Because of the hostility of the Romans to the Germans, he said, as exemplified by the Via Rasella attack, Rome had to be immediately evacuated. The neighborhoods infested with communism had to be emptied, especially such intensely populated districts as Trastevere, San Lorenzo, Testaccio, and certain areas in the suburbs. Aside from wiping out resistance to the occupation, the Obergruppenfuehrer pointed out, the deportations would ease the difficult and costly process of supplying Rome with German food. Further, the Roman men could contribute to alleviating the manpower shortage in the north. He asked for opinions from the Nazis in Rome.[8]

At the suggestion that so vast an operation was not possible, Wolff replied that this type of discussion was inadmissible. Since 1933, he said, the word "impossible" had not existed in Germany.[9]

Kappler, who would have to handle the technical aspects of the evacuation, was cautiously reserved. To Möllhausen, he appeared to be "a man who had had enough." [10] Dollmann noted that he had "fallen into a state of torpor . . . there was no fear of any enthusiasm on his part." [11]

The Gestapo man said that even if only the most dangerous neighborhoods were emptied, at least two or three full divisions would still be required for security and escort.[12]

Dollmann brought up the problem of "the world reaction [and] the position of the Pope . . ." [13] He was convinced that Pius would not remain silent in this case.[14] Möllhausen and Borch discussed the diplomatic repercussions. General Mälzer, who was not present at the meeting, had already been informed of the deportation plan at the dinner for General Wolff. The matter was of no concern to him, Mälzer had said. His representative at the conference, the Nazi officer in charge of transportation, said nothing all evening.[15]

The discussion continued on past midnight. The talk remained animated. Kappler, however, had become catatonic but managed to stay awake.

Sometime after one in the morning, Wolff decided to telephone Himmler in Berlin and report. While they waited for the call to be put through, Wolff and Dollmann went into the adjoining room to decide what had to be said to the Reichsfuehrer. Dollmann was to report first and then Wolff. The latter left Dollmann waiting at the telephone and rejoined the company of the others.

About 2 A.M. the connection was made. "Himmler wanted to be informed on the situation in the capital," Dollmann said later. The Standartenfuehrer obliged. About the deportations, "I undertook to convince him of the need for the expediency of representations at the Vatican by the Ambassador." The Pope would have to be apprised of the mass evacuation if the Germans were to have any hope of averting a papal protest. On one ground or another Weizsäcker would have to gain some kind of *de facto* approval for the exodus from the Pope's own diocese.

Himmler was not certain this was necessary. "Unwillingly, he agreed," Dollmann said. To this Himmler added the condition that the Vatican was to be made aware of the plan "only if everyone decides it is indispensable." [16]

When General Wolff took the telephone, Dollmann could hear only "innumerable *Mein Reichsfuehrers* here and *Mein Reichsfuehrers* there . . ." Himmler was irate. He continued to insist on the deportations, issuing "tremendous, outright Neronian threats against Rome." [17]

In the end, Himmler and Wolff agreed to go ahead despite the difficulties raised in Rome. Wolff was to enlist the cooperation of Kesselring, and Kappler would draw up a plan on paper.

When the call to Berlin had been completed, the meeting was adjourned. Dollmann stood at the threshold of the general's suite and bade his colleagues good-night. He said to Möllhausen as he shook his hand, "Have patience, we did everything we could." [18]

XXIV

In the meantime the communiqué had been released. It would not be made public until noon of the 25th, when *Il Messaggero* would come out on the kiosks of Rome. But at 10:55 P.M. it had been moved on the Fascist wire service Stefani to the newsrooms of occupied Italy and Vatican City.

It read:

> On the afternoon of March 23, 1944, criminal elements executed a bomb attack against a column of German police in transit through Via Rasella. As a result of this ambush, thirty-two men of the German police were killed and several wounded.
>
> The vile ambush was carried out by *comunisti-badogliani*. An investigation is still being made to clarify the extent to which this criminal deed is attributable to Anglo-American involvement.
>
> The German Command has decided to terminate the activities of these villainous bandits. No one will be allowed to sabotage with impunity the newly affirmed Italo-German cooperation. The German Command has therefore ordered that for every murdered German ten *comunisti-badogliani* criminals be shot. This order has already been executed.[1]

PART FOUR

The Aftermath

March 25–31, 1944

"[Name] *ist am 24.3.1944 gestorben. Evtl. zurückgelassene persönliche Gegenstände können bei der Dienststelle der Deutschen Sicherheitspolizei in Via Tasso 155 abgeholt werden.*

I.A. [*signed*]

SS-Hauptsturmführer."

–Text of form letter received after long delay by Roman families of men executed in the Ardeatine caves [1]

I

At dawn on the 25th, Consul Möllhausen drove the thirty miles to Monte Soratte to see Kesselring.[1] The political grouping of the Third Reich in Rome had little taste for so laborious a task as evacuating the Holy City as an encore to the atrocity in the Ardeatine caves. The idea of deporting the Romans had been studied by the occupiers months before Himmler's and Wolff's brainstorm. The Germans in Rome had quickly concluded that it was too complicated.[2] Men like Möllhausen, Dollmann, and Kappler had no interest in leaving a city in which they had reached the power summit of their careers and found a culture with which they were delighted. The farther one stood from the Nazi core, the more authority one could assume. When these three men finally were forced to go north, they were in fact reduced to secondary, functionary roles more commensurate with their ranks. But while they remained in Rome, where the depraved clown Kurt Mälzer was "king," they were the princes.

"Upset by the idea of the unheard-of consequences that could result from the effectuation of such a plan," Consul Möllhausen later wrote, "I rushed to Monte Soratte at the break of day to try to gain Kesselring's support." [3]

The Field Marshal was uninformed of the meeting held last night at the Excelsior, and Möllhausen undertook to report to him. He then painted a vivid picture of what such an exodus would be like—"hundreds of thousands of persons marching north on foot, as there would be no other means of transportation, with their belongings piled on carts, in their arms, or . . . on their shoulders . . ." The weaker ones would die, falling on the side of the road "without assistance." From a military point of view, Möllhausen said, the supply roads from north to south would be blocked by a "formidable human sea." The German troops themselves would be in danger. According to his own account, Möllhausen concluded by declaring that "Germany could not treat Rome like an agglomeration of savages. History would never forgive her."[4]

Kesselring expressed disapproval of the plan, at least in the terms put by the young diplomat. As a military officer, the Commander in Chief looked upon the activities of the SS with disdain. He was often in conflict with General Wolff, especially on matters of jurisdiction. The delineation of their separate powers was, by design, never clearly drawn.[5] Unless there was a superior order from Jodl or Hitler, Kesselring could be relied upon to oppose the evacuation, which had little to do with the war and his own plans for the eventual military withdrawal from Rome to a new defense line in the north.

Assuring Möllhausen of his coolness to Wolff's mission, the Field Marshal accompanied the Consul to his car.

"The weather was radiant," Möllhausen recalled. From the 2,000-foot mountain they could see in the early morning light the spectacular expanse to the south. The goatherds and their flocks circled below them. Still lower lay the little town named for an imaginary saint, Saint Oreste, and, beyond it, Via Flaminia, sticking like a spear into the distant city. "We stopped for a moment in silence and cast our eyes toward Rome. Then Kesselring said, 'How strange are the ways of this, my beautiful kingdom, and so much interference, and so much struggle!' "[6]

II

At 8:05 a.m. the German guide at the catacombs of Saint Calixtus, the Silesian named Szenik, heard a volley of small explosions from the vicinity of the Ardeatine caves. He interpreted this as a continuation of the gunfire which yesterday had crackled through the entire afternoon. These explosions were made, however, by the engineers who had returned to the caves to complete the sealing they had begun the night before. Out of curiosity Szenik crossed above the catacombs to Via Ardeatina. He spoke with two German guards who had been on sentry duty through the entire night, inviting them to visit him sometime for a tour of the ancient Christian burial grounds. He then asked why there was so much activity going on here.

"Thirty-two SS soldiers were killed," he was told, "but for every one of them, we killed ten Italians."

The other guard said, "This was still too few." [1]

Less than an hour later there was a powerful blast from the tunnels. At 10:30 a German NCO, carrying a submachine gun, entered the catacombs. He wanted to use the telephone. He returned a half hour later for the same purpose. The guides asked him if there was any danger to Saint Calixtus. There was none, the German replied. There would be, he said, possibly one further explosion.[2]

From the same point he had stood the day before, the hogkeeper Nicola D'Annabile watched the continual arrivals and departures of the same trucks he had seen yesterday. He thought the shootings had not yet ended, and he estimated that the Germans had killed about 700 men by now.[3]

In a few hours, D'Annabile and the guides in Saint Calixtus would hear the final explosion and watch the Germans withdraw. With the Ardeatine left unguarded, some of the people in the area would soon be driven to search for the victims.

III

Before the morning ended, funeral services were conducted for the German soldiers who died in Via Rasella. They were attended by Dollmann, Kappler, and Möllhausen, who had returned from Monte Soratte. The principal speaker was Obergruppenfuehrer Karl Wolff. According to Dollmann, he gave a "bold" and "soldierly speech . . . without having shown the text to anyone." [1] Kappler, however, recalled that the general said, "I promise you, my dead comrades, that you will be avenged beyond that which has already been done." [2]

With the SS policemen buried, Wolff and Dollmann went to General Mackensen's headquarters to secure the troops for the evacuation plan. While Wolff was conferring with the head of the Fourteenth Army, Dollmann dealt with Mackensen's chief of staff, Colonel Hauser, whom he considered "very level-headed." [3]

Beyond the hearing range of his superior, Dollmann sought Hauser's support in opposition to the Himmler-Wolff order. The Wehrmacht officer who yesterday had refused to assist in the Ardeatine massacre was now against detaching troops from the Anzio front.[4] Mackensen, too, was expressing his coolness. But later, when Wolff left, the Prussian said of his disapproval, "I don't know if this is enough." [5] Wolff, despite the solid front of reserve, seemed determined to deport the Romans.

In the light of this brilliant Saturday morning, Major Peter Tompkins was less resolved than the previous night to carry out the raid on the Pensione d'Oltremare. "I had a hangover," he would recall, ". . . and without benefit of exhilarating brandy, the operation to free Cervo seemed more problematical; nevertheless it was the best that we could hope for." He was awaiting word from Franco Malfatti of the hour that day the attack would be mounted.[6]

IV

NOT FAR from Via Rasella, a small group of Romans began to gather some minutes before twelve o'clock at the entrance to the *Il Messaggero* building. They waited at the display case in Largo del Tritone for the first edition of the newspaper, which was placed there every day at noon.

Among them was Vincenzo Florio, the Sicilian who had been released some days earlier from Via Tasso. Walking with his wife in Via Tritone, he recognized a man in civilian clothes as an officer of the Gestapo. He was an interpreter named Fritch. Florio guessed that he had been sent to mingle with the Italians of the Via Rasella district to learn what was being said.[1]

Rosario Bentivegna, who had spent the night at the *cantina*, had walked from Via Marco Aurelio to the *Il Messaggero* building and now he too stood waiting for the day's first newspaper to come out.[2]

Carla Capponi had slept in a hideout in the Centocelle suburb. She had an appointment to meet Bentivegna at noon. Now she was at his side.[3]

When an unfolded copy of the newspaper was placed behind the glass, it appeared at first very ordinary. The principal stories that occupied the heads of the nine columns on page 1 dealt with the "decimated" Anglo-Americans at Cassino, the war in Asia, and the continuing volcanic activity of Vesuvius. About halfway down the right side of the page, however, a two-column box in bold type grabbed the eye. It was without a headline and was signed only "Stefani." Seized by these three ugly-looking paragraphs of broken letters in smudgy print, Romans began to read: "*Nel pomeriggio del 23 marzo 1944, elementi criminali* . . ." [4]

Fifty seconds, 117 words later, the merciless communiqué had been read. Carla felt a "terrible desperation, anguish." [5] The aching realization struck her immediately that the Germans must have killed the partisans that had been captured in recent weeks. "And they were our friends, our comrades. They were the ones who had taught us how to hate the Fascists. They were the ones who had risked their lives with us. They were the ones whom we loved." [6]

Bentivegna was overcome with "wrath, pain, and outrage at so cowardly a reprisal. The first impulse was to take revenge, to kill, call it what you will, in sum, to react so as to show them that we had not been broken, that they had not destroyed the Resistance . . . At that moment, for the first time, I understood the ferociousness of the enemy we faced." [7]

The young partisans of Rome were new to the war. Only by rumor did they know of the genocidal policies of Italy's former ally, of the death camps north of the Alps. They had grown up in the era of the Fascist lie. When Adolf Hitler journeyed triumphantly to Rome in 1938, the children of fascism had been dressed by their mothers in their finest clothes and they had been led by their teachers and schoolmasters to stand at the railroad station and welcome the glorious Fuehrer. Only months ago these children had seen the lie bared. Now they were partisans, but they had never looked into the eyes of an *Einsatzkommando*. They had never seen the black smoke puffing from the chimneys of Auschwitz, or naked Jewish, Russian, gypsy women digging the ditches they would die in. They had never heard of Zyklon B, I. G. Farben, Krupp, *Sonderkommando*, *Endlösung*, and Dr.

Mengele. Others in Rome, more sophisticated men, knew of these and other things; and they knew where the Jews of Rome had gone. But they did not speak of it, or print it, or broadcast it. They did not tell these children who had become the *partigiani.*

Even their comrades were silent. They never returned from Via Tasso to tell their fellow partisans about the Germans. Only later would Bentivegna learn of the "sickening tortures, of being whipped to death, of fingernails being ripped away, eyes being blinded, of flesh branding with fiery irons." [8] But now, reading the communiqué that had been hammered out the night before in the Hotel Excelsior, "I understood how far Nazi bestiality could go." [9] For Bentivegna there could be but one reply to a tougher enemy: a tougher Resistance.

V

ALTHOUGH EIAR did not broadcast the German press release for another four hours, once the news appeared in print, it spread rapidly. With the tens of thousands of copies of *Il Messaggero* being disseminated throughout the city, the reaction of the people of Rome was immediate and permanent. They were stunned and lacerated with disbelief, hatred, fear, sorrow, immeasurable pain and paralytic terror: " . . . a shiver of horror ran through those who read this cold-blooded communiqué," the American woman hiding in a Catholic convent noted that day.[1] The majority of Romans would never during the occupation recover from this heaviest of blows.

The announcement that ten times the number of Germans killed in Via Rasella had already been shot immediately affected directly hundreds of thousands of people in the Eternal City. Nearly everyone knew of or had a father, mother, son, daughter, relative, or friend in the hands of the Germans and the Fascists. Who among them had been executed?

Almost at once bizarre rumors began to churn. They were to haunt and torment the people of this city for days, then weeks.

"Groans have been heard," people said when it became known during the day that the victims had been sealed in the abandoned sand mines of Via Ardeatina.[2] The Germans went back, found four men alive, and executed them a second time. "A youth with four bullet wounds in his legs escaped during the night." Now he was hiding in the south part of the city.[3] "Not 320, but more than 500 were shot . . ."[4] Of 550 killed, "300 were machine-gunned in the Colosseum."[5] According to one source, another 12 or 14 or 16 SS police wounded in Via Rasella died in the hospital so another 120 or 140 or 160 Italians were taken out and shot.[6] "That is the truth," foreign newsman de Wyss recorded in her diary with understandable credulity. "It is simple and natural enough for anybody who knows the Germans, but many Italians repeat naïvely that they would never have expected such a thing."[7]

This naïveté in the days ahead would be cruelly exploited by the enemies of antifascism.

VI

FROM UNDER the first wave of shock, the first reactions began to emerge that afternoon. The full directorate of the Military Junta of the Resistance, which included the right-wing parties, gathered hastily for an emergency meeting. One element of the right wing argued that the CLN should deny having anything to do with the attack in Via Rasella. Giuseppe Spataro, the military commander of the Christian Democrats, demanded that all future operations against the Germans in Rome be cleared through the Junta. Amendola, of the Communists, refused on the ground that the partisan activity would be bureaucratized and ultimately neutralized. He threatened to withdraw the Communists from the now leaderless CLN. Spataro's motion was defeated when he was unable to win any support for the proposal.[1] On the matter of disavowing the attack, Manlio Brosio, the military representative for the Liberals,* intervened in favor of the Via Rasella partisans. The CLN, he said, had to assume full responsibility for all its armed actions against the enemy.[2]

The calculated language of the Nazi communiqué was, however, doing its caustic work on the anti-Fascists. The new atmosphere in the Resistance was already clouded with charges and recriminations. A consensus seemed beyond reach.

For the *gappisti*, there was little to debate. They met and agreed at once to identify themselves as the armed partisan unit that carried out the attack. They issued the following statement, which was dated March 26:

> 1. Against the enemy who occupies our soil, sacks our wealth, provokes the destruction of our cities and our countryside, starves our children, deports our workers, tortures, kills, massacres, there is only one duty for all Italians: to strike him, without hesitation, at every moment, wherever he is found, in his men and in his things. To this duty the Groups for Patriotic Action have dedicated themselves.
>
> 2. All GAP actions are true and real acts of war which strike exclusively at German and Fascist military objectives, contributing in this way to sparing the capital from aerial bombardments, destruction, and casualties.
>
> 3. The attack of March 23 against the column of German police, which was marching in full battle dress through

* Currently Secretary General of NATO.

the streets of Rome, was accomplished by two groups of GAP, using the tactics of the partisan guerrilla: surprise, speed, and boldness.

4. The Germans, defeated in combat in Via Rasella, vented their hatred of Italians, killing women and children and shooting 320 innocent persons. Not one member of GAP fell into their hands nor into those of the Italian police.

The 320 Italians, massacred by German machine guns, disfigured and thrown into a common grave, cry for revenge. And it will be pitiless and terrible! We swear it!

5. In reply to today's lying and intimidating communiqué from the German Command, the GAP Command declares that the patriotic and partisan guerrilla actions in Rome will not cease until the total evacuation from the capital on the part of the Germans.

6. The activities of GAP will be increased until the armed national insurrection routing the Germans from Italy, the destruction of fascism, and the winning of Independence and Freedom! [3]

In the Vatican, judging from its official reaction, the expected German communiqué was met with singular equanimity. The cherished prestige of the Pope could not have been more affronted by this German crime against the people of the Holy City.* These were not Jews of a distant land, or Bolsheviks, or armed soldiers who were cut down in the Ardeatine caves, but innocent children of the Holy See, 253

* The papal image was in the forefront of the Vatican's wartime policy makers. When Rome was bombed by the Allies for the first time in the war, Monsignor Montini complained to the American Tittmann that "the Pope was desperately hoping Rome would not be bombed during [the] war since it would have meant so much to his prestige afterwards if it could be said that [the] city had been spared out of respect for [the] Common Father." (Telegram from Tittmann to Hull of July 26, 1944, *Foreign Relations of the United States, op. cit.*, p. 938.)

of whom were Catholics. Never had a Holy Father been so lightly regarded by a secular power in Rome. But the Church would not be offended. Its far-reaching aims could not be allowed to be lost in polemic.

The Vatican's attitude had already been sounded the day before. Nothing had changed. But now that the whole world knew what had yesterday been shared by a select few, the Holy See decided it could not be silent. Whereas twenty-four hours ago, while Romans were dying in the Ardeatine caves, the Vatican had called on the people of the city to repress their "violent urges," the police to keep public order, the clergy to pacify the faithful, *l'Osservatore Romano* this afternoon addressed itself to other elements of this unhappy *Urbe*. On page 1 it began with the heading "A Communiqué from Stefani on the Deeds in Via Rasella." [4] This was followed by the text of the German announcement and then, authoritatively italicized, the Vatican declared:

> In the face of such deeds every honest heart is left profoundly grieved in the name of humanity and Christian sentiment. Thirty-two victims on the one hand; and on the other three hundred and twenty persons sacrificed for the guilty parties who escaped arrest. Yesterday we addressed a sorrowful appeal for serenity and calm; today we repeat the same request, with more ardent affection, with more fervid insistence.
>
> Above and beyond the strife, moved only out of Christian charity, out of love of country, out of fairness to all "the facts" and to all the sons of "the only way of redemption" from the hatred that is nourished everywhere and the vengeance that is perpetrated everywhere; abhorring blood no matter where it is shed, conscious of the state of mind of the citizenry, persuaded by the fact that one cannot, one must not push things to the point of desperation, which makes for the most dreadful decisions and yet is the most

> dreadful of all forces, we call upon the irresponsible elements to respect human life, which they can never have the right to sacrifice, to respect the innocence of those who are their fatal victims; from the responsible elements we ask for an awareness of their responsibility toward themselves, toward the lives they seek to safeguard, toward history and civilization.[5]

With this gratuitous pronunciamento, the Vatican had now gone beyond placing itself on the side of all good and against all evil. Scarcely a moment after the bodies in the Ardeatine caves had stopped writhing, the Universal Church, before dusk of that day, had publicly declared not the Germans but the partisans of the Via Rasella the "guilty parties" ("*i colpevoli*"). Moreover, the language of the statement implied that the "guilty parties" not only were responsible for thirty-two victims, but somehow they, not the Germans, were fundamentally responsible for 320 who were sacrificed *for* the culprits "who escaped arrest."

Thus, suggesting that the partisans in escaping arrest were the cause of the sacrifice, the Vatican became the first to spread the germs of a controversy that would continue beyond two decades. Soon, from seeds such as these the false notion would grow that the German executioners had proposed to the Roman Resistance that the lives of the 335 prisoners would be spared if the combatants of the Via Rasella were to surrender.[6]

VII

By late afternoon the news had spanned the continents, diminishing in interest and impact with the distance it traveled. In Rome the German communiqué had appeared in *Osservatore* and in all of the Fascist evening papers. It had been broadcast by Radio Rome, and newspapers throughout occupied Italy, including *Corriere della Sera* of Milan and *La Stampa* of Turin, were carrying the Stefani dispatch on their front page.[1] German and Japanese correspondents in Rome had filed it for their domestic press and their occupied territories. The Swiss Telegraph Agency had reported the story throughout Europe and to the United States Office of War Information. And on West 43rd Street in New York, deskmen making up the Sunday *Times* were rewriting an English version of the Swiss dispatch, headlining the three-paragraph story "320 Hostages Killed by Germans in Rome —Nazis Exact 10–1 Penalty for Slaying of Occupying Police." [2]

Somehow, however, after the hour of sunset the American OSS spy in the center of Rome was still unaware of the news.[3] While waiting for word about the raid from Malfatti, Tompkins had been joined by some friends with whom he passed the afternoon. During the early evening a fuse burned out in his apartment. In the cellar of the building, while repairing the damage, he received from a refugee-tenant information "just heard from the maid of the bombed-out police commissioner who lived on the floor below us . . ." [4] The American's blood was chilled as he heard "the rumor" that 320 men had been shot by the Germans.

Tompkins returned to his flat, and Malfatti arrived shortly afterward.

"They have shot Cervo," the Italian said, "and eleven of our men."

Malfatti had learned that Giglio was seen, unable to stand, at Regina Coeli and was carried away with other prisoners.

"We will kill a lot of guilty Fascists," Malfatti said.

"All who are guilty," Tompkins replied.[5]

But he felt incapable of sadness. With admirable honesty, the youthful major would later recall that "I was a little scared, but more than anything—horrible as it may seem upon analysis—relieved." The death of the Italian lieutenant, Tompkins felt, was an escape for Giglio from the tortures he had suffered. For himself and his fellow agents it was a release "from the constant fear that he might not be able to refrain from giving us away." The American was filled with "the warm, glowing realization that a human being had achieved one of the highest peaks within his limits." [6]

It occurred to Tompkins that evening that at the moment Giglio had been slain "we, his friends, had been drinking brandy in the apartment of a Palatine count in the arms of beautiful girls . . ." But had they known this, "we might have but drunk deeper, danced later into the night." [7]

The plan to attack the Pensione d'Oltremare was not put aside. It would be a way to avenge their fallen comrades, Tompkins believed. In his diary that night he wrote "we are planning a little surprise for the brutes that torture people at Via Principe Amedeo 2, in the form of 80 pounds of dynamite . . ." [8]

Unfortunately, however, the operation would never be consummated.

In the north, another, more celebrated diarist, Donna Rachele Mussolini, recorded her evening of March 25. "My husband is furious about what happened in Rome," she said.[9] The Duce had been silent at supper, but Donna Rachele had subtly managed to make him speak his mind.

"What was done," said her husband, "was terrible. They think they can treat Italians as if they were Poles . . . I didn't have time to stop it, only to protest. Why is there so much hatred? That wretch who threw the bomb that killed some thirty German soldiers and provoked the awful reaction, which he himself escaped, did not change the destiny of the war. The Germans, for their part, will certainly not stop with this pitiless reprisal the repetition of such deeds." * [10]

VIII

In a German aircraft flying north from Viterbo through the night, Obergruppenfuehrer Karl Wolff was completing the last leg of his troubleshooting mission to Rome.

After his meeting with Mackensen and stops at two Roman hospitals to visit at the bedside of the German survivors of the Via Rasella incident, Wolff had returned to Monte Soratte. There, with Field Marshal Kesselring, he had resolved the differences between Rome and Berlin with regard to the evacuation plan.[1]

Kesselring, who had consulted with Mackensen, declared that in view of the situation at the front he could not at this time provide the large number of troops needed for the operation.

Wolff agreed to a temporary delay until such time as the Fourteenth Army could spare the men. He formally proposed that Obersturmbannfuehrer Kappler be assigned by Kesselring's command to draw up a detailed military plan to be operational for the designated neighborhoods. The Field Marshal was then to present Kappler's plan to Reichsfuehrer Himmler. Kesselring agreed.[2]

* Less than five months later the *Capo del Governo*, according to his wife, would also protest the German massacre of fifteen partisans whose bodies were thrown into Milan's Piazzale Loreto for public exhibition. In this case, he again did not "have time to stop it," although, as in Rome on Mar. 24, 1944, it was the Fascist police who turned over the victims to the Germans from an Italian prison. The Duce informed Hitler in Aug. 1944, Donna Rachele said, that no one could carry out reprisals on Italian soil without his permission. (R. Mussolini, *La mia vita con Benito*, Milan: Mondadori, 1948, p. 247.) In April of the following year, the Duce himself was exhibited in Piazzale Loreto. His body was hung there upside down for twenty-four hours on the day following his execution, Apr. 28, 1945.

With this, the forced exodus of the men of Rome was relegated to some other day. When the German storm that had burst with the bomb in Via Rasella finally subsided, the deportations were never spoken of again.

IX

ON SUNDAY, the 26th, two weeks before Easter, the 335 bodies in the Ardeatine caves began to issue a terrible, fetid odor. Like a cry for justice, it soon arose to permeate the air of the Appian Way, drawing increasing numbers of Romans to the tomb.[1]

A passing priest named Nicola Cammarota stopped that morning at the sealed entrances to the tunnels and began to pray. In the absence of information about whether the men had been afforded religious assistance, the priest imparted "conditional" absolution. The matter was then taken up by the Vatican, which had been informed, apparently by rumor, that the doomed men had been attended to by a Silesian priest. Monsignor Montini, the papal *Sostituto*, was said to have inquired of the Germans if this were true and received a denial.[2]

At the Saint Calixtus catacombs the German guide Szenik decided to make another visit to the caves. Accompanied by a clergyman from the catacombs, he investigated the area, collecting about sixty-five feet of electric wire. There was nothing else. Later a French guide came by with some flowers, which mysteriously disappeared during the day.[3]

X

WITH THE publication of *Il Messaggero* that noon, it was clear that the Vatican's "open city" negotiations had withstood the ordeal of the past days. The Germans had not carried out their threat to review their attitude. A new communiqué was issued by the German Command, outlining what steps had been taken to observe the open-city proclamation "in order to deprive the Anglo-American enemy of every pretext for the senseless bombardment of the city of Rome." [1]

It then declared:

> Through the city and in the city there is no military traffic of any kind. These measures have been taken by the German High Command in the interest of the city of Rome and for the good of the civilian population, despite the difficulties of a military character, which arise from them.
>
> If, therefore, *comunisti-badogliani* elements, as happened March 23, try to disrupt these far-reaching provisions and if other circles misinterpret these measures, the German High Command will be forced to take such military measures as it deems necessary in the interest of the conduct of war operations in Italy.
>
> *With this, the fate of Rome and its civilian population, apart from the conduct of the Anglo-Americans, is placed exclusively in the hands of the people of Rome.* [Italics in original.] [2]

In a separate statement handed to foreign correspondents "to lay responsibility for future outrages at their proper doors," the Germans said that troops and matériel had been forbidden to enter or pass through Rome. "This document," they concluded, "should not be considered a sign of weakness on our part, as should be amply demonstrated by the latest military developments in the fighting south of Rome. This decision was taken by the High Command merely with the aim of saving Rome from total destruction." [3]

Reading the German communiqué, anti-Fascist journalist Carlo Trabucco wrote that day: "To listen to them, they never set foot in Rome. It's the lies of enemy propaganda. . . . The Romans, in fact, do not have eyes to see what is happening in their streets and in their *piazze*. They have to listen to Radio London—the lies of enemy propaganda—to find out that the Germans are everywhere in Rome." [4]

The American woman hiding in a Roman convent commented equally as wryly: "The rumor about the Germans having agreed to withdraw to a point 20 kilometers beyond Rome so that there may be no more attacks from the air is repeated by everyone, high and low, wise and foolish, diplomats, market women, journalists, bus drivers, priests, shop girls. They are going, they say. Oh, yes, there is no doubt about it. Just a few would remain to police the city. And what might that mean? Well, they didn't know." [5]

The Pope had taken care of everything with the Germans, the rumor continued. Rome would be a "hospital city" only and Pius would take charge of the wounded. An international corps of neutrals would police the city. *Papa* Pacelli had already ordered 60,000 armbands bearing the word "Vatican" for them to wear.[6]

Nevertheless, in subsequent weeks the actual removal of some detachments from the city was accompanied by a pause in Allied air attacks. The German propaganda offensive represented a major tactical victory. The Eternal City not only remained occupied but in having been terrorized, it was becoming pacified.

To the extent that the bombings were halted, all factions of the Resistance and the Vatican could lay equal claim to the success of their policies—no matter how divergent they may have been. To the extent that the people of Rome would never rise up from under the German heel and with its own muscle throw out the Nazi-Fascist oppressor, it was a victory for the Roman Catholic Church alone.

XI

On this first Sunday of spring, the leaders of the Communist Party in Rome, assessing Bonomi's resignation, were beginning to realize that the CLN had been pushed too far and too hard by the left. In a secret document dated March 26, the directorate of the Roman Communists stated that "the crisis which has currently struck the National Liberation Committee of Rome poses the need . . . for a revision of our policies."[1]

The time had come, the Communists recognized, to make concessions to their political opponents and "to modify the positions we took in October and November with regard to the monarchy . . ."[2]

Such an about-face would break the solid front of the three left-wing parties. When it was announced in Naples the following week, it astounded the Socialists and Actionists, as well as many rank-and-file Communists. For the PCI, it meant the loss of friends and members and created permanent enmity and disillusion.

The party was apparently willing to risk cries of "betrayal" and "*possibilismo*" in order to combat what it discerned as a right-wing-monarchist conspiracy underlying the technical issues of a postwar government.

"There are evident signs," the March 26 situation report stated, "of a tendency to resolve the governmental problem with the expulsion from the Government of the parties of the left." The real purpose of the "reactionary-monarchist forces," according to the Communists, was not to find a *modus vivendi* with the CLN as a whole. These forces were only using the issue to provoke a crisis in the Committee. They sought to "rupture" the CLN in order to set up a right-wing government of the Liberals, Catholics (Christian Democrats), Democratic Laborites, Badoglio, "and all the other men and currents linked to the most reactionary cliques that are presently gathering closely around the monarchy." [3]

The PCI, which could hardly be accused of paranoia, foresaw that unless the breach in the CLN could be healed, the rightist "maneuver" would succeed. In this event the "demagogic" positions of the Socialists and the Actionists would tend to harden, and these two parties would gain the upper hand among the Italian left. The end result would be, the Communists believed, that the PCI "in particular" would be excluded from the future administration of the country.

The central task of the party had to be the prevention of this situation, it said. The unity of the CLN had to be preserved, "even at the cost of making some concessions to the right, in order to try to save what at this moment is really essential to our position: the need to bring about a decisive turn in the conduct of the war; and to have a government based on the anti-Fascist parties." [4] While most people thought the PCI was fighting for socialism, in reality it was worrying about being excluded from the Old Establishment.

The document did not indicate what the concessions should be, but in the meantime the Secretary of the PCI, Palmiro Togliatti, who had spent the past eighteen years living in exile in the Soviet Union, was secretly traveling westward from Moscow to return to Italy.

In a few days, on April 10, still using the code name Ercole Ercoli, he would unleash the dramatic announcement in Naples which would become known as Togliatti's *svolta*—his turn. Turning the entire political situation upside down, the Communist would announce that winning the war had to come first; he was ready to collaborate with the monarchy and form a "Government of National Unity" in order to intensify the fight for national liberation.*

XII

DURING THE week beginning Monday, March 27, while demoralizing rumors continued to plague Rome with the encouragement of the silent occupiers, the Fascist press picked up the antipartisan cudgel.

Monday afternoon's *Giornale d'Italia* came out with an article by its director, Umberto Guglielmotti, saying that all the victims of the Ardeatine massacre were responsible for the attack in Via Rasella. Those, he wrote, who were "taken by justice were actually directly or indirectly guilty of the attack . . . This is not then the shooting of hostages and a reprisal . . . but the strict and severe application of the laws of war." [1]

Bruno Spampanato, of *Il Messaggero,* called the atrocity "exemplary German justice." [2] In an editorial entitled "Clear Words to the People of Rome," he said that the British and the Americans had encouraged "irresponsible elements" to organize terror in the city. "On March 23," the Fascist wrote, "thirty-two soldiers of the Reich, who belonged to police forces operating in the interest and the tranquility of Rome, tragically lost their lives in the most ferocious of attacks.

* Togliatti's practical politics brought embarrassment and chagrin to many Communists and accusations, especially from the Actionists, that he had forsaken the aspirations of the people and had bowed to the will of the Russians, the British, and the Americans. In any case, within a month an Allied-approved "Government of National Unity" was formed with the six parties, with Badoglio at the head. The King announced that he would abdicate in favor of a lieutenancy of the realm until free elections decided the fate of the monarchy. Bonomi withdrew his resignation. For the first time in Italian history the Communist Party had entered the Government—a victory that would, however, prove to be of brief duration.

. . . These valorous *comunisti* and these gallant *badogliani*, who fight their war in the style of their Anglo-American, Bolshevik, Savoyard bosses, had until yesterday won the incautious consent of certain 'right-thinkers.' But these 'right-thinkers,' be they bourgeois or proletarian, know now that the criminals who have taken up arms had bombs and explosives in their homes instead of ideas in their head."[3]

The severe measures of the Germans, he said, were taken out of the necessity to maintain public order by any means. As the Germans had said, the people of Rome held their destiny in their own hands. Future attacks, he warned, would cause the Germans to react as they had on March 23 "against known guilty parties and their accomplices." Spampanato called for every citizen "to fight on the home front with good sense, in control of his nerves, with his patriotism, and also with an assiduous faith in a better tomorrow for the Nation." *[4]

In the middle of the week Luigi Barzini's Stefani news agency released the following brief item: "Women and Children Killed in the March 23 Attack in Via Rasella: In the attack perpetrated against German soldiers in Via Rasella, seven Italians, almost all women and children who were passing through the street, also lost their lives."[5]

This figure, which was never substantiated, soon was inflated to higher numbers, with the implication that the civilians had been killed as a result of the bomb blast.

The clandestine press tried to galvanize public opinion into a single will to strike back against the Germans. The Action Party newspaper *l'Italia Libera* came out with the headline "We Shall Not Bow to the Nazi Terror."[6]

* After the war, Spampanato would find it more convenient to refer to the Nazi reprisal as "cruel." Guglielmotti of *Giornale d'Italia*, after fleeing Rome, would call the Ardeatine crime "pitiless." (*Cf.* B. Spampanato, *Contromemoriale*, Vol. 2, Rome: L'Illustrato, 1951–52, p. 179; U. Guglielmotti, *L'Assedio di Roma*, Milan: Mondadori, 1944, p. 75.)

"From the grave where the bodies of the still unvindicated martyrs are amassed," the paper wrote, "a solemn and imperious cry is raised in a single word: 'Fight!' Fight for the Italy for which they dreamed and so nobly consecrated with their blood."[7] They had died for an Italy of free men, *partigiani*, workers, and peasants who were fighting for their nation and the salvation of Europe.

L'Unità, the Communist Party's underground newspaper, was published on Thursday, March 30, with the headline "Eternal Glory to the 320 Shot at Rome. Avenge Our Martyrs–Liberate Our Country." The newspaper gave the first full account of the Via Rasella attack and the reprisal. It was sparse and somewhat inaccurate in detail, but generally was correct. Calling for a war against the Germans "to the death," the paper said that the Romans would be "neither deceived, nor blackmailed, nor intimidated" by the Germans and the Fascists.[8]

In an unsigned article, Giorgio Amendola, the Junta leader, said that in their martyrdom, the men who had been executed had from that day "the right to demand from us that no sacrifice be too great, that no risk be judged too serious, that no effort be considered too hard in order that they might be avenged."[9]

The appeals of the Resistance served only to intensify the people's hatred of the Germans and the Fascists. But this did not find expression in mass action against the enemy. The anguished Romans had but a single overriding concern: They sought desperately to learn who among them had been executed.

The Germans, poking the open wounds of the people in whatever way they could, were withholding the list of Ardeatine victims. While increasing numbers of Romans took up a vigil at Via Tasso Gestapo headquarters to wait for the release of the names, many others began to turn to the Vatican and to Padre Pancrazio.[10] They appealed to him to intercede at the German offices. Weeks later, Vatican Secretary of State Cardinal Maglione queried the German Embassy in behalf of the families who had asked the help of the Holy See. The reply was that the Embassy wanted to maintain its position of having nothing to do with the matter and could do no more than refer inquiries to the Via Tasso.[11]

Even a request by the Fascist police for the list of executed men brought the cryptic reply from the untrusting Kappler that he could not reveal the names to anyone since it would prejudice investigations being conducted by the Gestapo.[12]

In the meantime a list of about 200 names of men said to have been among those shot in the Ardeatine caves began to circulate secretly in the city. Of doubtful authenticity, it nevertheless became a hot item for speculators, who were selling the list for 10,000 lire ($100) a copy.[13] Of the purchasers of the list, one Roman noted at the time: "Many [names] were missing, but whoever did not find the name of his own loved one, still could hope . . ."[14]

The Germans were unrelenting in tightening their stranglehold on the Romans.

In the early part of the week of March 27, someone who lived near the Appian Way called the police to report the terrible stench of death that was thickening the air throughout the district. The information was passed to the chief of a sectional bureau, who in turn told Questore Caruso.

"I notified Kappler," Caruso said later. "He replied that he would have the inconvenience eliminated."[15]

The action taken was an order to dump the city's garbage at the sealed entrances to the Ardeatine caves, presumably to mask the cadaverous odors with a more conventional smell.[16]

XIII

UNSATISFIED WITH the coverage given the events by the Fascist press, Stadtkommandant Mälzer called a press conference, which featured a personal report from Obersturmbannfuehrer Kappler.[1]

It was held at General Headquarters of the German Command in Corso d'Italia and was attended by the daily newspapers, Stefani, EIAR, and an undersecretary from the Fascist Ministry of Popular Culture, which was the official instrument of news censorship, and Borch, the press attaché at the German Embassy.

General Mälzer opened the meeting with some brief remarks. He advocated a "coordination" of the Roman press "so as to avoid misunderstandings which could lead to unfavorable consequences." [2] Then, speaking as if the Germans planned to be in Rome for the duration of the thousand-year Reich, he said that in the future, press conferences such as this one would be held periodically for an exchange of views and to regulate the news. Now the "King of Rome" gave the floor to Kappler, declaring that the Gestapo officer had an interesting statement which would be useful to the Roman press. The newspapers would, as a result of what Kappler had to say, be able to enlighten the people of Rome and "convince them of the opportuneness and the necessity of collaborating with the Germans." [3]

When Kappler stood, Bruno Spampanato of *Il Messaggero* greeted the German with an obsequious bow and a smile. Most of the other Italians present regarded Kappler with about the same amount of esteem he held for them. The German spoke for about thirty minutes, dealing exclusively with the Via Rasella attack and the German answer.

From a folder of anti-Fascist newspapers, he withdrew a copy of the March 30 edition of *l'Unità* and held it up for all to see. "*L'Unità*," he said, "has arrived at the point of elevating the 320 men shot in Rome to the ranks of heroes and of equating the Germans to ferocious beasts."[4] Such articles were "deplorable," he said. This and other evidence demonstrated that the people of Rome, by their conduct, supported the carrying out of the Via Rasella attack. If such acts are repeated, he declared, the German Command will have to take even harsher measures. It was up to the Fascist press to combat Communist propaganda.

The purpose of his statement today, Kappler said, should not in any way be construed as an attempt to justify the measures taken in the Ardeatine caves. Rather, it was to get "the Roman population to collaborate, in full awareness, in the suppression of attacks against the Germans."[5] He deplored, he said, the essentially passive attitude of the people. This could not go on or the German Command would be forced to use "very severe methods."

At this point, Kappler unfolded a chart which purported to illustrate how the Via Rasella attack took place. The detachment was made up from a company of the Bozen Regiment and was returning from military exercises. Despite his investigation, he had been unable to learn, he stated, whether the bomb had been detonated on the right or the left flank of the column. He had learned that it was a "very powerful" explosive device, although no fragments had been found. He then went on to give a reasonably accurate account of what took place, considering that it was reconstructed from information given by his own men.* He described the Italian mortar shells used by the partisans and revealed the fact that many pistol and rifle shots were fired against the windows of the houses in Via Rasella, although he maintained that such

* Despite incorrect figures and a highly tendentious presentation, Kappler's statement was remarkably truthful. Many future chronicles of these events–Germans, Italians, and others–would fail to maintain even Kappler's level of objectivity. The outright lies, although already being nurtured, had yet to be born.

fire had been returned. Kappler said that the number of attackers was unusually high and they had not been captured. He blamed the Romans for this, since they did not cooperate with the German authorities.

General Mälzer followed Kappler's statement with rapt attention. At what he felt were appropriate moments, he grunted his approval.

Speaking, as always, in his vacuous monotone, Kappler described the scene in Via Rasella after the attack. He said that of the persons rounded up from the houses in the street, 129 were detained, of whom eleven were later shot in the caves because they were "known Communists."

The German repeatedly insisted that the action had been carried out with at least the complicity of people in the neighborhood. For example, he said, the women who hung out their clothes on the terrace early that afternoon must have noticed something unusual going on in the street below. Another instance of this noncooperation, he said, occurred prior to the Via Rasella incident when the Germans had received a tip that some "Communists" were going to carry out an armed attack. The Gestapo spotted them boarding a tram. They stopped and surrounded it, but when they searched the attackers no arms were found. Under one of the seats in the tram, Kappler recounted, they recovered four hand grenades and two revolvers. "Is it possible," Kappler asked, "that when the Communists became aware that the tram was surrounded by the SS, they could have hidden the arms without any of the passengers seeing them?" [6] Not one passenger, he complained, admitted seeing the arms being hidden.

"It is this attitude," Kappler asserted, "that authorizes the taking of hostages." [7]

In the case of the Ardeatine reprisal, however, it was inexact to refer to it as "shooting of hostages," since the victims had been political prisoners for "a long time." They were, according to Kappler's version, for the most part already tried and sentenced, or had been arraigned before the German Military Tribunal. Admitting that there had not been enough persons in these categories, Kappler said that the remaining victims were selected from among prisoners at his disposition and some were handed over by the Italian authorities. He maintained, however, the fictitious figure of 320 as the number of men who had been executed.

It was not true, as had been rumored, that the men had been blown up inside a cave. They were shot first, then the entrances to the caves were mined to cut off access to the bodies. Without specifying when, he said that the families of the victims would be notified.

Concluding his report, the Gestapo officer pointed out that the severity of the Via Rasella attack would have justified an even tougher German reply. He called on the Fascist press of Rome to mount a campaign portraying the dangers of noncollaboration. To help them do this, which he said would augur well for the future, he invited them to publish his statement of today.

According to captured stenographic notes found in the Ministry of Popular Culture after the liberation of Rome, Kappler received the following reply: "It would be better to suspend publication of this news since this is not the most suitable moment to rekindle in the hearts of the Romans—especially during the Easter season—a pain which has scarcely subsided." [8]

XIV

ON MONDAY afternoon, March 27, a priest from the catacombs of Saint Calixtus, Michele Valentini, and Don Cammarota, the priest who on Sunday had stopped at the Ardeatine caves and imparted conditional absolution, went to the site and found an entrance to the tunnels.

They walked the length and the width of the passageways, but about thirty feet from the entrance the trail ended, obstructed by soft piles of sand, freshly accumulated from the caved-in walls. They could find no trace of the victims.[1]

On Tuesday, a cold and rainy day, the priests made several visits to the caves. They tried to locate the source of the cadaverous odor, which was becoming more and more acute. On Wednesday, Don Valentini went back with the German guide Szenik to the tunnels he had explored on Monday. "We succeeded in establishing that the stench came from the vicinity of the entrances," Don Valentini said later, "while from inside the tunnels it weakened in such a way as to become barely perceptible at the rear. That oriented the search around the exit, but without any result." [2]

During these days increasing numbers of Romans were learning that the massacre had been committed in the sand pits of Via Ardeatina. Mourners of the unknown dead made pilgrimages to the caves, only to lay their flowers and wreaths on a field of garbage.

Some of the people, tormented by grief and outraged at the insult dumped at the site of the massacre, tore through the garbage and piled it to the side to make room for their flowers and a place to pray.[3]

In the early afternoon of the 30th, a band of some twenty boys from the poverty-stricken Garbatella district were scavenging the area of the Ardeatine caves for booty. They found a hat, two shoes, and a length of electric wire which ran along the ground above the tunnels. They followed the trail of the wire. It led to a swarm of giant flies. The insects were clustered just over the caved-in entrances, darting and buzzing in and out of a large hole through the ceiling of one of the tunnels.

Some of the priests from Saint Calixtus were nearby and

the boys told them what they had found. Gathering around the hole, the boys and the clergymen looked down. They saw a wooden ladder, which they removed. The electric wire ran into the opening. They pulled it up. The end of the wire was covered with a greasy substance. It was human fat.[4]

The priests did not descend into the tunnel, but instead returned to the catacombs, where they informed their colleagues. Don Valentini and Don Fernando Giorgi, of the Silesian Institute at Saint Calixtus, and another clergyman, Don Perinella, who had been at the hole, rushed to the caves.

In the meantime the band of young scavengers had been joined by another twenty boys, but no one had yet gone through the hole. The priests chased the boys back from the opening. Then, Don Valentini and Don Giorgi lit a torch and went down.

"We entered through the hole in the tunnel," Don Valentini recounted. "At about six feet from the opening we stumbled upon a pile of corpses." [5]

They lay beyond an accumulation of earth. By the light of the torch, Don Giorgi saw that the bodies were "covered with a thick mold." [6]

"Six were plainly visible," according to Don Valentini, "although they lay face down. The tunnel extending behind them was completely filled by cadavers lying in awkward positions.

"In front of one of the cadavers we found an old man's cane and a can of sulfur. The victims had their hands tied behind their backs with heavy cord. One had his left hand free: an aristocratic hand." [7]

Don Valentini and Don Giorgi immediately notified Monsignor Respighi at the Vatican.[8]

At eight o'clock the next morning, the young priest Don Giorgi returned to the caves. With him were a man who believed his son to be among the victims, two brothers in search of their father, and a young woman physician. The brothers,

Nino and Francesco Collarello, were members of the Action Party. They brought with them masks with headlamps, the type used by miners.[9]

The party went down through the hole and into the tunnel. They remained there for three hours.

They explored the tunnels and found the two piles of corpses, the layers of which were covered with a "sticky material . . . caustic to the touch." [10] Attempting to find the bodies of the men they were looking for, they tried to remove from the pile some of the corpses, all of whom were lying face down. Failing that, they examined the cadavers as closely as possible.

Of the four who lay at the top of one heap, "one was a tall, distinguished-looking man with a black handlebar moustache and gold-framed eyeglasses; the second was a youth with his face unrecognizable, riddled by machine-gun fire; * the third was a youth wearing an army jacket and black-and-white-checkered pants; the fourth was a youth who was easily recognizable once the material that was covering him had been removed." [11]

Another victim, about twenty-five years old, they estimated, had his hands and his forearms bandaged. Three fingers from his right hand protruded, lacerated from previous torture. One body was that of a young man whose hands were clutching the wall of the tunnel, his fingers embedded in the sand. Another dead man seemed to them to be in a position "almost as if he were trying to get up." [12]

At the back of another tunnel they discovered the skeletonized body of the man who had mysteriously died in the caves some months before. But they could identify no one. They came up through the hole in the tunnel. One of them,

* According to rumor, the victims were said to have been machine-gunned, and, indeed, the body described here must have appeared as a confirmation of that. But all fatalities except the man killed by a blow from a blunt object were caused by the German *Maschine Pistole* in the manner already recounted.

for no apparent reason, took the old man's walking stick that had been found there yesterday.

Later, the boys who had searched for their father learned that he was not among the victims; the father who had sought his son would one day soon see his name listed among the dead.[13]

XV

AT 10:30 that Friday morning Don Michele Valentini was received at the Vatican. He was told that the Vicariate—the office of the Pope's Vicar for Rome—would be informed at once of the news he had brought about the discovery of the hole and the investigations he and the other priests had made at the Ardeatine caves.[1]

Some hours later Monsignor Respighi, accompanied by an official inspector for the catacombs of Rome, went to the *Governatorato*, a high office of the Vatican Government.[2] In his capacity as a representative of the Pontifical Commission for Sacred Archeology, the Vatican prelate tried to learn if it would be possible for the Holy See to make diplomatic representations in order that the victims might be interred in some appropriate manner. There was no reply, only an ambiguous shrug of the shoulders.[3]

Learning of Monsignor Respighi's mission from the inspector, Roman journalist Carlo Trabucco wrote in his diary that day:

> Again the massacre of the catacombs of Domitilla. The people speak of it every day, even aloud. The horror is such that at one week's distance one cannot yet come to oneself. . . . So near to the dead of the catacombs who for 2,000 years have slept in peace, there are now 320 patriots who lie without burial, without a sign of pity,

without a name. Little boys come by there, however, and scatter flowers. With them, men and women come to pray. Human compassion is stronger than the outrageous bestiality of the enemy. When we will be able to honor the 320 martyrs—still unidentified because up until now there has not been a single official notification given to the families—a pilgrimage without end will go to *le Fosse Ardeatine*.* [4]

During this same day, the Germans had somehow been informed of the breach in the Ardeatine caves and all the details learned by the priests of the Appian Way, including the name and activities of Don Giorgi. The following morning they sent a truckload of soldiers to close up the hole.

At four, five, and six o'clock in the afternoon powerful explosions shook the area, breaking the windows of nearby homes. Some of the tunnels were collapsed.[5] The earlier failure of the Germans to seal the caves had now been corrected. Kappler, who had wanted to create a "sepulchral chamber," had, in the end, buried the victims under a landslide of earth, sand, and garbage. Now, at last, they were interred. As long as the Germans ruled Rome, the bodies would not be reached again.

Having done this work, the Germans ordered Don Giorgi's arrest.[6]

XVI

RADIO LONDON, early in that week of March 27, broadcast a German-language report on the incidents in Rome. It was

* Trabucco's is probably the earliest recorded use of the term "*le Fosse Ardeatine*," which was to become the byword characterizing for all Italians the entire episode of the massacre in the caves of Ardeatine. While it may be translated as "Ardeatine caves," "*le Fosse Ardeatine*" is a more expressive rendering in Italian of the literal "*Cave Ardeatine*." "*Le fosse*" is the Italian equivalent of pits, or holes, or graves.

totally incorrect and did more harm than good. According to the BBC transmission, which was beamed toward central Europe, the Germans had shot 550 Romans, 300 of whom were machine-gunned in the Colosseum. "Among the persons shot were the son of Badoglio, ex-head of the Italian Government eighty-three-old [Vittorio Emanuele] Orlando and Grand Admiral Taon de Ravel [Paolo Thaon di Revel]." More than 1,000 persons, mostly women, were said to have been rounded up at Stazione Termini, and many of these women were taken by truck to the Colosseum, where they were immediately executed. The item ended by saying that Rome had been declared "in a state of siege." [1]

A similar report was broadcast for Allied-liberated southern Italy and appeared in the Italian newspapers there, including the southern edition of *l'Unità*.[2] In Rome this was used swiftly and effectively as ammunition by the Fascist press to ridicule "enemy propaganda." [3]

Before long, however, the BBC received accurate data and corrected its transmissions. In Rome, the familiar voice of a Briton known to Italian BBC listeners as "Colonel Stevens," who would open his nightly broadcasts with a British-accented "bwona sarah," spoke favorably of the attack in Via Rasella and, of course, condemned the German atrocity.[4] Allied broadcasts spoke of the Via Rasella partisans as "Italian patriots" [5] and apparently sought to arouse the wrath of the monarchists and the anti-Fascist right. They emphasized the arrest in Via Rasella of eighty-year-old Donna Bice Tittoni and the execution of monarchist Resistance leader Colonel Montezemolo, as well as the Army generals and diplomat Filippo de Grenet.[6]

This was the only public reaction of the Allies, but it did not go unnoticed by the parties in the Resistance who wanted to disclaim the Via Rasella attack. For this and other reasons, opposition in the CLN to taking collective responsibility waned. On March 31, Bonomi recorded that Socialist Party leader Nenni met with him and said that he would like to see "a note of protest and indignation" issued by the CLN.[7]

"He wants me to write it," Bonomi said, "even though I am no longer president. I agreed. It will be published in our underground press." [8]

To mask the dissension and hesitation in the CLN, the date of its protest was set back to March 28.* It was long and fiery in language. It read:

> *Italian men and women!*
>
> *A crime without name has been committed in your capital. Under the pretext of a reprisal for an act of war by Italian patriots, in which it lost 32 of its SS, the enemy has massacred 320 innocent persons, snatching them from the prisons where they had been languishing for months. Men whose only guilt was love of country—none of whom had any part either directly or indirectly in that act of war—were killed on March 24, 1944, without any kind of trial, without religious assistance or comfort from their family: not executed but murdered.*
>
> *Rome is horrified by this unprecedented slaughter. It rises in the name of humanity and condemns to abomination the murders, and equally their accomplices and allies. But Rome will be avenged. The atrocity that has been consummated within its walls is the extreme reaction of the beast that feels itself about to fall. The armed forces of all free people are on the march on all continents in order to give it the final blow. When the monster has been brought down and Rome is secure from any return to barbarism, it will celebrate its liberation on the tombs of its martyrs.*

* The predating of the communiqué of Mar. 28 can be surmised from the following: 1) Bonomi's record of his talk with Nenni is dated Mar. 31; 2) the Mar. 30 edition of *l'Unità* did not contain this document of utmost significance, although it did print the less important GAP statement; and 3) the CLN protest did not appear in the underground press until the Apr. 13 edition of *l'Unità* and the Apr. 15 edition of *Risorgimento Liberale*, the Liberal Party's paper, which published it without any date.

Italian men and women:

The blood of our martyrs must not have flowed in vain. From the grave where the 320 Italians—of every social class, of every political creed—lie united for all time in their sacrifice, a solemn call is raised to each of you:

All for the liberation of the fatherland from the Nazi invader!

All for the reconstruction of an Italy worthy of its fallen sons!

Rome, March 28, 1944.

Il Comitato Centrale di Liberazione Nazionale.[9]

This was the first and only official CLN statement on the armed Resistance during the occupation of Rome. Almost certainly it was not written by Bonomi, who never expressed himself in such terms and who on March 31 referred privately to the "Italian patriots" cited in the statement as "extremist elements." [10] The anonymous author of this eloquent document expressed the teeth-gritting sentiment felt by all Italians, but, unfortunately, all the calls for unity and action melted in the personal suffering of every Roman.

In Rome, the Ardeatine massacre produced no battle cry like "Remember Pearl Harbor" or the Alamo, although it steeled the Italians for the brutal, all-out partisan war in the north that was to follow the liberation of the capital. It was not the blood of their brothers slain in their own house that brought a measure of unity among the men of the CLN in Rome, but the political expediency of the Communist Party. Togliatti's concession to the monarchists and the right-wing parties of the CLN would be better understood by the sophisticated politicians of Rome than the meaning of the Nazi murder. The *svolta* of the Communists, announced in April, would be applauded by Bonomi as "wonderful." [11] The Liberals would see it as opening the way for "the first act of reconstruction of a new Italian life." [12] The Christian Democrats and the monarchists would be equally delighted. Indeed, there is evidence that the CLN statement on the massacre in support of the partisans represented a tactical concession by the right to the concession of the PCI.*

The reality of the division in the CLN was the reality of the division among the Romans. It could not be bound by the martyrdom of the Ardeatine, least of all by the power of the pen. The majority of Romans would never during the occupation pick themselves up from the staggering blow of the massacre. Once down, they would be unable to rebuff the Nazi-Fascist domination. The continuing efforts of the partisans to mobilize the uncommitted segment of the population against the oppressors—hated as they were—succeeded only in separating the one from the other.

A few days before Easter, the first of the notifications to the families of the Ardeatine victims went out through the Appio post office. It was posted in a square envelope, bearing two defaced 25-centessimi stamps of the "traitor King," Vittorio Emanuele.[13] In May they were still being mailed. Having written and sent the notice in a language known to almost none of the recipients, the Germans had found yet another way to tear at the hearts of the Romans. Soon, however, it required no translation. For the receiver, the return address on the envelope was sufficient. The message inside varied only in the name of the victim. In one Roman household in the Prati district, where German was understood by

* The evidence is: 1) the setting back of the date of the statement to one day *prior* to the convening of the National Council of the PCI in Naples, at which the Togliatti *svolta* was adopted by the party; 2) the surprising about-face of the parties who wanted to disavow the Via Rasella attack—a right-wing *svolta* which cannot be explained simply by the BBC propaganda broadcasts; 3) the Mar. 28 statement of unanimity changed nothing within the CLN, which remained split until one month after the formation of the Government of National Unity; and 4) the right-wing parties did not sustain their support of the Via Rasella action and continued to oppose the strategy of armed Resistance in Rome.

a member of the family, a mother read the letter from the Gestapo to her husband and her daughter.

> Maurizio GIGLIO died on March 24, 1944.
>
> Personal belongings, if any, may be recovered at the office of the German Sicherheitspolizei in Via Tasso, 155, where they are being held.

The name of the signer was illegible.[14]

In the Giglio home, however, this notice had not brought news. The lieutenant's father, an officer in the Fascist secret police, had already gone to see Questore Caruso in an attempt to free his son.[15] But he had been too late. Maurizio was already dead. On March 31 the family had published its own notice in *Giornale d'Italia:*

> Lt. Dr. Maurizio Giglio, at only twenty-three years of age. Volunteer, wounded in action, and decorated for military valor, he died on the 24th last most suddenly . . .[16]

XVII

THE PARTISAN actions against the Germans continued. The only way to stop reprisals, many believed, was to demonstrate by deed that the Resistance would not be intimidated. In this, they were successful. The Germans never again in Rome and in any of the cities of Italy where the armed resistance was strong and active repeated such a massacre—although they burned and sacked scores of defenseless villages. Following a partisan attack on Easter Monday, April 10, in which German soldiers were killed in the peripheral Cinecittà district, the occupying command was forced to admit that as far as the reprisal was aimed at terminating armed resistance it had failed.

"The hard German reply," the occupiers announced, "which, unfortunately, had to follow the crime committed in Via Rasella, evidently in some circles has found . . . little comprehension . . ." [1] The Germans, instead, raided the district to round up "all the Communists" for labor service, but they did not risk another reprisal.[2]

Nevertheless the partisans could not maintain the earlier tempo of activities against the enemy. Of the forty-six GAP operations carried out in Rome during the occupation, only three occurred after the Via Rasella attack.[3] The military organizations of the Socialists, the Actionists, and the monarchists had suffered heavy losses in manpower and leadership in the Ardeatine caves.

Yet it was not reprisal but the antipartisan police work of the Gestapo and the Fascists that won a major victory over the partisans, virtually destroying the most militant organization, GAP Central. In the middle of April, the *gappista* Guglielmo Blasi, who had taken part in the Via Rasella attack, was picked up by the Koch band in the course of a routine roundup. Rather than be shipped to the north for labor service, he purchased a new destiny by betraying his comrades.[4] Blasi, a former thief and a daring partisan, had earned a place for himself in GAP by a single qualification: twenty years older than his comrades, he had long been a member of the working class. To the youthful Communist intellectuals of GAP Central, no man in Fascist Italy could have had more impressive credentials.

"To us students," one whom Blasi betrayed would later recall, "any member of the working class was incorruptible." [5]

But Blasi told all he knew of the Via Rasella—which was everything—and then went to work for Pietro Koch. Within days GAP commander Carlo Salinari, Franco Calamandrei, Raoul Falcioni, the caretaker Duilio Grigion, and other *gappisti* were arrested, brought to Koch's prison and then to Via Tasso, and tortured. Carla Capponi and Bentivegna were not named by Blasi because he knew them only by their code names, Elena and Paolo. Calamandrei escaped through a bathroom window of the Oltremare, but Salinari and Falcioni were sentenced to death—a fate from which they were spared several weeks later when the Allies arrived only hours before their scheduled execution.[6]

With the successes of the enemy political police the forms of anti-Fascist activity underwent a change. Protests and demonstrations involving thousands of Romans arose in piazza after piazza. Some were in commemoration of the Ardeatine victims, but for the most part the single rallying cry that brought the people into the streets was "*Pane!*"—"Bread!" [7]

It was smeared in paint on the walls of Rome, printed in bold headlines in the underground press, and shouted by desperate mothers outside the city's bakeries. If the Ardeatine massacre had paralyzed some sectors of Rome society, the collateral action, taken on the same day, of reducing the bread ration brought others to life.

Hunger, the worsening food shortage, the flood of counterfeit ration books, and the incredible prices on the black market—which had undergone a tenfold increase in six months—posed a far greater threat to public order than anti-Fascist politics. Many of the poorer districts in the periphery of the city were in open rebellion. The Vatican stepped up its operation "soup for the people." [8] Even the Germans, who had to supply a large part of the food, increasd their effort. But they could not keep pace with the exasperated population.

For a time during April the possibility of insurrection loomed again. Once more the partisans sought to give political direction to the unrest and antifascism to unite the socially stratified Romans. Calling for "bread and freedom," various Resistance committees, mostly on the left, attempted to organize a general strike for May 3.[9] It was to be a show of strength, and many looked upon it as a test of whether Rome would rise up when the Allies advanced on the city.

In being successful only in the periphery of Rome and failing in the center of the city, the general strike of May 3 once again demonstrated that the Romans would not transcend the lines that kept them apart.[10]

In the end, heroism, sacrifice, martyrdom, and privation brought few changes in occupied Rome. The reality of power—represented in the presence of the Vatican, the rigid, established structure of Roman society, and the political ambitions of right and left—triumphed over the dreams of mere men of every persuasion who yearned for freedom—now. The policy of *attesismo*—waiting peacefully for the Germans to leave, waiting with forbearance for the Allies to come—which was advocated by the Church and the Old Order, was the policy that prevailed.

It was not until after the liberation of Rome that the people of Italy united temporarily under a strong, Allied-recognized CLN for the north with full governmental status and a powerful Corps of Freedom Volunteers. Then a land army of 150,000 *partigiani*, brigades of Christian Democrats, Liberals, Actionists, Socialists, and Communists took to the mountains and the *campagna* to fight alongside the United Nations. And in city after city, in Florence, Genoa, Milan, Turin, and Venice, the Italians rose up in insurrection to expel the Germans and subdue the Fascists in the name of the short-lived *Resistenza.*

PART FIVE

Epilogue

"While a mere episode in the wretched chain of ignominies that has scarred the face of humanity [the Ardeatine massacre] has become a clear symbol of two worlds, opposed to each other and irreconcilable in moral conception: on the one hand, the world of the oppressors, ferocious, intoxicated with power and criminal ideological aberrations; on the other, the world of justice . . . of free men, of pride, of dignity."

—Written twenty-one years after the crime in the Ardeatine caves by Giuseppe Saragat, President of Italy [1]

I

At sunset on Sunday, June 4, 1944, advance patrols of the United States Fifth Army entered Rome through the Porta Maggiore wall in the west part of the city and Porta San Giovanni in the south. At the same moment the last tired troops of the Wehrmacht were trudging across the Ponte Milvio, headed beyond the north limits of the city. Rome, which had lived and died for 268 days under Nazi rule, was free of the Germans.

At the sight of the first American soldiers, the city, which had watched the German departure with mute, lowered eyes, was suddenly jubilant and gay. But in the midst of the festive days that followed, a poster appeared on the walls of the city. It read:

> At the tombs of the Christian Martyrs, there are new tombs for the Martyrs of the Nation. The former and the latter died for dignity of the spirit and freedom from the pagan tyranny of brute force.[1]

Rome had not forgotten. It would never forget. Almost immediately, United States occupation forces, at the request of the Romans, established a commission of American and Italian officials to investigate the Ardeatine crime and open the caves. A technical committee was set up by the commission to exhume the bodies and attempt to identify them.

The committee, headed by Dr. Attilio Ascarelli, a specialist in forensic medicine from the University of Rome, began its work inside the Ardeatine caves at the beginning of July.[2]

Dr. Ascarelli wrote in his report:

At the entrance to the caves there were numerous wreaths, and the walls were decorated with writings and relics placed there out of compassion by the people.

Entering those somber tunnels, the visitor was overcome with a sense of coldness and, even worse, by an offensive odor, which was difficult to tolerate—a stench that was so nauseating it made one vomit. There was no one who having once entered that place of sadness and martyrdom did not experience an unforgettable sense of horror, of pity for the victims, and of execration for the murderers. . . . The members of the commission were terrified. They inspected the caves, passing through the sloping tunnels by the light of torches, and arrived at the sacred site of the massacre.

. . . To give an exact idea and a representative description of the appearance of those two piles of human remains is something I do not know how to express in words. The sense of horror and of pity that gripped the visitor is beyond any imagination. Two enormous, shapeless heaps of cadavers, from which arose an unbelievable smell of rottenness, of rancid and decomposed fat. It penetrated and permeated one's clothes to the point that it became necessary to take precautions by wearing special garments, gloves, and boots, and to shield the respiratory tract with gauze masks soaked in deodorant. And even that was not enough.

. . . Little could be seen of the bodies, but through the mixture of volcanic dust, soil, and the decomposed cadaverous fat that covered the corpses there emerged a foot, here and there a pair of shoes, there a skull, whole or crushed, now a limb, now a piece of tattered clothing. Insects swarmed among the scattered limbs. Myriads of larvae fed on the rotting flesh. Numerous large rats darted from the unburied and unguarded remains, and even from the fragmented heads. . . .[3]

The arduous work of properly assembling the parts of bodies and attempting to identify them occupied a team of scientists for six months. Visual identification by the families of the victims was not possible. Through questionnaires, however, and primarily through items found on the bodies, such as watches, rings, articles of clothing, labels, etc., Dr. Ascarelli's group succeeded in establishing the identities of 322 of the 335 victims.*

To accomplish this remarkable work of identification, Dr. Ascarelli notes that he undertook the task with "religious fervor." A Roman Jew and the uncle of two who were killed in the Ardeatine caves, he sought to foil any German hopes that the gruesome details of the crime might never come to light or at least that in the anonymity of the victims, the massacre might be more readily forgotten. Such hopes were in vain, he records in his monograph: "Their names are no longer unknown; passed on to eternal glory, they will remain forever engraved in the minds and hearts of every Italian . . . they will echo for all time among the valleys and mountains of Italy." †[4]

* Two other bodies were subsequently identified. One man, identified as a victim, was reported years later to be alive. His name is Alexy Kubjsckin, a Russian who was arrested in occupied Rome and marked for execution in the Ardeatine caves. He somehow succeeded in avoiding that fate and is said to be living now in the Soviet Union.

† On Mar. 24, 1949—the fifth anniversary of the massacre—the Ardeatine caves were consecrated as a national monument. The area is dominated by three tortured figures sculptured in marble by Francesco Coccia, a representation of three men bound together at the wrists, approaching their death. They stand above and behind a gate sculptured in bronze by Mirko Basaldella. A mausoleum inside the caves, containing 335 sarcophagi, holds the remains of the victims. On the twentieth anniversary of the Ardeatine massacre, Dr. Ascarelli was posthumously decorated by the President of Italy, receiving the *Medaglia d'Argento* for his work in identifying the bodies.

At about the same time as the Ardeatine Caves Commission began its investigations, the new administration in liberated Rome empowered a civilian judiciary system "for the punishishment of Fascist crimes."[5]

The first war criminal to fall into the hands of the people he had outraged in the Ardeatine caves was ex-Questore Pietro Caruso. Caruso had bolted from Rome on the morning of June 4. Driving north in a powerful Alfa Romeo, he was at the head of a column of cars filled with Italian spies, informers, and Fascist policemen. Above them was a formation of Allied fighter planes, which were strafing the roads to impede the flight of the enemy. In the confusion, Caruso wandered off the main road, lost his way, and finally, rushing blindly from his pursuers, crashed into a tree near Lake Bracciano. He and the others in his car were taken to a hospital in Viterbo, which momentarily was still in German hands. Caruso had suffered a fractured leg and other injuries.

Unable to move on his own, he was refused transportation by the escaping Germans. Then, while under anesthesia, he was deserted by his Fascist colleagues, from whom he had minutes before extracted a promise that they would not leave him alone in the hospital. The oafish Neapolitan was nevertheless unrecognized by the hospital personnel—he was carrying false documents identifying him as an official of the national telegraph company, Italcable. But when he emerged from the operating room and learned he was alone and nonambulatory, Caruso promptly announced his true name, apparently out of fear of receiving something less than the best medical care. When the Allies advanced on the Latium town, local partisans turned him in and the ex-Questore was remanded to a cell in Regina Coeli.[6]

When arrested, he had in his possession two diamonds, two lady's gold evening bags, six gold ingots, five men's watches, three diamond pins, one lady's diamond wristwatch, one diamond ring, one pearl necklace, two pearl earrings, one pearl ring, nine gold sterling coins, one silver coin, 453,000 lire, thirteen 20-pound British banknotes, one 10-pound note, two checks totaling 6,000 lire, three 100-franc French banknotes, and one 50-franc banknote.[7]

Caruso was brought to trial on September 20, 1944, but not before tragedy claimed another man who had played a role on the day of the Ardeatine massacre, although he was innocent of any crime. On September 18, the day originally scheduled for the opening of Caruso's trial, an incensed mob of Romans stormed the Palace of Justice. Joined by some members of the families of the Ardeatine victims, they were out to get Caruso. Failing that, they blindly seized Donato Carretta, former director of Regina Coeli, who on the day of the massacre had resisted the German removal of the prisoners on Caruso's list.

Carretta, who was to have appeared as a prosecution witness, was dragged from the courtroom and lynched. All the hatred that for nine month had festered in Rome was heaped on this one man. The shouting horde of thousands mauled and beat him. They tried to have him run over by a tram, after pinning him to the tracks. When the driver refused Carretta was thrown into the Tiber, where he regained consciousness and attempted to get back to shore. But the lynchers prevented him from coming out of the water. With blows from the oars of a rowboat, they forced his bobbing head under the surface until he finally drowned. Then they hauled the body through the streets to the Carretta home, delivering the dead man to his wife.[8]

Two days later, under the tightest security, the Caruso trial opened. It lasted a single day. The following morning he was found guilty as charged and sentenced to death. That afternoon he was driven in a gray police wagon to Forte Bravetta and executed by a firing squad of twenty Carabinieri, fourteen of whom aimed at his back and six at his head. An American eyewitness, *The New York Times* correspondent Herbert Matthews, said that Caruso's last words were a ringing cry to his executioners: "*Mirate bene!*" ("Aim well!")—a dispensation not accorded the men he had sent to the Ardeatine caves. "They did," wrote the American, ". . . it sounded like one shot." [9]

In the end, it was said, Caruso repented. He was photographed in his cell reading the Bible. A bishop was called to testify at his trial to his good character. To his wife, Caruso wrote from Regina Coeli: "I atone with my life the harm that I have done to society. Tell my children not to curse their father." [10]

But Herbert Matthews, observing Caruso on those final days, was convinced that he "was not conscious of having done wrong . . . His excuse was that he was simply obeying orders and carrying out the job to which he had been assigned by the State." [11] And another American who was among the liberation forces in Rome was moved to ask, "Is it not a trifle tardy, this remorse? This late conscience dashing up like a man about to miss his train? . . . And I confess these sketches of his humble spirit leave me singularly unmoved. Still, still, on the warm wind, where the road forks on the Street of the Seven Churches, I smell that terrible odor . . ." [12]

On May 2, 1945, the war in Italy ended. Germans and Italians incriminated in the Ardeatine crime were taken into custody and interrogated in Nuremberg, Milan, Rome, and London.

Pietro Koch, who had gone north after the liberation of Rome, was brought back to the capital. In Milan he and his band had compiled a record of crimes equally as infamous as in Rome. Taken before the High Court of Justice, he refused legal assistance. He was defended despite his wishes and, on June 4, 1945, convicted on six counts. One of these—a charge he denied—dealt with his role in the Ardeatine crime. He was sentenced to death. His last request, two days later at Forte Bravetta, was to shake hands with the officer who was to command the firing squad that was about to execute him. It was granted and the thirty-seven-year-old torturer was shot.[13]

General Eberhard von Mackensen, ex-Commander of the Fourteenth Army, was taken to England and held for questioning. After making a statement about his part in the Roman war crime, he was informed that he would have to stand trial before a British military tribunal. The old, white-haired nobleman, once so prideful of his Prussian heritage, was astonished. He leaped to his feet and with a look of shock on his face muttered, "Thank God my father is no longer alive." [14]

When his trial opened in Rome, November 18, 1946, he pretended to quite another demeanor. Eyewitnesses saw only the veneer of haughtiness stretched tightly over a rigid frame. Mackensen's codefendant was the "ex-King of Rome," General Kurt Mälzer. He tried to imitate his former superior's indifference, but succeeded only in revealing his incorrigible churlishness.[15]

Mackensen and Mälzer were jointly charged with committing a war crime—namely, the massacre in the Ardeatine caves. The principal witness for the defense was Field Marshal Albert Kesselring; for the prosecution, Obersturmbannfuehrer Herbert Kappler.

The defense claimed that Kappler completely misled the defendants. He told them, it was said, that he had enough prisoners under a sentence of death to make up a list of 320 men to be shot. Mackensen and Mälzer pleaded that they had believed that Hitler's order for the reprisal was justified. They disclaimed any knowledge of how the crime was carried out. The prosecution maintained that Kappler told both the accused that he did not have enough prisoners who had been sentenced to death, that he would instead compile a list of persons "worthy of death." Citing the Hague Convention of 1907 on rules of land warfare and British and American military law, the defense contended that the reprisal was legal.[16]

On November 30, Mackensen and Mälzer stood before the court to hear the verdict. They were found guilty and sentenced "to suffer death by being shot."[17] Neither German, when he heard he was to die, moved from the military posture taken before the judges. A surge of blood reddened Mälzer's neck, but he said nothing. Mackensen slowly removed the monocle from his left eye and placed it in his vest pocket. Italian men and women burst into tears and shouted cries of abuse at the convicted Germans as they were led from the court. The prosecutor, Colonel R. C. Halse, was surrounded by women dressed in black, widows' garments. They kissed his hands and thanked him and expressed their belief that the verdict had been fair and that justice had been done.[18]

The sentences handed down in the Mackensen-Mälzer case were not carried out.

They were commuted to life imprisonment, later reduced, and finally canceled. Mälzer, however, did not live long enough to gain his freedom. He died in prison. Mackensen was released in 1952. Today, almost ninety years old, he lives in seclusion in the north-German city of Kiel.

In Venice, February 17, 1947, Albert Kesselring was brought to trial in a British military court on two charges, one of which was "being concerned in the killing as a reprisal of some 335 Italian nationals." The second, unrelated count was "inciting and commanding . . . forces . . . under his command to kill Italian civilians . . ." which led to the slaughter of 1,078 unarmed persons, including schoolchildren and babies.[19]

On the first charge, the defense argued that following the Fuehrer's order for the reprisal, a second command was issued by OKW: the execution was to be carried out by the SD. Kesselring declared that Kappler had told him personally on the night of March 23 that there were enough persons already sentenced to death to carry out the reprisal and that no innocent persons would have to be killed. Therefore, according to the defense, Kesselring acted humanely in ascertaining that all who would be killed were already convicted of capital crimes and that, in any case, he was not responsible for the reprisal since the "second order" relieved him of any role in the massacre other than passing the communication to the proper party. Moreover, Kesselring's lawyers said, the Ardeatine reprisal was not a war crime, but rather a legal act sanctioned by international law.

The judge advocate advised the court that if it felt that on the evidence the shootings were the responsibility of the SD "then to my mind you are bound to acquit the accused." [20]

Kesselring was not acquitted; the court found that the executions constituted a war crime. On May 6, Kesselring was declared guilty. He was also convicted on the second count —that of inciting his troops to kill civilians. He was sentenced to death.[21]

The Field Marshal was perplexed by the verdict. He found it "incomprehensible" that "the sworn testimony of my officers was considered untrustworthy . . ." He had not committed any reprisal on his own, he said later. His responsibility had been "relieved by Hitler's order." In obeying orders, said Kesselring, he "tried to achieve a deterrent effect by the execution of those who were so liable according to international law." Such work should have been regarded by the court "as an honest effort to exercise humanity." [22]

According to Kesselring: "both von Mackensen and I did all we could to prevent reprisals . . ." [23]

Kesselring simply could not understand the Americans, the British, and especially the Italians. Even before his trial he felt himself to be subjected to "utterly unjustifiable persecution." Late in 1945, at about the time the full horrors of what Kesselring's armies had done to Italy were being revealed, the Field Marshal wrote to Prime Minister De Gasperi, asking him "to use his high office to publish the true facts." [24]

The truth was, Kesselring confided to the Italian, "I sympathize with the grief of Italian fathers and mothers at the death of their sons. I bow my head in silent respect for their sorrow and for all those who died for their country, insofar as they were not the instruments of an alien communism . . ." Italians had to understand, he told the former CLN leader, that it had been his duty to protect his soldiers from the Resistance.[25]

The sentence of the British court handed down in the Kesselring case was "death by shooting." [26]

It was not, however, carried out. Two months after his conviction, it was commuted to life imprisonment. Later, it was cut to twenty-one years. Finally, it was canceled. In October, 1952, despite mass protests in Italy, he was released by the British from the war-crimes prison in Wehrl, Germany. The demonstrations went on for days, but to no avail, and the Italians fell silent. In Germany, Kesselring's release was applauded as a "great step toward Anglo-German understanding." [27]

The old soldier retired to a villa near Munich to write *Soldat bis zum letzten Tag*. Later he became head of a veterans' organization. He was honored by his countrymen, including Chancellor Konrad Adenauer, who received him sometime after his release from prison.[28] In July, 1960, Kesselring died at the age of seventy-four. Childless and a widower, he had adopted a son in order that the family name might live beyond his death.

His testament to the German people may be found on the final page of his memoirs. Suggestions, he said, that there was something basically wrong with the German Army of Nazi and pre-Hitler times and that it be reorganized in accordance with democratic principles "is more than I can take."

". . . let us keep our national character and respect our traditions," he counseled. "Let us beware of becoming a people without roots." As for his account of the war, he had wanted to contribute in whatever way he could "towards a truthful record of a good piece of German history, to the raising of a monument to our magnificent soldiers and to helping the world recognize the face of war in its grim totality." Looking ahead, he concluded, "To the young I would say that the meaning of life lies in the endeavor to do right . . ." [29]

Kesselring was buried in a small cemetery in Bad Wiessee; on his tombstone: his name and his rank.

In July, 1947, under the terms of the Moscow Declaration on German Atrocities, Herbert Kappler was turned over by the British to the Italians. The declaration, signed in November, 1943, by Roosevelt, Churchill, and Stalin, provided that German war criminals involved in massacres "will be brought back to the scene of their crimes and judged on the spot by the peoples whom they have outraged." [30] The Obersturmbannfuehrer was placed in a cell in Regina Coeli.

The Kappler trial opened before the Tribunale Militare di Roma on May 3, 1948. Named as codefendants were Sturmbannfuehrer Durante Domizlaff, Hauptsturmfuehrer Hans Clemens, Hauptsturmfuehrer Kurt Schutz, Hauptscharfuehrer Johannes Quapp, and Scharfuehrer Karl Wiedner. They were charged with homicide, provoking "with premeditation" the death of 335 persons. Kappler alone was cited as aggravating the circumstances of the crime by having "promoted and organized" and directed the massacre in the Ardeatine caves.* [31]

* Kappler was also charged separately for having extorted fifty kilograms of gold from the leaders of the Jewish community of Rome. Demanded on the threat that failure to pay would result in the taking of hostages among the Roman Jews, the money was turned over to the German State, according to Kappler's orders from Berlin. The Jews, of course, were rounded up anyway and shipped to Auschwitz and other extermination centers.

Taking the witness stand on May 31, Kappler gave testimony that lasted eight full days. He spoke with the precision of a scientist and conducted himself with stoical reserve. Kappler described his role in the crime in the minutest detail. Though he was fluent in Italian, he chose to speak in German, presumably to sharpen the accuracy of his presentation.

At times his anatomical rendering of the atrocity brought cries of pain from the courtroom audience, many of whom were family members of the victims. At one point, an Italian journalist noted, "only crying could be heard in the courtroom . . . The crying of the crowd now grows stronger and more convulsive. The president of the military tribunal, himself disturbed by the macabre recollection, warns that if there is not silence he will empty the courtroom. They answer that they cannot contain their emotions." [32]

Kappler's defense sought to demonstrate that the attack in Via Rasella was illegal and that the reprisal was a legitimate act of "collective repression." The military court, while declaring the Via Rasella action courageous and an act of patriotism, upheld its illegitimacy. It explained that in March, 1944, the partisan movement out of necessity had to act "in the orbit of illegality." It was not until later in the war, said the court, that the partisan movement became a legal armed force under international law. Thus the attack in Via Rasella was said to justify a reprisal. Nevertheless, in the opinion of the Italian military judges, the reprisal in the Ardeatine caves was not legitimate under international law, particularly since ten of the 335 persons killed were outside the authority of an order by the German State and five others were put to death by error.[33]

On July 20, the tribunal handed down its verdict. Kappler was found guilty and sentenced to life imprisonment—the severest penalty under the laws of the new Italian republic. His five codefendants were acquitted.

A series of appeals took the Kappler case before the highest court in Italy, the Supreme Court of Cassation. In December, 1953, the final appeal was denied.

Serving his time in the Italian penitentiary at Gaeta, a coastal town between Rome and Naples, Kappler in 1957 addressed an appeal to the State for a pardon:

> The order for a reprisal for the attack in Via Rasella was given by Adolf Hitler, passed from Field Marshal Albert Kesselring to the commander of the German Fourteenth Army, General von Mackensen, and was transmitted to General Mälzer, Commandant of Rome. I was only an executor of orders, which, as a soldier, I could not evade. It was Hitler who stated that ten Italians had to die for every fallen German soldier. That afternoon of March 24, 1944, the hardest task that the terrible war was to demand of us fell to me and my men. I could see that my men, who had already many times been spectators to the most horrible aspects of the conflict, left that cave of death with their eyes filled with emotion. The memory of those hours remained with almost all of my officers and men, and myself, too, for a long time.[34]

His plea was denied.

In 1959, Kappler sent a letter to the President of Italy, asking for authorization that he might make a "pilgrimage of penitence to the shrine of the Ardeatine and stay there as long as necessary in order to render homage" to the victims.[35]

This was denied.

A year later, Kappler applied to the highest military court for an amnesty. This was rejected with the finding that Kappler in 1944 had acted out of ambition, "hoping that through this action the highest leaders would see in him a man of ready initiative capable of striking and suppression with maximum rigor." [36]

Kappler today remains in the Gaeta prison. He is fifty-nine

years old. He receives a small pension from the Bonn Government which augments his prison standard of living.[37] His time is his own. He spends a great deal of it raising pet fish, which are sold by a local vendor and for which he earns a percentage of the sales. He is said to have become very religious, and often he receives the prison chaplain in his cell for coffee and spiritual discussions. At Christmastime he receives packages from some of his former colleagues, including ex-Consul Möllhausen, who is now a businessman living in Milan.[38] The former Gestapo chief still spends long periods drafting appeals for clemency to the State. He hopes to come out of Gaeta alive, to see Germany once again.

Encouraged by neo-Fascist propaganda and the reluctance of the military tribunal in the Kappler case to declare the Via Rasella attack legitimate, a small group of relatives of five of the Ardeatine victims filed a civil action in 1948 against some partisans and members of the CLN.

Named as defendants in the indemnification suit were Carla Capponi, Rosario Bentivegna, Carlo Salinari, Franco Calamandrei, Giorgio Amendola, Sandro Pertini, and Riccardo Bauer—the latter three forming the directorate of the Military Junta that operated in Nazi-occupied Rome.

The action was rejected virtually out of hand. The Roman court stated flatly that the Via Rasella attack was a "legitimate act of war" for which "neither those who organized it or carried it out can be made to answer for the massacre committed by the German Command in the name of a reprisal." [39]

In September, 1949, by Presidential decree, Carla Capponi was decorated with the *Medaglia d'Oro* for Military Valor. By then she had become the wife of the Roman physician Dr. Rosario Bentivegna and the mother of their daughter, Elena. Before a full military review, she was cited for her "heroic deeds." The citation continued: "With gun in hand, first among the first, she participated in tens of actions, distinguishing herself . . . by her spirit of sacrifice toward her comrades in the face of danger." [40]

Some months later Rosario Bentivegna and Franco Calamandrei, who commanded the Via Rasella action, were awarded the *Medaglia d'Argento* for Military Valor, which was signed by Prime Minister De Gasperi. Bentivegna's medal bears the following:

> During the Nazi-Fascist occupation of the capital he rose to command a group for patriotic action by virtue of his organizational abilities, unrelenting activities, his fearlessness and daring. In the streets and in the *piazze* of the *Urbe*, and particularly on December 18, 1943, and March 23, 1944, he fought against the *nazifascisti* . . .* [41]

Notwithstanding the prestige gained by the partisans in postwar Italy and the fact that Carla Capponi was elected to Parliament, the group that had filed suit against them in Rome took its case to higher courts. The Roman Court of Appeals in May, 1954, confirmed the earler ruling. It declared the Via Rasella attack an "act of war," sanctioned by the State, which recognized the partisan formations "as valid organs, accepted their deeds as acts of war, and assumed responsibility for them within the limits permitted by law and for their consequences. Thus there can be no guilt of any kind . . ." [42]

The case was then taken to the Supreme Court of Cassation. The lawyers for the five families offered a new argument.† Rome during the occupation had been an open city,

* Dec. 18, 1943, is the date of a GAP attack on the Germans in front of the Barberini movie theater. Mar. 23, of course, refers to the Via Rasella attack.

† Most of the families of the Ardeatine victims supported the partisans, with whom they have maintained a close relationship through their organization, the National Association of Italian Families of the Martyrs (ANFIM). In some cases friendships between the ex-partisans and the relatives have developed. Dr. Bentivegna, for example, became and remains today the family physician of several of the victims' survivors.

they said, and therefore could not be the site of legitimate partisan actions. This was, indeed, new. The open-city thesis had until now been employed by many as a polemical tool to celebrate Vatican diplomacy and to discredit the Roman Resistance as being *ipso facto* and fundamentally illegal. But it had never been tested in the courts. The Supreme Court was now asked to rule on both the legitimacy of the Via Rasella attack and the open city.

Handing down its judgment on August 3, 1957, the court stated that Rome was never an open city because of German military concentrations within its territory—a fact which precluded Allied recognition of open-city status.[43] As for the attack in Via Rasella, the court declared, in rejecting the claims of the families, that it was an "act of war" committed at a time when Rome was but a few miles from the battlefront.[44]

"Every attack against the Germans," concluded the highest court in Italy, "was a response to appeals from the legitimate government . . . and therefore constituted an act of war reportable to that same government." [45]

Powerful sectors of Italian postwar society did not, however, let up in their efforts to denigrate the Resistance, the partisans, and particularly the attack in Via Rasella. With the publication of war memoirs and "histories" by political opportunists, ex-Fascists, neo-Fascists, and unrehabilitated Nazis, a protracted defamation campaign was launched. It has not yet ended.

Books, newspaper articles, handbills, and speeches sought to portray the Via Rasella partisans as cowardly massacrers guilty of slaughtering innocent men, women, and children in carrying out a sinister plot against the people of Rome on orders from Moscow.

The mating of distortions with a will to deceive gave birth to the monstrous, naked lie which is still believed by perhaps hundreds of thousands of uninformed Italians: that the Germans, before executing 335 men in the Ardeatine caves, addressed an appeal to the Via Rasella partisans to give themselves up so that the innocent victims might be spared. This is totally unfounded. It has been promulgated in the absence of any evidence and despite testimony to the contrary by the Germans themselves.

In the Kappler trial, the ex-Gestapo chief, as has been shown, stated that secrecy about the Ardeatine crime had been decided upon for security reasons—a fear of an attempt by the partisans to stop them from carrying out the reprisal. Asked point-blank by the president of the court if any "specific appeal" was made to the partisans to surrender, Kappler replied, "I had no authority to make such appeals." At another point he declared, "I had no time to do it . . ."[46]

Further, in each of the other Ardeatine caves trials, none of the defendants, who had more authority than Kappler, claimed to have addressed any appeal to the partisans to surrender. However, in books published in Italy as recently as 1965 and 1966, one can read that such an appeal was made.[47]

The Roman Catholic Church—first to announce the "guilt" of the partisans—did nothing to unravel the web of distortions around the Via Rasella story. From the day following the Ardeatine massacre until today the Vatican and its semi- or nonofficial spokesmen have maintained that the Via Rasella partisans were guilty of a crime equal to—if not greater than—the German slaughter in the caves. The authoritative Roman Jesuit journal *La Civiltà Cattolica*, for example, referred in 1946 in the same sentence to the "Via Rasella massacre" and the Ardeatine "reprisal"—the latter word bestowing a higher status to the German action.[48] The *Enciclopedia Cattolica*, which is published by the Holy See, has defined the events as "the double massacre of the Via Rasella and of *le Fosse Ardeatine* . . ."[49] This judgment appeared after the Rome court's legitimate-act-of-war ruling about the Via Rasella attack and after the State had conferred its highest decorations on the Via Rasella partisans.

Such hardened and unjustified attitudes served only to polarize the politically charged Italian society. In the process, the truth was discarded and finally was lost from view.

"Even today," says Carla Capponi, "I receive anonymous letters from Fascists, with insults, with atrocious vulgarities, with grotesque but violent threats of death."

Sometimes the threats come by telephone. "One hears at the other end an absurd, cavernous voice, which says: 'Hello. We are the martyrs of the Ardeatine speaking. Is the murderer Bentivegna there, and his worthy comrade?' Or else a voice speaks in German, which I do not understand. But then I hear one word, '*Rasellenstrasse*.' "

Sometimes a picture of Mrs. Bentivegna, torn from a newspaper, comes in the mail. There are holes punched through the eyes; the ears are cut off, the mouth bloodied with red ink. "This is what we will do to you," the correspondent warns.

In Parliament, Mrs. Bentivegna, a former member of the Chamber of Deputies, has been the object of obscene gestures and catcalling. "During Parliamentary debates," she says, "right-wing Deputies have cried to me, 'Whore!' "[50]

On a slightly more sophisticated level, it also became fashionable in Italy and abroad to speak of the Via Rasella attack as militarily useless, as cowardly and without meaning, as the unconsidered act of misguided youths; in sum, as being, at best, an error. The partisans should have known, it is said even now, that the Germans would commit the Ardeatine atrocity in one form or another.

Obviously, the direction of this argument leads to submission and finally to abject surrender to all forms of tyranny and intimidation, including an implied threat of force. It is difficult to locate a middle ground between submission and resistance which is not merely a more complex form of submission. Even noncollaboration or passive resistance—historical experience has repeatedly shown—can provoke extremely hostile acts by a force bent on having its own will prevail.

With the benefit of the same hindsight used by those who assert that the partisans should have anticipated the Ardeatine massacre and consequently should have abstained, one might well say that the execution of so bestial a massacre—which was unprecedented in Italy—demonstrates the correctness of the partisans in opposing with all the power they could command such a ruthless occupation. It was, in reality, the nonpartisans who "should have known" that the Germans would sooner or later commit an atrocity in Rome, and they should have stood united against the occupation. Atrocities are the bane of only the weak and helpless.

The "error" of the Via Rasella was that in the context of the long-range objectives of the Resistance in Rome it did not succeed.

In any case, it is absurd to single out one attack from a genuine resistance movement, which is guided by strategies and developed through various forms of tactics, and declare in disparaging terms that this was the battle that should not have been fought. This is the equivalent of a rejection of armed resistance to armed aggression, since any one of a hundred partisan actions in Rome might have brought on the Ardeatine crime. It rejects as meaningless and dishonors as cowardly those who fought and died for freedom from Nazism in the resistance movements of France, Belgium, the Netherlands, Norway, Denmark, Poland, Russia, Czechoslovakia, Rumania, Greece, Yugoslavia, and Italy. To dishonor them is to disarm the freedom fighters of tomorrow.

II

> POPE: *Certainly the terror . . . is loathsome,*
> *but we must not allow it to incense Us so*
> *that We forget the duties that devolve*
> *upon the Germans for the immediate future*
> *as the present protectors and rulers of Rome.*
> —Rolf Hochhuth, *The Deputy* [1]

The campaign—unconscious or otherwise—to deprecate the Via Rasella attack and the partisans had, and continues to have, as its primary aim to gain support for the idea that the Ardeatine massacre could somehow have been prevented by the partisans had they so chosen. Therefore, it is said, they betrayed Rome and their country.

In the postwar period of hysterical anticommunism, the success of such an effort was fraught with opportunities. Today, only the diehards can derive satisfaction in their unrelenting work to misinform the Italian people. The main contestants have moved on to other, more complex arenas. Nevertheless, the controversy whether the crime in the Ardeatine caves might never have occurred occupies an important place in the contemporary affairs of men.

Unquestionably, the massacre could have been prevented. It took place, we have seen, against the will of almost everyone involved. Ignited by anger, it was consumed in the cold flames of bureaucracy. A single drop of humanity would have sufficed to dampen and douse the entire conflagration. But in the Holy City of Rome, among those in a position to act, the well of humanity had run dry.

By way of review, the first mention of any kind of reprisal was broached by General Mälzer when he arrived in a state of intoxication at the scene of the Via Rasella attack, at about four o'clock on the afternoon of March 23. Not too many hours later, however, when the Stadtkommandant had regained his sobriety, he lost interest in revenge. It had become more important for him to apologize for his unconventional behavior. On the 24th, on the heels of Dollmann's mission to Consul Möllhausen as an "angel of peace," Mälzer went personally to the young diplomat with whom he had argued and threatened in Via Rasella. "He said," Möllhausen later recalled, "he had lost control of his nerves at the sight of his stricken soldiers . . ." [2] What Mälzer would have done had he not been drunk or had he not been at the scene of the battle is impossible to say. It is certain, however, that his lust for revenge was short-lived, a characteristic consonant with his personality.

If Mälzer's reaction was hotheaded and unenduring, the same must be said of Hitler's. Both men, interestingly, made the same wild demands: that the houses in Via Rasella be blown up and that a large number of civilians be shot.

Clearly, after Hitler barked his first response on hearing the news from Rome, he too lost interest in the matter, which was turned over to General Jodl's office of operations at OKW. Nowhere is there any record, testimony, or document indicating that Hitler ever again expressed any interest in the incident or its outcome.

Aside from a general feeling that the Romans ought to be punished, every other German concerned with bringing the massacre to a successful conclusion did so without any special enthusiasm or eagerness, but merely because he was part of the administrative machinery. There were no prior German plans to commit wholesale atrocities in Rome. A program of massacres, such as those performed in Poland and Russia, had no place in the German occupation of Rome or, by March 23, in the plans for the inevitable withdrawal from the city. There were no compelling military or political reasons for the Germans to slaughter 335 Romans until such reasons were attributed to it in a room of the Hotel Excelsior after the deed had been done. It was not, as the Roman Resistance said, "the extreme reaction of the beast that feels itself about to fall," but rather the *ex machina* result of a wretched but impersonal array of live components.

The written order for the reprisal, it will be recalled, was issued by Kesselring. This occurred after Jodl had taken OKW out of the picture, deferring to the Field Marshal's judgment as to the number of men to be killed. Kesselring's role in the crime came to an end as he passed the order to Mackensen, who in turn passed it on to Mälzer. Mälzer attempted to pass it to Major Dobbrick, the nonvindictive commander of the Bozen Battalion. Failing that, he tried to pass it back to Mackensen, through Fourteenth Army Chief of Staff Colonel Hauser. Unsuccessful again, Mälzer passed the order to Kappler, who suggested that he would pass it to his men, but finally had to take charge.

The Gestapo in Rome worked more or less efficiently during the hours that followed, but without relish. Kappler felt it necessary to repeatedly threaten his officers and men with immediate death unless they cooperated in the executions. But hardly anyone was prepared to stand up against the system. And when one officer refused to take part, Kappler, with sincere tenderness, did not carry out his threat. Furthermore, the fact that the executioners had to drink their way through their dirty work and that the victims offered almost no resistance to the killers conveys the feeling that both murderer and murdered were somehow embarrassed to find themselves as participants in such a horrible mess. Both found ways to get the thing over with as quickly as possible.

And when Kappler executed an extra ten persons by extrapolation of the Fuehrer's order, and when he erred in killing an additional five, no one reprimanded him or congratulated him. His colleagues and superiors merely chose a path of conduct which would isolate Kappler and his blunder should it ever be the subject of an accounting by a higher authority.

As it turned out, in fact, it was this mistake that proved to be Kappler's downfall. His reputed ambition and cruelty notwithstanding, Kappler must be considered among the most impersonal of neutrals in this crime. Except in that one hasty decision, he went to extremes to avoid responsibility for a direct role in the reprisal. In making up the list, he was scrupulous in obtaining the necessary authorizations from the German military judges. He took care to report in detail to his superior officer in Verona, General Harster, who provided a solution to Kappler's dilemma in choosing names for the death roster by empowering him to "take as many Jews as you need." Kappler surely must have felt himself to have fully shifted any onus of guilt when the general said, "The important thing is to complete the list." [3]

Had he not been among "neutrals" who were as formidable as he was in achieving release from responsibility through paper and ink, Kappler might not be in prison today. The judges in the Kappler trial, while acquitting his co-defendants, were greatly influenced by the fact that Kappler did not have the legal "competence" to order the death of the ten last-minute victims. This had been *unauthorized.*[4]

On the side of the Italian Fascists, the same trite corporatism characterized those two days in March. The morally gutted Questore Caruso sent out his men to make arrests and sack the houses in Via Rasella that evening of the 23rd for no other reason—as he tells us—than "to demonstrate that we too were carrying out an investigation . . ." [5]

And it was anything but initiative that brought him to Buffarini-Guidi's bedside the following morning. He simply needed authorization from the State to discharge the "great responsibility" requested of him by Kappler. "Having obtained this authorization, rather this order," Caruso later said, "I felt relieved." [6]

Once he had "legalized" his own actions, Caruso left his men to find their means of experiencing that bureaucratic orgasm. Questioned at the Caruso trial about the list prepared by the Questore, Commissar Alianello said, "The list was an order . . . and I was only a messenger." After Carretta and he had substituted the names of the men taken at random—because the Germans had to meet an arbitrary deadline—"Carretta said to me, 'Since there have been some changes, put your signature to them.' I said I had no official authority and I didn't sign." [7]

On such bearings the machine ground on.

The momentum that produced the Ardeatine crime could have been broken at almost any point during the hours between 4 P.M. of the 23rd and 8 P.M. of the 24th, when the last man was executed. The method that could have been used to prevent the massacre was a relatively simple one, for which there are an infinite number of precedents on all levels of human relations. Indeed, we have seen an excellent example on the foregoing pages.

When General Karl Wolff arrived in Rome on the afternoon of March 24, he had every intention of executing Himmler's order for what would have been one of the most astounding and dramatic events of the twentieth century: the exodus of the male population of Rome.

In many respects the genesis and development of this idea parallels the Ardeatine crime. It was born from the same burst of anger. Had it taken place, it would have employed the same personnel and machinery that carried the massacre to its intended conclusion. The deportation plan, however, had an even greater forward thrust than its diminutive twin. Unlike the Ardeatine massacre, the evacuation had been previously studied in Rome and there were military and political grounds for doing so (*i.e.*, shortage of labor power in the north; difficulty in supplying Rome with food; antipartisan operations). Despite these reasons, the exodus did not take place, not because it was unsound or infeasible—which it may very well have been—but because it was *delayed.*

Through the intervention of various Nazis in Rome who found life in the Italian capital too complex or too comfortable to undertake the organization of so vast an operation as evacuating the city, consummation of the plan was forestalled. With everyone having found an "out"—an excuse for why it could not be done or for why his own role was nonessential—it was finally forgotten, never, once the ire aroused by the Via Rasella attack had burned itself out, to arise again.

Thus, given a motive—however mundane or ignoble—to remain comfortably inert, the Nazi hierarchy in Rome, employing the age-old tactic of delay, eschewed a disaster of immense proportions.

In this way, too, by all that is known of those two days in March, 1944, delaying and stalling almost certainly would have prevented the war crime in the Ardeatine caves. Mussolini, for example, surely could have had the massacre postponed for, let us say, twenty-four hours. During this interlude the hotheads would have cooled—which they did anyway. It is doubtful that the rhythm that lent an inexorable quality to the crime, once interrupted, could have been struck up again. In a less pressured atmosphere, a less violent response—perhaps along the lines set down by Dollmann—would have prevailed.

It is difficult to see how, in the city of Rome, the Ardeatine massacre could have taken place in any other way than in the nonstop manner in which it actually happened. But to expect Mussolini or any of the high Fascists or Nazis to have intervened is to attribute to these men a quality of humanness they neither deserve nor possessed. It would be tantamount to asking for a supernatural occurrence.

A miracle was not necessary to save the 335 men doomed to die in the Ardeatine caves. There was one man who could have, should have, and must be held to account for not having acted to at least delay the German slaughter. He is Pope Pius XII.

Four preconditions were necessary before a papal intervention would have been possible and advisable. These were: a) knowledge that the reprisal was going to take place; b) a channel of communications between the Pope and the massacrers; c) some chance of succeeding; and d) a will to act in behalf of the doomed men.

Pius knew reasonably in advance of the Ardeatine crime of the German intention to commit a reprisal in Rome. This is evidenced by the testimony of Dollmann, who has described his mission to Padre Pancrazio on the evening of March 23; by the German writer Prince Konstantin, who independently of Dollmann learned from Vatican sources of that mission; * by Kappler, who noted the unusual absence of Padre Pancrazio from his offices on the 24th; by Monsignor Giovannetti, the Vatican diplomat who has recorded the German threat "to reexamine their attitude" toward the so-called open-city negotiations; by Albrecht von Kessel, the aide to Weizsäcker who has reported the Ambassador's March 24 telephone contacts with Kesselring; † and, finally, but primarily, the Vatican statement that appeared in *l'Osservatore Romano* on the evening of the 24th, which could only have been written before the first men of the 335 victims were put to death in a tunnel of the Ardeatine caves.

As for the second precondition, at least two means of communications between the Pope and the murderers were open on March 23–24, 1944: through Padre Pancrazio and

* In a communication through a third party to the author (Feb. 18, 1966), Konstantin recalls that his source "very probably" was Monsignor Ludwig Kaas, the high German prelate who served in the Vatican as Secretary of the Sacred Congregation of the Fabric of Saint Peter's. See also "Notes on Chapters," p. 288, Chapter XXVII, note 3.

† See "Notes on Chapters," p. 294, Chapter XI, note 1.

through the German diplomatic mission to the Holy See. The third precondition—a possibility that intervention by the Pope might be effective—existed in the form of many precedents. When Caruso and Koch, for example, raided the extraterritorial church of San Paolo early in February, 1944, the Pope protested the intrusion. The German diplomats in Rome and in the north then interceded successfully to forestall or to at least *delay* any further actions in violation of the Vatican's rights.[8] The Germans, from the moment they marched into Rome, went to great lengths to promote good relations with the Vatican, a fact which was acknowledged by the Holy See in word and in deed. Pius himself publicly or privately expressed his gratitude to influential Germans for their cooperation with the Vatican.[9] For various reasons, not the least of which was the desire to have the Pope mediate a separate peace between the Germans and the Western Allies, many highly placed Nazis in Italy were very responsive to the Pope's wishes.*

Surely Pius, working quietly through German channels, without having to break his well-known silence on other questions, could have won at the minimum a twenty-four-hour stay of the mass executions. Surely such a possibility existed and was worth at least a try. Failing that, he could have spoken out not as the Pope but as the Bishop of Rome —as he had when American bombers threatened the security of the Vatican. There was no need to sacrifice or compromise his principle of silence. Further, this was not a "Jewish question," about which he had decided long before not to raise his voice in protest. This was a question of the extermination of his own Catholic children in his own Catholic diocese—the diocese of Saint Peter. Surely a word from the

* General Karl Wolff, for example, was asked by Pius in a secret audience to demonstrate good faith by releasing an Italian being held by the Gestapo in Rome. The prisoner was freed immediately. (S. Bertoldi, *I tedeschi in Italia,* Milan: Rizzoli, 1964, p. 157; *cf.* also, Konstantin, *The Pope,* New York: Roy Publishers, 1956, pp. 231–247.)

Bishop of Rome—other than calling on the Romans to control their "violent urges"—was in order.

What does the Vatican have to say about this? On May 20, 1965, I went to Vatican City, seeking information and clarification about the position of the Holy See with respect to the events of March 23–24, 1944. I was received cordially by a high lay official of the *Servizio della Stampa*, a bureau of the Holy Office. Outlining in general terms the questions I hoped to have answered, I was directed to a source within the Vatican, with the invitation to return should I meet with any difficulty. Such difficulty arose when I was advised by the second party, who did not wish to respond to my questions, to consult a third source, a clergyman associated with *La Civiltà Cattolica*. Since this Jesuit journal, however authoritative, is not an *official* organ of the Vatican, I declined and returned to the *Servizio della Stampa*, as directed. I was then asked to submit my questions, in English, in written form and to provide documentation to confirm that I was a bona fide professional writer. Having fulfilled these requests, I was assured that I would receive a reply within twenty-four to forty-eight hours.

The principal question, of a total of three, was:

> I have read that the Vatican, represented by Padre Pancrazio Pfeiffer, was able to achieve certain successes in behalf of prisoners held by the German occupiers of Rome. Was it possible to take any action, in this connection, on 23 or 24 March 1944? If so, how was this initiative received on the part of the Germans? *

* The source confirming Padre Pancrazio's successful liaison work between the Pope and the Germans is the Vatican itself (see footnote, p. 102). The two other questions I submitted asked if the Vatican would clarify or comment on material I had gathered from other sources with regard to the Pope's reaction to the Via Rasella attack and to representations said to have been made by the Holy See in behalf of Don Pietro Pappagallo during his imprisonment at Via Tasso but not necessarily on the day of his execution in the Ardeatine caves.

None of the questions was ever answered.*

Given the existence of the first three of the four preconditions stated above, and given the absence of any intervention by the Pope, one can hardly escape the conclusion that Pius XII lacked the will to attempt to save the men destined to die in the Ardeatine caves.

In other words, it must now be said, Pope Pius XII *chose* to do nothing in full awareness that action by him might prevent the reprisal. In making this choice, he consented.

This is not surprising, considering that:

—the Pope felt the Vatican to be under the guardianship of the Nazi occupation forces;

—he was in the midst of the "open-city negotiations" to provide for the orderly transfer of power in Rome from the Germans to the Allies;

—he was opposed to the Roman Resistance; †

—he feared a popular insurrection, the establishment of radically left-wing anti-Fascist power in Rome, and—with an incredulousness explainable only if Pius believed himself already too compromised with fascism—the possible destruction of the Vatican City State.

Viewed in this light, it is not, then, surprising that when public knowledge of the horrendous crime was imminent, the Vatican was calling on the people of Rome to exercise restraint.

* The author remained in Rome ten days after the forty-eight hours in which the reply was to have been received. Further, the same questions were resubmitted on June 23, 1965, in correspondence from the United States, again without eliciting response.

† Pope Pius XII was not against armed resistance in general. This had already been made clear with the Fascist victory in 1939 of Franco's rebels in Spain. At that time he sent notice of his "immense joy" and congratulated Spanish Catholics for a "victory with which God has deigned to crown the Christian heroism of your faith and charity, proved through such great and generous sufferings." (Radio address by the Pope, Apr. 16, 1939; quoted in G. Lewy, *The Catholic Church and Nazi Germany*, New York: McGraw-Hill, 1964, p. 312.)

How anxious the Holy See must have been during those hours of murder! While the people of Rome moved about the city in ignorance of what was taking place in Via Ardeatina, the Vatican was anticipating the worst of eventualities. Who could know how the Romans would react tomorrow? The Gestapo itself, as Kappler has told us, felt insecure.

Today, rereading *l'Osservatore* of that sad spring afternoon, the panic leaps from the page: "Our appeal is made directly to the conscience . . ." Maintain a "spirit of sacrifice," counseled the Vatican, and control any impulse to violence. "Every ill-considered act would have no other result than to end by injuring many innocent people . . ." "All those upon whom it is incumbent to maintain public order have the task of assuring that it is not disturbed . . ." "All those . . . who can and know how to effectively influence the minds of the citizenry—above all the clergy—have the high mission of persuasion, pacification, and giving comfort."

And how astute was the American woman in Rome, the pseudonymous Jane Scrivener, who noted that evening: "The writer of this . . . must already know something of the consequences of yesterday's occurrence in Via Rasella. Perhaps we shall know tomorrow."

Thus, it cannot, finally, evoke surprise that on the following day the Vatican reacted to the news of the massacre by declaring the Via Rasella partisans guilty, by calling on the "irresponsible elements" to respect human life, and the "responsible elements" to be mindful of the "lives they seek to safeguard" and of "history and civilization."

There is cause for wonder, however. The Vatican for more than twenty years has claimed for Pope Pius XII the awesome title of *defensor civitatis*—the defender of Nazi-occupied Rome—and has demanded appropriate and unending tribute from the Romans and the world.

On the afternoon of June 5, 1944—the first full day of

Rome's liberation by the Allies—loudspeaker trucks criss-crossed the city. The amplified voices urged the people to gather at Saint Peter's. The Pope would offer his blessings to the *Urbi* and *Orbi.* All the church bells pealed. By nightfall more than 100,000 Romans stood in Piazza S. Pietro. All eyes lifted toward the central loggia above the entrance to the great Basilica. Pius appeared alone in a simple white cassock. He was greeted with tears, elated cries of jubilation, and prolonged and repeated applause.[10]

When at last he could speak and be heard, the Pope gave thanks to the "mutual collaboration" of the Nazis and the Allies for having spared Rome from physical damage. According to one of the Pope's biographers, who has been blessed by Pius for having written his book, the Holy Father carefully avoided reference to "his own struggle in defense of Rome . . . But the common people of Rome had understood the Pope's role, and they were deeply grateful. Their tribute to Pius XII as defender of Rome left no doubt about how they felt." [11]

Twenty years later, however, when some Romans were feeling somewhat less grateful, the Vatican was being a great deal less modest. On February 13, 1965, a private performance of Rolf Hochhuth's play *The Deputy* in an improvised cellar theater in Rome was banned. The Vatican had immediately intervened, declaring that presentation of the drama in Rome, the city Pope Pius XII had helped to save, constituted "objectively a grave offense." Aside from the content of the play, performing it, said the Holy See, "has the sad flavor of ingratitude toward him [Pius] to whom many of today's denigrators and many of their sympathizers owe their safety." [12]

In reality, Pius' "concern" for the safety of Rome and the Romans never arose as an issue in Vatican diplomacy until the Italians had already suffered twenty years of fascism. More precisely, it became a subject of major papal interest only after the fall of El Alamein and the battle of Stalingrad; that is, when it became clear that the Axis would be defeated and events would sooner or later change the *status quo* in the Eternal City.

It was then, early in 1943, that the Vatican began to insist that Rome be spared from the impending Allied advance against the Axis. In a spate of notes from Vatican diplomats —none of which mentioned the safety of the people of Rome —the Holy See emphasized again and again that "Vatican City itself would have little chance of escaping damage . . ."; [13] "the grave danger to Vatican City"; [14] and the difficulties it would face in order "to guarantee the security of the Vatican itself." [15]

The Pope, speaking privately, appealed to the Allies on a more personal level. He warned, according to a telegram from American diplomat Tittmann to the State Department, that "Allied bombardment of Rome might provoke popular uprising against diplomats residing Vatican City . . ." The people of Rome, Tittmann was told, regarded the Vatican as a "nest of spies." The Holy See would not be able to give Tittmann and the other diplomats in the Vatican "adequate protection if such an uprising occurred." [16] Where the Romans fit into this overdrawn and rather desperate view is hard to say.

Any question that the Pope's primary interest was in the safety of Vatican City and its extraterritorial property rather than the safety of the people of Rome should have been clarified on the day Rome was bombed by the Allies for the first time in the war. The air attack killed about 1,000 men, women, and children. But the Pope did nothing extraordinary for the Romans.

"Several hours after all clear had sounded," Tittmann's telegram following the July 19, 1943, air raid reported, "His Holiness in his capacity of Bishop of Rome with Monsignor Montini [now Pope Paul VI] as sole attendant proceeded by automobile to devastated quarters city mingled with faithful there discharging his pastoral duties *just as any other Bishop would have done.*" [*Italics added*] * [17]

During the occupation of Rome by the Germans, Pius probably did not do *as much* as any other bishop would have done.

In view of the assurances given to him by Hitler and Ribbentrop that the occupiers would not violate Vatican rights, it is difficult to see how the Pope could have done less for the Romans.

As Hochhuth dramatized in *The Deputy*, Pius failed to protest the roundup of Roman Jews for deportation to Auschwitz. He did not protest German military movements through the city to the Cassino front and the Anzio beachhead. He did not protest the brutalities of the SS prison in Via Tasso. He said nothing about the outrages of the Fascist police. He had nothing to say about the mass roundups of Roman men for forced labor in Germany. There was not a word about the Fascist torture chambers in Via Principe Amedeo and later in the Pensione Jaccarino. And, above all, he looked on in grotesque silence at the massacre of the 335 men in the Ardeatine caves.

The most prominent of Pius' defenders is the present Pope, Giovanni Battista Montini. For many years, and especially during the German occupation of Rome, he worked very closely with Pius XII as Undersecretary of State—although at the time of his election as Supreme Pontiff, he managed to publicly disassociate himself from the wartime Pope's diplo-

* Other than draft a letter of "lament"—described privately by the Vatican as customary whenever a catastrophe occurs in Rome, the Pope did not protest in behalf of the Romans. The Holy See, however, declared to the Allies that the attack, which damaged the extraterritorial Basilica San Lorenzo, proved that despite good intentions Rome could not be bombed without bringing destruction to Vatican property. (Tittmann's telegram of July 26, 1943; *Foreign Relations of the United States, op. cit.*, p. 937.)

matic policies (Montini, defending Pius: "It is true that the precise scope of my duties did not include foreign affairs . . .").[18] He nevertheless felt himself qualified to speak on this subject. In his own words, "It was my good fortune to be drawn into close contact with Pius XII . . . serving him day by day . . ." Further, the nature of this non-foreign-affairs work gave him access "to the mind, and I would add, to the heart of this great Pope." [19]

Pope Paul VI has explained Pope Pius XII's position in the following terms: "An attitude of protest and condemnation . . . would have been not only futile but harmful: that is the long and the short of the matter." [20]

In the case of the Ardeatine caves, such a position, it would seem, was not only wrong but immoral.

Another close wartime associate of Pius XII, Eugène Cardinal Tisserant, the present Dean of the College of Cardinals, has spoken otherwise of Pacelli. In a confidential letter written at the time of the German atrocities in Poland, Cardinal Tisserant woefully related, "I fear that history will reproach the Holy See with having practiced a policy of selfish convenience and not much else." [21]

Both Montini and Tisserant were inside the Vatican on March 23 and 24, 1944. Perhaps they were even in consultation with the Pope about the tragedy unfolding at that very moment in Rome. While Pius himself kept neither diaries nor personal notebooks, it is known that Monsignor Montini often drafted the minutes of meetings considered important by the Pope. With the recent announcement by the Vatican that Pope Paul has authorized publication "wholly and completely" [22] of all documents in its archives concerning World War II, one looks forward for further word on the unfinished story of the Via Rasella and *Le Fosse Ardeatine*.

Appendix

THE LIST OF MEN KNOWN TO HAVE DIED IN THE ARDEATINE CAVES

(Including Ages and Occupations)

Agnini, Ferdinando, 19	*medical student*
Ajroldi, Antonio, 37	*major*
Albanese, Teodato, 39	*lawyer*
Albertelli, Pilo, 36	*professor of philosophy*
Amoretti, Ivanoe, 23	*lieutenant*
Angelai, Aldo, 36	*butcher*
Angeli, Virgilio, 44	*painter (artist)*
Angelini, Paolo, 34	*chauffeur*
Angelucci, Giovanni, 19	*butcher*
Annarumi, Bruno, 22	*tinsmith*
Anticoli, Lazzaro, 26	*peddler*
Artale, Vito, 62	*general*
Astrologo, Cesare, 41	*polisher*
Aversa, Rafaele, 37	*captain, Carabinieri*
Avolio, Carlo, 48	*clerk*
Azzarita, Manfredi, 31	*captain*
Baglivo, Ugo, 27	*lawyer*
Ballino, Giovanni, 38	*farmer*
Banzi, Aldo, 23	*clerk*
Barbieri, Silvio, 41	*architect*
Benati, Nino, 30	*banker*
Bendicenti, Donato, 36	*lawyer*
Berardi, Lallo, 38	*laborer*
Bernabei, Elio, 36	*railroad engineer*
Bernardini, Secondo, 35	*merchant*
Bernardini, Tito, 45	*warehouseman*
Berolsheimer, Aldo * †	‡
Blaustein, Giorgio, 49	*banker*
Bolgia, Michele, 49	*railroad worker*

* Unidentified.
† Age unknown.
‡ Occupation unknown.

Bonanni, Luigi, 34	*chauffeur*
Bordoni, Manlio, 23	*clerk*
Bruno di Belmonte, Luigi, 24	*landlord*
Bucchi, Marcello, 22	*surveyor*
Bucci, Bruno, 23	*designer*
Bucci, Umberto, 51	*clerk*
Bucciano, Francesco, 49	*clerk*
Bussi, Armando, 47	*railroad clerk*
Butera, Gaetano, 19	*painter (artist)*
Buttaroni, Vittorio, 38	*chauffeur*
Butticè, Leonardo, 23	*mechanic*
Calderari, Giuseppe †	*farmer*
Calò, Cesare * †	*factory worker*
Camisotti, Carlo, 41	*road worker*
Campanile, Silvio, 48	*merchant*
Canacci, Ilario, 17	*busboy*
Canalis, Salvatore, 35	*professor of literature*
Cantalamessa, Renato, 40	*carpenter*
Capecci, Alfredo, 19	*mechanic*
Capozio, Ottavio, 21	*postal clerk*
Caputo, Ferruccio, 21	*student*
Caracciolo, Emanuele, 31	*film technician*
Carioli, Francesco, 65	*fruit vendor*
Carola, Federico, 28	*captain, Air Force*
Carola, Mario, 23	*captain*
Casadei, Andrea, 31	*carpenter*
Caviglia, Adolfo, 45	*clerk*
Celani, Giuseppe, 42	*civil servant*
Cerroni, Oreste, 69	*typographer*
Checchi, Egidio, 51	*mechanic*
Chiesa, Romualdo, 21	*student*
Chiricozzi, Aldo, 18	*clerk*
Ciavarella, Francesco, 27	*seaman*
Cibei, Duilio, 15	*carpenter's apprentice*
Cibei, Gino, 19	*mechanic*
Cinelli, Francesco, 45	*clerk*
Cinelli, Giuseppe, 42	*food deliverer*

* Unidentified.
† Age unknown.

Cocco, Pasquale, 24	‡
Coen, Saverio, 33	*merchant*
Conti, Giorgio, 41	*engineer*
Corsi, Orazio, 52	*carpenter*
Costanzi, Guido, 29	*clerk*
Cozzi, Alberto, 19	*mechanic*
D'Amico, Cosimo, 36	*theatrical producer*
D'Amico, Giuseppe, 39	*student*
D'Andrea, Mario, 32	*railroad worker*
D'Aspro, Arturo, 60	*accountant*
De Angelis, Gerardo, 49	*captain*
De Carolis, Ugo, 45	*major, Carabinieri*
De Giorgio, Carlo, 34	*clerk*
De Grenet, Filippo, 39	*diplomat*
Della Torre, Edoardo, 50	*lawyer*
Del Monte, Giuseppe, 39	*clerk*
De Marchi, Raoul, 28	*clerk*
De Micco, Cosimo * †	‡
De Nicolò, Gastone, 18	*student*
De Simoni, Fidardo, 45	*factory worker*
Di Capua, Zaccaria, 44	*chauffeur*
Di Castro, Angelo, 26	*shop clerk*
Di Consiglio, Cesare, 30	*peddler*
Di Consiglio, Franco, 17	*butcher*
Di Consiglio, Marco, 19	*butcher*
Di Consiglio, Mosè, 74	*merchant*
Di Consiglio, Salomone, 45	*peddler*
Di Consiglio, Santoro, 18	*butcher*
Di Nepi, Alberto, 64	*merchant*
Di Nepi, Giorgio, 24	*salesman*
Di Nepi, Samuele, 36	*merchant*
Di Nola, Ugo, 43	*business agent*
Diociajuti, Pier Domenico, 64	*merchant*
Di Peppe, Otello, 53	*cabinetmaker*
Di Porto, Angelo, 25	*shop clerk*

* Unidentified.
† Age unknown.
‡ Occupation unknown.

Di Porto, Giacomo, 53	*peddler*
Di Porto, Giacomo, 48	*peddler*
Di Salvo, Gioacchino, 30	*clerk*
Di Segni, Armando, 30	*merchant*
Di Segni, Pacifico, 22	*peddler*
Di Veroli, Attilio, 54	*merchant*
Di Veroli, Michele, 15	*merchant's apprentice*
Drucker, Salomone, 39	*furrier*
Duranti, Lido, 24	*factory worker*
Efrati, Marco, 36	*merchant*
Elena, Fernando, 24	*artist*
Eluisi, Aldo, 45	*housepainter*
Ercolani, Giorgio, 26	*lt. colonel*
Ercoli, Aldo, 27	*painter (artist)*
Fabri, Renato, 55	*merchant*
Fabrini, Antonio, 44	*tinsmith*
Fano, Giorgio, 36	*scientist*
Fantacone, Alberto, 27	*lawyer*
Fantini, Vittorio, 25	*pharmacist*
Fatucci, Amadio, 66	*peddler*
Felicioli, Mario, 42	*technician*
Fenulli, Dardano, 54	*general*
Ferola, Enrico, 42	*blacksmith*
Finamonti, Loreto, 43	*merchant*
Finocchiaro, Arnaldo, 22	*electrician*
Finzi, Aldo, 52	*landowner*
Fiorentini, Valerio, 25	*auto mechanic*
Fiorini, Fiorino, 63	*music teacher*
Fochetti, Angelo, 28	*clerk*
Fondi, Edmondo, 49	*merchant*
Fontana, Genserico, 26	*lieutenant, Carabinieri*
Fornari, Raffaele, 49	*merchant*
Fornaro, Leone, 22	*peddler*
Forte, Gaetano, 24	*merchant*
Foschi, Carlo, 51	*merchant*
Frasca, Celestino, 32	*bricklayer*
Frascà, Paolo, 45	*clerk*
Frascati, Angelo, 56	*merchant*

Frignani, Giovanni, 46	*lt. colonel, Carabinieri*
Funaro, Alberto, 24	*merchant*
Funaro, Mosè, 55	*merchant*
Funaro, Pacifico, 54	*chauffeur*
Funaro, Settimio, 27	*peddler*
Galafati, Angelo, 46	*factory worker*
Gallarello, Antonio, 59	*cabinetmaker*
Gavioli, Luigi, 42	*clerk*
Gelsomini, Manlio, 36	*physician*
Gesmundo, Gioacchino, 35	*professor of literature*
Giacchini, Alberto, 36	*insurance agent*
Giglio, Maurizio, 23	*lieutenant*
Gigliozzi, Romolo, 35	*chauffeur*
Giordano, Calcedonio, 27	*metal worker*
Giorgi, Giorgio, 23	*accountant*
Giorgini, Renzo, 56	*industrialist*
Giustiniani, Acitano * †	‡
Gorgolini, Giorgio, 20	*accountant*
Gori, Gastone, 30	*bricklayer*
Govoni, Aladino, 35	*captain*
Grani, Umberto, 46	*major*
Grieco, Ennio, 29	*electrician*
Guidoni, Unico, 20	*student*
Haipel, Mario, 32	*warrant officer*
Iaforte, Domenico, 50	*shoemaker*
Ialuna, Sebastiano, 23	*landowner*
Imperiali, Costantino, 35	*wine salesman*
Intreccialagli, Mario, 22	*shoemaker*
Kereszti, Sandor, 29	*military officer*
Landesmann, Boris, 43	*merchant*
La Rosa, Salvatore * †	‡
La Vecchia, Gaetano, 42	*cabinetmaker*
Leonardi, Ornello, 18	*shop clerk*
Leonelli, Cesare, 37	*lawyer*
Liberi, Epimenio, 23	*industrialist*

* Unidentified.
† Age unknown.
‡ Occupation unknown.

Lidonnici, Amedeo, 26	*industrialist*
Limentani, Davide, 53	*merchant*
Limentani, Giovanni, 58	*merchant*
Limentani, Settimio, 36	*merchant*
Lombardi, Ezio, 40	*clerk*
Lopresti, Giuseppe, 24	*lawyer*
Lordi, Roberto, 49	*general*
Lotti, Giuseppe, 40	*plasterer*
Lucarelli, Armando, 24	*typographer*
Lucchetti, Carlo, 44	*metal worker*
Luna, Gavino, 48	*clerk*
Lungaro, Pietro, 33	*Public Security agent*
Lunghi, Ambrogio, 50	*road worker*
Lusena, Umberto, 39	*major*
Luzzi, Everardo, 24	*steelworker*
Maggini, Alfredo, 19	*shoemaker*
Magri, Mario, 48	*captain*
Manca, Candido, 37	*brigadier, Carabinieri*
Mancini, Enrico, 47	*merchant*
Marchesi, Alberto, 43	*merchant*
Marchetti, Remo, 24	*chauffeur*
Margioni, Antonio, 43	*carpenter*
Marimpietri, Vittorio, 26	*clerk*
Marino, Angelo, 31	*salesman*
Martella, Angelo * †	‡
Martelli Castaldi, Sabato, 47	*general*
Martini, Placido, 64	*lawyer*
Mastrangeli, Fulvio, 41	*clerk*
Mastrogiacomo, Luigi, 40	*usher*
Medas, Giuseppe, 35	*lawyer*
Menasci, Umberto, 37	*merchant*
Micheli, Ernesto, 46	*housepainter*
Micozzi, Emidio, 43	*merchant*
Mieli, Cesare, 53	*peddler*
Mieli, Mario, 28	*shopkeeper*

* Unidentified.
† Age unknown.
‡ Occupation unknown.

Mieli, Renato, 30	*shopkeeper*
Milano, Raffaele, 48	*salesman*
Milano, Tullio, 44	*clerk*
Milano, Ugo, 38	*clerk*
Mocci, Sisinnio, 40	‡
Montezemolo, Giuseppe, 42	*colonel*
Moretti, Augusto, 39	*farmer*
Moretti, Pio, 40	*bank clerk*
Morgani, Sandro	*electrician*
Mosca, Alfredo, 53	*technician*
Moscati, Emanuele, 29	*salesman*
Moscati, Marco * †	‡
Moscati, Pace, 44	*peddler*
Moscati, Vito †	*electrician*
Mosciatti, Carlo, 20	*clerk*
Napoleone, Agostino, 25	*lieutenant*
Natili, Celestino, 23	*merchant*
Natili, Mariano, 56	*merchant*
Navarra, Giuseppe, 58	*farmer*
Ninci, Sestilio, 48	*tram driver*
Nobili, Edoardo, 50	*mechanic*
Norma, Fernando, 37	*cabinetmaker*
Orlandi Posti, Orlando, 18	*student*
Ottaviano, Armando, 24	*student*
Paliani, Attilio, 52	*merchant*
Pappagallo, Pietro, 55	*clergyman*
Partiti, Michele * †	‡
Pasqualucci, Alfredo, 40	*shoemaker*
Passarella, Mario, 39	*carpenter*
Pelliccia, Ulderico, 39	*carpenter*
Pensuti, Renzo, 25	*student*
Pepicelli, Francesco, 37	*warrant officer*
Perpetua, Remo, 38	*merchant*
Perugia, Angelo, 37	*peddler*
Petocchi, Amedeo †	‡

* Unidentified.
† Age unknown.
‡ Occupation unknown.

Petrucci, Paolo, 26	*professor of literature*
Pettorini, Ambrogio, 48	*landowner*
Piasco, Renzo, 18	*railroad worker*
Piattelli, Cesare, 43	*peddler*
Piattelli, Franco, 20	*shop clerk*
Piattelli, Giacomo, 46	*salesman*
Pierantoni, Luigi, 38	*physician*
Pierleoni, Romolo, 23	*blacksmith*
Pignotti, Angelo, 34	*shopkeeper*
Pignotti, Umberto, 29	*clerk*
Piperno, Claudio, 20	*merchant*
Piras, Ignazio, 64	*farmer*
Pirozzi, Vincenzo, 26	*accountant*
Pisino, Antonio, 26	*naval officer*
Pistonesi, Antonio, 19	*waiter*
Pitrelli, Rosario, 26	*mechanic*
Polli, Domenico, 36	*construction worker*
Portieri, Alessendro, 19	*mechanic*
Portinari, Erminio, 30	*surveyor*
Primavera, Pietro, 19	*clerk*
Prosperi, Antonio, 34	*clerk*
Pula, Italo, 28	*blacksmith*
Pula, Spartaco, 24	*housepainter*
Raffaelli, Beniamino, 39	*carpenter*
Rampulla, Giovanni, 49	*lt. colonel*
Reicher, Marian * †	‡
Rendina, Roberto, 51	*lt. colonel*
Renzi, Egidio, 43	*factory worker*
Renzini, Augusto, 45	*Carabiniere*
Ricci, Domenico, 31	*clerk*
Rindone, Nunzio, 31	*farmhand*
Rizzo, Ottorino, 44	*major*
Roazzi, Antonio, 46	*chauffeur*
Rocchi, Filippo, 35	*merchant*
Rodella, Bruno, 26	*student*

* Unidentified.
† Age unknown.
‡ Occupation unknown.

Rodriguez, Pereira Romeo, 25	*lieutenant, Carabinieri*
Romagnoli, Goffredo, 19	*railroad worker*
Roncacci, Giulio, 49	*merchant*
Ronconi, Ettore, 46	*farmer*
Saccotelli, Vincenzo, 46	*carpenter*
Salemme, Felice, 22	*clerk*
Salvatori, Giovanni, 48	*clerk*
Sansolini, Adolfo, 38	*merchant*
Sansolini, Alfredo, 26	*merchant*
Savelli, Francesco, 53	*engineer*
Scattoni, Umberto, 42	*painter (artist)*
Sciunnach, Dattilo, 63	*merchant*
Semini, Fiorenzo, 23	*lieutenant*
Senesi, Giovanni, 19	*clerk*
Sepe, Gaetano, 36	*tailor*
Sergi, Gerardo, 25	*lieutenant, Carabinieri*
Sermoneta, Benedetto, 39	*peddler*
Silvestri, Sebastiano, 28	*farm owner*
Simoni, Simone, 63	*general*
Sojke, Bernard * †	‡
Sonnino, Angelo, 29	*merchant*
Sonnino, Gabriele, 34	*shop clerk*
Sonnino, Mosè, 40	*peddler*
Sonnino, Pacifico, 52	*merchant*
Spunticchia, Antonino, 63	*mechanic*
Stame, Nicola Ugo †	*musician*
Talamo, Manfredi, 49	*lt. colonel, Carabinieri*
Tanzini, Giovanni Carlo, 49	*bricklayer*
Tapparelli, Mario, 52	*merchant*
Tedesco, Cesare, 31	*shop clerk*
Terracina, Sergio, 18	*shop clerk*
Testa, Settimio, 33	*farmer*
Trentini, Giulio, 33	*grinder*
Troiani, Eusebio, 50	*agent*
Troiani, Pietro, 35	*peddler*

* Unidentified.
† Age unknown.
‡ Occupation unknown.

Tuchman, Heinz Erich * †	‡
Ugolini, Nino, 25	*electrician*
Unghetti, Antonio, 38	*laborer*
Valesani, Otello, 19	*shoemaker*
Vercillo, Giovanni, 35	*clerk*
Villoresi, Renato, 37	*captain*
Viotti, Pietro, 34	*merchant*
Vivanti, Angelo, 49	*merchant*
Vivanti, Giacomo, 32	*merchant*
Vivenzo, Gennaro †	‡
Volponi, Guido, 36	*clerk*
Wald, Pesach Paul, 23	‡
Wald, Schra †	‡
Zaccagnini, Carlo, 30	*lawyer*
Zambelli, Ilario †	*telegraph operator*
Zarfati, Alessandro, 29	*merchant*
Zicconi, Raffaele, 32	*clerk*
Zironi, Augusto, 23	*lieutenant*

* Unidentified.
† Age unknown.
‡ Occupation unknown.

NOTES ON CHAPTERS

(*All translations from Italian-language sources are by the author.*)

(Abbreviations used)

Carretta dep.	Deposition of Donato Carretta, Aug. 7, 1944; published in *Caruso proceedings.*
Caruso proceedings	Z. Algardi, ed., *Il processo Caruso,* Rome, 1945 (transcript of TPC).
CDS	*Corriere della Sera,* Milan newspaper.
Deakin collection	Copies of captured Italian documents held by F. W. Deakin, Warden, Saint Antony's College, Oxford, England.
De Gasperis statement	Statement of Andrea De Gasperis, published in *l'Italia Libera,* Sept. 24, 1944.
Dollmann ms.	Copy given to author of unpublished manuscript written by Eugen Dollmann in 1948.
FRUS	*Foreign Relations of the United States, 1943, Vol. II, Europe,* Washington, 1964.
INQ	Inquest of the Ardeatine Caves Commission. (The Commission was set up by the US Fifth Army immediately after the liberation of Rome. It was composed of scientists, civic leaders, and American military administrative officials. Its purpose was to investigate the Ardeatine crime and provide for the exhumation and identification of the bodies in the caves.)
Lavagnino dep.	Deposition of Eleanora Lavagnino in INQ.
MLI	Istituto Nazionale per la Storia del Movimento di Liberazione in Italia (Archives of the Resistance), Milan, Italy.

NA	National Archives, Washington, D.C.
Pers. int. CC	Interviews with Carla Capponi, conducted in Italian, Rome, May 27 and 29 and June 1, 1965.
Pers. int. CD	Interview with Carmello De Stefanis, conducted in Italian, Rome, May 22, 1965.
Pers. int. CS	Interview with Carlo Salinari, conducted in Italian, Rome, May 29, 1965.
Pers. int. DG	Interview with Duilio Grigion, conducted in Italian, Rome, May 29, 1965.
Pers. int. ED	Interview with Eugen Dollmann, conducted in Italian, Munich, June 10, 1965.
Pers. int. FC	Interview with Franco Calamandrei, conducted in Italian, Rome, June 1, 1965.
Pers. int. GA	Interview with Giorgio Amendola, conducted in Italian, Rome, June 1, 1965.
Pers. int. MF	Interview with Mario Fiorentini, conducted in Italian, Rome, May 27, 1965.
Pers. int. NN	Interview with two unidentified nuns at Bambin Gesù convent, conducted in Italian, Rome, May 19, 1965.
Pers. int. PT	Interview with Peter Tompkins, conducted in English, Washington, D.C., Nov. 26, 1965.
Pers. int. RB	Interviews with Rosario Bentivegna, conducted in Italian, Rome, May 23 and 27, 1965.
Pers. int. RF	Interview with Raoul Falcioni, conducted in Italian, Rome, May 27, 1965.
Raider statement	Statement dated Rome, June 10, 1944; published in L. Morpurgo, *Caccia all' uomo*, Rome, 1946.
Scottu dep.	Deposition of Giovanni Scottu, in journal of MLI, Sept., 1950.

TAK	Trial of Field Marshal Albert Kesselring.
THK	Trial of Herbert Kappler.
TMM	Trial of Generals Eberhard von Mackensen and Kurt Mälzer.
TMR	Tribunale Militare di Roma, Processo Kappler, *Sentenza.* (This 30,000-word document represents the final sentence in THK, handed down by the Military Tribunal of Rome, Jan. 10, 1954, after a number of appeals by Kappler and five codefendants.)
TPC	Trial of Pietro Caruso.
UNWCC	United Nations War Crimes Commission, *Law Reports of Trials of War Criminals.*
Valentini statement	Statement of Michele Valentini published in G. Stendardo, *Via Tasso,* Rome, 1965.

PART ONE: *The Eve / March 1–22, 1944*

1. Quotation from Allied leaflet taken from original in Italian, on display at Museo Storico della Lotta di Liberazione di Roma, 145 Via Tasso, Rome.

I

1. *Pers. int. MF. Cf.* also "Morire a Roma" in *L'Europeo,* Apr. 12, 1964, pp. 32–42. This valuable source for details about the attack is comprised of a series of textual statements by Carla Capponi and Rosario Bentivegna in response to a series of questions.
2. I. Insolera, *Roma moderna,* Turin, 1962, p. 52.
3. G. Caputo, "*La Resistenza della scuola romana*" in: *Movimento di Liberazione in Italia* (historical journal of MLI), Apr.–June, 1962.
4. P. Monelli, *Roma 1943,* 3rd ed., Rome, 1945, p. 404. (This book has gone through several editions and revisions; the earlier editions, including the 3rd, have some very serious factual errors, which were later corrected.)
5. *Pers. int. MF.*
6. The Germans and Fascists later denied that this formation be-

longed to the SS. This and other allegations sought to picture the column as a group of harmless old men. Details on the column's history and its place in the German police organizations are given in Pt. One, Chap. V of this book. The principal source is noted.

7. *Pers. int. MF.*

II

1. The sources for this crucial and still-debated period are very numerous and the full history has yet to be written. *Cf.* F. W. Deakin, *The Brutal Friendship*, New York, 1962; C. Delzell, *Mussolini's Enemies*, Princeton, 1961; R. Zangrandi, *1943: 24 luglio –8 settembre*, Milan, 1964.
2. *Cf. supra*, Pt. One, Chap. III.
3. *Cf. supra*, p. 17.
4. The most vivid descriptions of life in occupied Rome are to be found in: Monelli, *op. cit.*, pp. 397–434; C. Trabucco, *La prigionia di Roma: Diario dei 268 giorni dell' occupazione tedesca*, Rome, 1945. For a bibliography on this aspect, *see* R. Battaglia, *Storia della Resistenza italiana*, Turin, 1953, pp. 590–593.
5. F. Onofri, "*GAP di zona*," in *Rinascita*, Apr. 1945, pp. 117–119.
6. *Ibid.*
7. Text quoted in E. Piscitelli, *Storia della Resistenza romana*, Bari, 1965, p. 252.
8. *Pers. int. GA.* The Junta's strategy was also given in testimony by Amendola and other leaders of the Junta and the CLN in THK; *cf.* testimony quoted in R. P. Capano, *La Resistenza in Roma*, Vol. II, Naples, 1963, pp. 291–295; also Z. Algardi, *Processi ai fascisti*, Florence, 1958, pp. 110–121.
9. *Cf.* Piscitelli, *op. cit.*, Chaps. VI and VII.

III

1. *FRUS*, p. 926.
2. Aside from the Pope's displeasure, which can be ascertained in telegrams to the State Department from the American diplomat in the Holy See, Roosevelt's message provoked a diplomatic embarrassment for the Vatican. (*Cf. ibid.* pp. 927–931.) The German Ambassador to the Holy See also recorded the Vatican's negative reaction to the President's message. (Telegram from Weizsäcker

to Berlin of July 12, 1943; text in S. Friedländer, *Pio XII e il Terzo Reich*, Milan, 1965, p. 166.)

3. Letter of Pius XII to President Roosevelt; text in *FRUS*, p. 931.
4. Piscitelli, *op. cit.*, p. 13.
5. Memorandum of Apostolic Delegation at Washington to State Department, Aug. 20, 1943; text in *FRUS*, p. 946.
6. Telegram from Weizsäcker to Berlin, Aug. 3, 1943; text in Friedländer, *op. cit.*, p. 170.
7. Telegram to Berlin, Aug. 4, 1943; text in *ibid.*, pp. 170–171.
8. Telegram from Churchill to Roosevelt, Aug. 4, 1943; text in *FRUS*, p. 940, and *passim.*
9. Memorandum of Apostolic Delegation at Washington to State Department, Aug. 18. 1943; text in *ibid.*, p. 944.
10. Memorandum of Apostolic Delegation at Washington to State Department, Aug. 20, 1943; text in *ibid.*, p. 945.
11. *Cf.* article by secretary to Pius XII, Father Robert Leiber, S.J., "*Der Papst und die Verfolgung der Juden*" in F. Raddatz, ed., *Summa Inuria oder Durfte der Papst Schweigen?*, Reinbeck bei Hamburg, 1963, p. 104; cited in G. Lewy, *The Catholic Church and Nazi Germany*, New York, 1964, p. 305. Lewy writes, "Father Leiber . . . recalls that the late Pope always looked upon Russian Bolshevism as more dangerous than German National Socialism."
12. Telegram to Berlin, Oct. 8, 1943; text in Friedländer, *op. cit.*, p. 178.
13. Telegram to Berlin, Sept. 24, 1943; text in *ibid.*, p. 175.
14. Telegram from Weizsäcker to Berlin, Sept. 10, 1943; text in *ibid.*, p. 180. The matter was taken up by Hitler, according to Goebbels. *Cf.* L. P. Lochner, ed. and trans., *The Goebbels Diaries*, Garden City, 1948 (paperback ed.), p. 505 (entry for Sept. 11, 1943).
15. Goebbels in *ibid.*
16. Telegram from Ribbentrop to Weizsäcker, Oct. 4, 1943; text in Friedländer, *op. cit.*, p. 182. Weizsäcker was received on Oct. 9 by the Pope, who was given Ribbentrop's message. *Cf. ibid.*, p. 182.
17. Telegram to Secretary of State Hull, Oct. 25, 1943; text in *FRUS*, p. 951.
18. Telegram to Berlin, Oct. 8, 1943; text in Friedländer, *op. cit.*, p. 178.
19. Telegram to Berlin, Oct. 14, 1943; text in *ibid.*, p. 178.
20. Telegram to Hull, Oct. 19, 1943; text in *FRUS*, p. 950.
21. Report of Kaltenbrunner to Ribbentrop, Dec. 16, 1943; text in Friedländer, *op. cit.*, p. 194.

22. *Cf.* Deakin, *op. cit.*, pp. 654–664.
23. *Ibid.*, p. 530.
24. Vatican Secretary of State Maglione to Tittmann, Aug. 15, 1943; text in *FRUS*, pp. 941–943, and *passim.*
25. *The New York Times*, Apr. 2, 1944, p. 19.
26. *Ibid.*

IV

1. *Pers. int. DG.*
2. *Ibid.*
3. *Ibid.*
4. *Il Messaggero*, Mar. 9, 1944.
5. *Pers. int. MF.*
6. *Ibid.*
7. *Ibid.*
8. *Pers. int. CC; cf.* also *L'Europeo, op. cit.*
9. *Pers. int. MF.*
10. *Pers. int. CC; cf.* Piscitelli, *op. cit.*, p. 287.
11. *Pers. int. RB; cf.* also *L'Europeo, op. cit.;* testimony of R. Bentivegna, June 12, 1948, in THK, partial transcript in *CDS*, June 13, 1948, p. 3.
12. Caputo, *op. cit.*
13. *Ibid.*
14. *L'Europeo, op. cit.*
15. *Ibid.*
16. *Pers. int. MF.*
17. *Pers. int. CS.*
18. *Pers. int. MF.*

V

1. The source of these two paragraphs is a letter to the author from the Austrian Bundesministerium für Landesverteidigung (Ministry of Defense), signature illegible, Feb. 25, 1965.
2. Deakin, *op. cit.*, pp. 654–664.
3. *Ibid.*
4. *Ibid.*
5. *Ibid.*

VI

1. E. F. Möllhausen, *La carta perdente*, Rome, 1948, p. 213.
2. *Il Messaggero*, Feb. 19, 1944.
3. *Giornale d'Italia*, Mar. 22, 1944.
4. Piscitelli, *op. cit.*, p. 281.
5. *Ibid.*, p. 287.

VII

1. Möllhausen, *op. cit.*, p. 213.
2. *Ibid.*
3. S. Bertoldi, *I tedeschi in Italia*, Milan, 1964, p. 221.
4. Möllhausen, *op. cit.*, p. 139.
5. Telegram to Ribbentrop, Oct. 6, 1943; text in Friedländer, *op. cit.*, p. 184.
6. Möllhausen, *op. cit.*, p. 116.
7. *Ibid.*, pp. 196–197.
8. *Ibid.*, p. 213.
9. *Ibid.*, p. 174. *Pers. int. ED.* The sources for background material about him are many. *Cf.* E. Dollmann, *Roma nazista*, Milan, 1949. Bertoldi, *op. cit.*; Deakin, *op. cit.*
10. Dollmann, *op. cit.*, p. 241.
11. Möllhausen, *op. cit.*, p. 214.
12. Testimony of Herbert Kappler, May 31, 1947, in THK; partial transcript in *CDS*, June 1, 1948, p. 1.
13. Among the sources for biographical material on Kappler are his testimony and others, in THK, TMM, TAK; Bertoldi, *op. cit.*; Möllhausen, *op. cit.*
14. Möllhausen, *op. cit.*, p. 133.
15. *Ibid.*, p. 214; for biographical material on Mälzer, *see* "Il Re di Roma" in *ibid.*, pp. 133–142.
16. *Ibid.*, p. 215.

VIII

1. Testimony of Sandro Pertini, member of the Military Junta, July 3, 1948, in THK; partial transcript in *Il Messaggero*, July 4, 1948.
2. Trabucco, *op. cit.*, p. 173 (diary entry for Mar. 1, 1944).

3. Monelli, *op. cit.*, p. 418.
4. *Pers. int. CS.*
5. Testimony of Sandro Pertini, July 3, 1948, in THK, *op. cit.*

IX

1. *Pers. int. MF.*
2. *Pers. int. CS; cf. l'Unità*, June 5, 1948, p. 3.
3. A rough diagram was drawn for the author by Rosario Bentivegna. Refinements were made as a result of subsequent interviews with Bentivegna and other partisans; *cf.* also *l'Unità*, June 5, 1948, p. 3.
4. The reconstruction that follows is based on the previously cited interviews with Mario Fiorentini, Carlo Salinari, Carla Capponi, Rosario Bentivegna, and Giorgio Amendola; also on interviews cited below of Franco Calamandrei and Raoul Falcioni. *Cf.* also account of Via Rasella partisan Pasquale Balsamo in *l'Unità*, June 5, 1948, p. 3; testimony of partisans, June 12 and 18, 1948, in THK; partial transcripts in *CDS*, June 13 and 19, 1948.

X

1. M. de Wyss, *Rome Under the Terror*, London, 1945, p. 204 (diary entry for Mar. 22, 1944); *cf.* also Trabucco, *op. cit.*, p. 190.
2. Pope's speech quoted in A. Giovannetti, *Roma città aperta*, Milan, 1962, p. 240.
3. *Ibid.*
4. *Keesing's Contemporary Archives*, Vol. V, London, 1943–1946, p. 6363.
5. *Ibid.*, p. 6326.
6. Trabucco, *op. cit.*, p. 182.
7. Giovannetti, *op. cit.*, p. 251.
8. Quoted in J. Scrivener, *Inside Rome with the Germans*, New York, 1945, p. 142 (diary entry for Mar. 22, 1944).
9. *Ibid.*
10. De Wyss, *op. cit.*, p. 204.
11. E. Weizsäcker, *Memoirs*, Chicago, 1951, p. 292.
12. Hitler's speech of Sept. 10, 1943; text in F. Watts and N. Ausubel, eds., *Voices of History*, New York, 1944, p. 343.
13. Möllhausen, *op. cit.*, p. 243.
14. *Ibid.*, p. 244.

XI

1. *Pers. int. CC.*
2. Historical Division, Department of the Army, *Anzio Beachhead*, Washington, 1947, p. 116.
3. *Pers. int. RF.*
4. *Pers. int. CC.*
5. *L'Europeo, op. cit.*
6. Quoted in *ibid.*
7. Letter to author from Carla Capponi, Aug. 20, 1965.
8. Onofri, *op. cit.*
9. Quoted in *L'Europeo, op. cit.*
10. *Pers. int. RB.*
11. *Ibid.*
12. *Ibid.; cf.* also *L'Europeo, op. cit.*

XII

1. I. Bonomi, *Diario di un anno*, Milan, 1947, p. 161 (diary entry for Mar. 22, 1944).
2. Piscitelli, *op. cit.*, p. 62.
3. Bonomi, *op. cit.*, p. 160 (diary entry for Mar. 18, 1944).
4. *Ibid.*, p. 161.
5. *Ibid.*

PART TWO: *The Attack in Via Rasella / March 23, 1944*

1. Quotation attributed to Kesselring by Möllhausen, *op. cit.*, p. 235.

I

1. This account is based on press reports in *Giornale d'Italia*, Mar. 24, 1944, p. 1.

II

1. Quoted in Piscitelli, *op. cit.*, p. 296.
2. *Giornale d'Italia*, Mar. 23, 1944, p. 1.

3. Monelli, *op. cit.*, p. 418.
4. Historical Division, Department of the Army, *op. cit.*, p. 113.
5. *Giornale d'Italia*, Mar. 23, 1944, p. 1.
6. *Ibid.*
7. *Ibid.*, p. 2.
8. *Ibid.*
9. *Ibid.*
10. *Ibid.*

III

1. *Pers. int. DG.*

IV

1. *Giornale d'Italia*, Mar. 24, 1944, p. 1.
2. Testimony of Pietro Caruso, Sept. 20, 1944, in TPC; *Caruso proceedings*, p. 142.
3. Pretrial interrogation of Caruso, Aug. 8, 1944, in *ibid.*, p. 56.
4. *Giornale d'Italia*, Mar. 24, 1944, p. 1.
5. B. Mussolini, *Opera omnia*, Vol. 32, Florence, 1960, p. 75.
6. *Ibid.*
7. *Ibid.*
8. Quoted by G. Bottai, *Venti anni e un giorno*, Milan, 1959, p. 302.
9. *Giornale d'Italia*, Mar. 24, 1944, p. 1.
10. *Ibid.*

V

1. *Scottu dep.*
2. P. Tompkins, *A Spy in Rome*, New York, 1962 (paperback edition), p. 44, and *passim.*
3. A. Fumarola, *Essi non sono morti*, Rome, 1945, p. 149.
4. *Cf.* report of Rome police chief Morazzini, Aug. 11, 1944, in *Caruso proceedings*, pp. 37–50.
5. *Scottu dep.*
6. *Ibid.*
7. Tompkins, *op. cit.*, p. 49; *cf.* also Capano, *op. cit.*, Vol. II, p. 490.
8. *Scottu dep.*

VI

1. Tompkins, *op. cit.*, p. 187. Also *pers. int. PT.*
2. *Ibid.*, pp. 44–49.
3. *Ibid.*, p. 20.
4. *Ibid.*, p. 187.

VII

1. *Giornale d'Italia*, Mar. 24, 1944, p. 2.
2. Capano, *op. cit.*, Vol. I, p. 210.
3. *L'Osservatore Romano*, Mar. 24, 1944, p. 1.
4. *Ibid.*
5. Giovannetti, *op. cit.*, p. 255.
6. *L'Osservatore Romano*, Mar. 25, 1944, p. 2.

VIII

1. *Pers. int.* CC and *pers. int. RB.*
2. Trabucco, *op. cit.*, p. 187.
3. *Giornale d'Italia*, Mar. 25, 1944, p. 2.
4. *Pers. int. CS.*
5. *Pers. int. RF.*
6. *Pers. int. RB.*
7. *L'Europeo, op. cit.*
8. *Ibid.*
9. *Pers. int. RB.*
10. *Pers. int. CC.*

IX

1. *Scottu dep.*
2. Quoted in *l'Italia Libera*, June 24, 1944, p. 2.
3. *Scottu dep.*

X

1. Kappler's testimony, June 3, 1948, in THK; partial transcript in *CDS* and *Il Messaggero*, June 4, 1948.

2. Quoted by A. Mellini Ponce de Leon, *Guerra diplomatica a Salò*, Bologna, 1950, pp. 69–70 (diary entry for Feb. 16, 1945).
3. Kappler's testimony, May 31, 1948, in THK; partial transcript in *CDS*, June 1, 1948, p. 1.
4. Kappler's testimony, June 4, 1948, in THK; *ibid.*, June 5, 1948, p. 3.
5. *Ibid.*
6. *Lavagnino dep.* in INQ, p. 76. Documents of INQ appear in the report of Professor Doctor Attilio Ascarelli, who directed the work of INQ's technical committee–the exhumation and identification of the bodies in the Ardeatine caves. He published his findings in a work titled *Le fosse Ardeatine*, Rome, 1945. Page numbers for INQ refer to this report.
7. Capano, *op. cit.*, Vol. II, p. 506.
8. Kappler's testimony, June 3, 1948, in THK; partial transcript in *CDS*, June 4, 1948.

XI

1. *Pers. int. CC.*
2. *Ibid.*
3. *L'Europeo*, *op. cit.*
4. *Il Messaggero*, Mar. 23, 1944.
5. *Pers. int. CC.*
6. *Ibid.*
7. *Pers. int. RB.*
8. *L'Europeo*, *op. cit.*
9. *Pers. int. CC.*

XII

1. *Giornale d'Italia*, Mar. 25, 1944, p. 1.
2. Möllhausen, *op. cit.*, p. 215.
3. *Ibid.*
4. *Ibid.*
5. *Ibid.*, p. 216.
6. *Giornale d'Italia*, Mar. 25, 1944, p. 1.
7. *Ibid.*
8. Möllhausen, *op. cit.*, p. 215.
9. *Ibid.*, pp. 215–216.
10. *Giornale d'Italia*, Mar. 25, 1944, p. 1.

11. *Ibid.*
12. Figure and attitude of troops given in Deakin, *op. cit.*, p. 664.

XIII

1. *L'Europeo, op. cit.*
2. F. Ripa di Meana, *Roma clandestina*, Rome, 1944, p. 283.
3. R. Mussolini, *My Life with Mussolini*, London, 1959, p. 60.
4. R. Mussolini, *La mia vita con Mussolini*, Milan, 1948, p. 237. (This is the original Italian edition of the above-cited English translation.)
5. C. Hibbert, *Il Duce*, Boston, 1962, pp. 36–37.
6. P. Levi Cavaglione, *Guerriglia nei Castelli Romani*, Rome, 1945, pp. 144–145.
7. *Ibid.*

XIV

1. *Pers. int. CC.*
2. *L'Europeo, op. cit.*
3. Möllhausen, *op. cit.*, p. 216.
4. *Pers. int. GA.*
5. *L'Europeo, op. cit.*
6. *Ibid.*
7. *Pers. int. RB.*
8. *Ibid.*
9. *Ibid.*
10. *Pers. int. FC.*

XV

1. L. Morpurgo, *Caccia all' uomo*, Rome, 1946, p. 240.
2. De Wyss, *op. cit.*, p. 204 (diary entry for Mar. 23, 1944).
3. Kappler's testimony, June 3, 1948, in THK; partial transcript in *CDS*, June 4, 1948, p. 1.
4. V. Florio, *4 giorni in Via Tasso*, Palermo, 1947 p. 43.
5. *Giornale d'Italia*, Mar. 26, 1944, p. 2.
6. INQ, pp. 13–15.
7. *Ibid.*

8. Möllhausen, *op. cit.*, p. 216.
9. *Ibid.* (This is the moment when Möllhausen heard the explosion.)
10. *Cf.* P. Balsamo in *l'Unità*, June 5, 1948, p. 3.; Dollmann, *op. cit.*, pp. 241–255; article by Herbert Kappler in *Incom*, Mar. 1959, pp. 48–52; INQ, pp. 13–15.
11. *Pers. int.* CS and *pers. int. RB.*
12. *Pers. int. GA.*
13. De Wyss, *op. cit.*, p. 204.
14. Möllhausen, *op. cit.*, p. 216.
15. *Ibid.*
16. Balsamo in *op. cit.*
17. *Pers. int. GA.*
18. *L'Europeo, op. cit.*

XVI

1. Pretrial interrogation of Caruso, Aug. 9, 1944, in *Caruso proceedings*, p. 64.
2. *Ibid.*
3. Dollmann, *op. cit.*, p. 241
4. *Ibid.*
5. *Dollmann ms. Cf.* also Dollmann, *op. cit.*, pp. 241–255.
6. *Sommario dell' incidente del 23 marzo 1944*, Document No. 2, in INQ, p. 74.
7. *Ibid.*
8. Pretrial interrogation of Caruso, Aug. 9, 1944, in *Caruso proceedings*, p. 65.
9. Möllhausen, *op. cit.*, p. 218.
10. The exchange between Möllhausen and Mälzer is quoted by Möllhausen in Bertoldi, *op. cit.*, pp. 223–224; a similar account is in Möllhausen, *op. cit.*, pp. 218–219; *cf.* also Dollmann, *op. cit.*, p. 241; Monelli, *op. cit.*, pp. 402–404.
11. Möllhausen, *op. cit.*, p. 219.
12. Kappler, *Incom, op. cit.*
13. Möllhausen, *op. cit.*, p. 219.
14. Kappler's testimony, June 3, 1948, in THK; partial transcript in *CDS*, June 4, 1948, p. 1.
15. *Ibid.*
16. Kappler, *Incom, op. cit.*
17. Kappler's testimony, June 3, 1948, in THK; partial transcript in *CDS*, June 4, 1948, p. 1.

XVII

1. *Pers. int. CC and pers. int. RB; cf.* also, *L'Europeo, op. cit.*

XVIII

1. Möllhausen, *op. cit.*, p. 219.
2. Dollmann, *op. cit.*, p. 245.
3. A. Hitler, *Hitler's Table Talk*, London, 1953, pp. 716–717 (entry for midday, Mar. 23, 1944).
4. *Ibid.*
5. Quoted in Dollmann, *op. cit.*, p. 245. Möllhausen says that it later became known in Nazi circles that Hitler demanded a reprisal that would "make the world tremble." (Möllhausen, *op. cit.*, p. 229.)

XIX

1. S. Derry, *The Rome Escape Line*, New York, 1960, p. 174.
2. NA, Microcopy T-586, Roll 479, Frame 045206.
3. Kappler's testimony, June 3, 1948, in THK; partial transcript in *CDS*, June 4, 1948, p. 1.
4. Kappler's testimony, June 3, 1948, in THK; partial transcript in *Il Messaggero*, June 4, 1948.
5. Kappler, *Incom, op. cit.*
6. *Dollmann ms.*
7. Möllhausen, *op. cit.*, p. 219.
8. *Pers. int. ED.*
9. TMR, p. 176. (Page numbers for TMR refer to copy which appears as an appendix to a twentieth-anniversary edition of Dr. Ascarelli's work. This edition by A. Ascarelli also is titled *Le fosse Ardeatine* [Bologna, 1965].)
10. *Ibid.; cf.* also Kappler's testimony of June 4, 1948, in THK; partial transcript in *CDS*, June 5, 1948, p. 3.
11. TMR, p. 176; *cf.* also Bertoldi, *op. cit.*, p. 243.
12. TMR, p. 176.
13. Quoted by Kappler in his testimony, June 4, 1948, in THK; partial transcript in *CDS*, June 5, 1948, p. 3.
14. TMR, p. 177; *cf.* also TMM in *UNWCC*, Vol. 8, London, 1949, Case No. 43, p. 1.

15. TMR, p. 177.
16. *Ibid.*
17. Pretrial interrogation of Caruso, Aug. 9, 1944, in *Caruso proceedings*, p. 65.
18. *Ibid.*

XX

1. Pretrial interrogation of Siegfried Westphal, Nuremberg, Oct. 23, 1945; in *Nazi Conspiracy and Aggression*, Suppl. B, Washington, 1948, pp. 1651–1652. (Westphal himself was never tried; nor was he implicated in the Ardeatine crime.)
2. S. Westphal, *Heer in Fesseln*, Bonn, 1950, pp. 246–247.
3. Quoted in Dollmann, *op. cit.*, p. 245.

XXI

1. *Dollmann ms. Cf.* also Dollmann, *op. cit.*, p. 242.
2. Möllhausen, *op. cit.*, p. 220.
3. *Ibid.*, p. 221.
4. *Pers. int. ED.*
5. Dollmann's conclusions are from *ibid.;* Möllhausen's from Möllhausen, *op. cit.*, p. 231.
6. *Dollmann ms. Cf.* also Dollmann, *op. cit.*, p. 242.
7. *Ibid.*
8. *Pers. int. ED.*

XXII

1. *Scottu dep.*
2. Tompkins, *op. cit.*, p. 187.
3. *Ibid.*
4. *Ibid.*
5. *Ibid.*

XXIII

1. *Giornale d'Italia*, Mar. 24, 1944.
2. *L'Osservatore Romano*, Mar. 24, 1944, p. 2.

3. *Ibid.*
4. *Ibid.*

XXIV

1. Bonomi, *op. cit.*, p. 162 (diary entry for Mar. 23, 1944).
2. *Ibid.*
3. *Ibid.*
4. *Ibid.*
5. *Ibid.*

XXV

1. Caruso's testimony, Sept. 20, 1944, in TPC, *Caruso proceedings*, p. 136.
2. *Ibid. Cf.* also TMR, p. 177.
3. Kappler's testimony, June 4, 1948, in THK; partial transcript in *CDS*, June 5, 1948, p. 3; *cf.* also TMR, p. 177.
4. Caruso's testimony, Sept. 20, 1944, in TPC, *Caruso proceedings*, p. 136.
5. *Cf.* "Moscow Declaration on Italy," Nov. 1, 1943, in *World War II International Agreements and Understandings Entered into During Secret Conferences Concerning Other Peoples*, Washington, 1953.
6. Caruso's testimony, Sept. 20, 1944, in TPC, *Caruso proceedings*, p. 136.
7. TMR, p. 177.
8. Caruso's testimony, Sept. 20, 1944, in TPC, *Caruso proceedings*, p. 136.
9. *Ibid.*

XXVI

1. Historical Division, Department of the Army, *op. cit.*, p. 105.
2. *Ibid.*
3. TAK, in *UNWCC*, Vol. 8, Case No. 44, p. 9; *cf.* also Bertoldi, *op. cit.*, p. 244.
4. *Ibid.*
5. A. Kesselring, *A Soldier's Record*, New York, 1954, p. 355.
6. Bertoldi, *op. cit.*, p. 244.

7. Pretrial interrogation of Westphal, in *Nazi Conspiracy and Aggression*, *op. cit.*, pp. 1651–1652.
8. Kesselring, *op. cit.*, p. 355.
9. TAK, in *UNWCC, op. cit.*, Vol. 8, p. 9.

XXVII

1. *Pers. int. ED* and *Dollmann ms.*
2. Giovannetti, *op. cit.*, p. 256.
3. Konstantin, *The Pope*, Diana Pike, trans., New York, 1956, p. 217. This is the English translation of Konstantin, Prinz von Bayern, *Der Papst: Ein Lebensbild*, Bad Wörishofen, 1952. A panegyrical biography of Pius XII, it is based in great part on personal interviews held at the Vatican with high prelates, including the outspoken Monsignor Ludwig Kaas, and an audience with Pius himself. The Prince, however, apparently abused his privileges, presumably because he revealed more than was discreet. In a note to me (Mar. 24, 1965), Rolf Hochhuth, the author, says that the Vatican looks upon Konstantin's book with disfavor—although Father Leiber quoted from it in his eulogy at the papal tomb at the time of Pius' death. On pp. 226–227 of the English translation, Konstantin, independently of Dollmann, corroborates Dollmann's urgent trip to Padre Pancrazio on the afternoon of Mar. 23—the details and results of which have hitherto not come to light. Dollmann in *pers. int. ED* told me that he had not wanted to disclose his meeting with Padre Pancrazio in order to avoid any possibility of personal embarrassment to the prelate. Some time after publishing his memoirs, however, Dollmann learned that Padre Pancrazio had been killed in an automobile accident.
4. Kappler's testimony in THK, quoted in Algardi, *op. cit.*, p. 114.
5. *Pers. int. ED.*
6. *Ibid.*
7. *Ibid.*
8. *Ibid. Cf.* also Dollmann, *op. cit.*, pp. 243–244; *Dollmann ms.*
9. Quoted by Dollmann in *pers. int. ED.*
10. *Ibid.*

XXVIII

1. A. Troisio, *Roma sotto il terrore nazi-fascista*, Rome, 1944, p. 25.
2. *Il Quotidiano*, June 24, 1944, quoted in Capano, *op. cit.*, Vol. II, p. 471.

3. Seen in Rome by the author at Museo Storico della Lotta di Liberazione di Roma, 145 Via Tasso.
4. *Pers. int. NN. Cf.* also Capano, *op. cit.*, Vol. II, pp. 468–473; A. Alessandrini, "*Carlo Zaccagnini e Monsignor Pappagallo*," in *Mercurio*, Dec., 1944, pp. 185–188.
5. Quoted by Alessandrini, in *ibid.*
6. Kappler's testimony, June 8, 1948, in THK; partial transcript in *Il Messaggero*, June 9, 1948, p. 1.
7. *Pers. int. NN.*
8. *Il Quotidiano*, June 24, 1944, in Capano, *op. cit.*, Vol. II, p. 471.
9. *Raider statement.*
10. *Cf.* Troisio, *op. cit.*, p. 17.

XXIX

1. TMR, p. 177.
2. Quoted by Kappler in his testimony, June 4, 1948, in THK; partial transcript in *CDS*, June 5, 1948, p. 3; *cf.* also TMR, p. 177.
3. Kappler's testimony, June 4, 1948, in THK; partial transcript in *CDS*, June 5, 1948, p. 3.
4. *Ibid.*
5. Quoted by Kappler in *ibid.*
6. *Ibid.*
7. Kappler, *Incom*, *op. cit.*
8. Kappler's testimony, June 4, 1948, in THK; partial transcript in *CDS*, June 5, 1948, p. 3; *cf.* also TMR, p. 177.
9. *The New York Times*, January 14, 1966, p. 10.
10. Quoted by Kappler in his testimony, June 4, 1948, in THK; partial transcript in *CDS*, June 5, 1948, p. 3.
11. TMR, p. 178.
12. *Ibid.*
13. *Ibid.*
14. Kappler's testimony, June 4, 1948, in THK; partial transcript in *CDS*, June 5, 1948, p. 3.

XXX

1. G. Dolfin, *Con Mussolini nella tragedia*, Milan, 1949, p. 291 (diary entry for Mar. 23, 1944).
2. Hitler's speech of Sept. 10, 1943, in *Voices of History*, *op. cit.*, p. 343.

3. Dolfin, *op. cit.*, p. 291.
4. *Ibid.*

XXXI

1. *Scottu dep.*
2. *Ibid.*
3. *Ibid.*
4. *Ibid.*

XXXII

1. Kappler's testimony, June 4, 1948, in THK; partial transcript in *CDS*, June 5, 1948, p. 3.
2. Möllhausen, *op. cit.*, p. 223.
3. Quoted in *ibid.*
4. Möllhausen quoted by Bertoldi, *op. cit.*, p. 245.
5. *Ibid.*

XXXIII

1. *Pers. int. CS.*
2. BBC Italian-language broadcast of Mar. 23, 1944, quoted in Appendix to P. Badoglio, *L'Italia nella seconda guerra mondiale*, Milan, 1946, pp. 243–244.
3. *Pers. int. CC.*
4. *Pers. int. RB.*
5. P. Malvezzi and G. Pirelli, eds., *Lettere di condannati a morte della Resistenza europea*, Turin, 1954, p. 452. *Cf.* also G. Caputo in *Patria Independente*, Mar. 18, 1962.
6. Letter of Mar. 4, 1944, in Malvezzi and Pirelli, *op. cit.*, pp. 452–453.
7. Calendar preserved on wall of cell no. 3 at Museo Storico della Lotta di Liberazione di Roma, 145 Via Tasso.

XXXIV

1. Dollmann, *op. cit.*, p. 243 and *pers. int. ED.*
2. Wolff was convicted of this charge on Sept. 30, 1964, by a West German court. *Cf. The New York Times*, Oct. 1, 1964, p. 1.
3. Möllhausen, *op. cit.*, p. 239 and Dollmann, *op. cit.*, p. 248.

PART THREE: *The Massacre in the Caves of Ardeatine / March 24, 1944*

1. In Italian: *La morte è brutta per chi la teme.*

I

1. *Pers. int. ED; cf.* also Dollmann, *op. cit.*, p. 242.
2. Kappler's testimony, June 7, 1948, in THK; partial transcript in *CDS*, June 8, 1948, p. 3.
3. TMR, p. 168.
4. For biographical material on Bordoni and Gesmundo *see* Capano, *op. cit.*, Vol. II, pp. 478, 490; for Lucchetti, *see* Piscitelli, *op. cit.*, p. 102.
5. TMR, p. 168.
6. Kappler's testimony, June 7, 1948, in THK; partial transcript in *CDS*, June 8, 1948, p. 3.
7. Kappler's testimony, June 7, 1948, in THK; partial transcript in *Il Messaggero*, June 8, 1948.
8. Troisio, *op. cit.*, p. 25.
9. *Cf.* Capano, *op. cit.*, Vol. II, p. 503; Piscitelli, *op. cit.*, p. 241.
10. Testimony of Dr. Raffaele Cardente, June 15, 1948, in THK; partial transcript in *Il Messaggero*, June 16, 1948. For the dramatic story of Montezemolo's career as a Resistance leader, see G. Lombardi, *Montezemolo e il fronte militare clandestino di Roma*, Rome, 1947; for biographical material, Delzell, *op. cit.*, p. 278; Capano, *op. cit.*, Vol. II, pp. 504–505.
11. Kappler's testimony, June 7, 1948, in THK; partial transcript in *CDS*, June 8, 1948, p. 3.

II

1. *Il Quotidiano*, June 24, 1944; quoted in Capano, *op. cit.*, Vol. II, p. 471.
2. TMR, p. 179.
3. Aliancllo's testimony, Sept. 20, 1944, in TPC, *Caruso proceedings*, p. 168.
4. *Ibid.*

5. TMR, p. 178.
6. Kappler's testimony, June 7, 1948, in THK; partial transcript in *CDS*, June 8, 1948, p. 3; *cf.* also Caruso's testimony, Sept. 20, 1944, in TPC, *Caruso proceedings*, p. 136.

III

1. Caruso's testimony, Sept. 20, 1944, in TPC, *Caruso proceedings*, p. 136.
2. *Ibid.*
3. *Ibid.*
4. *Ibid.*
5. Kappler's testimony, June 7, 1948, in THK; partial transcript in *CDS*, June 8, 1948, p. 3.
6. Caruso's testimony, Sept. 20, 1944, in TPC, *Caruso proceedings*, p. 136.
7. TMR, p. 178.

IV

1. Bonomi, *op. cit.*, p. 163 (diary entry for Mar. 24, 1944).
2. *Ibid.*, p. 164.
3. *Ibid.*, p 171.

V

1. TMR, p. 178.
2. *Ibid.*, p. 179.
3. *Ibid.*
4. *Ibid.*
5. *Ibid.*
6. Kappler's testimony, June 7, 1948, in THK; partial transcript in *CDS*, June 8, 1948, p. 3.
7. *Ibid.*

VI

1. *Ibid.*
2. *Ibid.*

3. *Ibid. Cf.* also partial transcript in *Il Messaggero*, June 8, 1948.
4. *Ibid.*
5. *Ibid.*
6. *Ibid.*
7. *Ibid.*
8. S. Negro, *Roma, non basta una vita,* Venice, 1962, pp. 227–228.
9. TMR, p. 179.
10. Kappler's testimony, June 7, 1948, in THK; partial transcript in *CDS*, June 8, 1948, p. 3.
11. *Ibid.*
12. *Ibid.*
13. *Ibid.*
14. *Ibid.*
15. *Ibid.*
16. TMR, p. 176.

VII

1. Troisio, *op. cit.*, p. 25. (Troisio was an eyewitness to the events described here in cell no. 7.)
2. *Ibid.*
3. *Ibid.*
4. *Ibid.*
5. *Ibid.*
6. *Ibid.*
7. *Ibid.*
8. *Il Quotidiano*, June 24, 1944; quoted in Capano, *op. cit.*, p. 471.
9. *Raider statement.*
10. Troisio, *op. cit.*, p. 26.

VIII

1. *Valentini statement.* Michele Valentini was a Silesian priest at the catacombs of Saint Calixtus on the Appian Way. Don Valentini and other priests of the Silesian Institute at the catacombs were eyewitnesses to some of the activities outside the Ardeatine caves on Mar. 24 and subsequently. Don Valentini's account written in the form of a diary was originally published soon after the massacre in the anti-Fascist newspaper *Risorgimento Liberale.* It was signed "Observer." Later it was reprinted in Troisio, *op. cit.* I

have used a copy of the document which identifies its author and appears as an appendix to a privately published guide to the Via Tasso museum, G. Stendardo, *Via Tasso,* Rome, 1965, pp. 45–48.
2. TMR, pp. 179–180.
3. Kappler's testimony, June 7, 1948, in THK; partial transcript in *Il Messaggero,* June 8, 1948.
4. Negro, *op. cit.*, p. 226.
5. *Ibid.* For an eyewitness account see also testimony of Attilio Ascarelli, Sept. 20, 1944, in TPC, *Caruso proceedings,* pp. 159–162.
6. INQ, pp. 27–29.
7. Kappler's testimony, June 8, 1948, in THK; partial transcript in *CDS,* June 9, 1948, p. 3.
8. Diagram of the caves is based on a copy which appears in INQ, Table IV, with modifications made as a result of my personal inspections in Mar., 1964, and May, 1965.
9. TMR, p. 180.

IX

1. *De Gasperis statement.*
2. *Ibid.*
3. *Ibid.*
4. *Lavagnino dep.*
5. *Ibid.*
6. *De Gasperis statement.*

X

1. *Scottu dep.*

XI

1. Statement of Albrecht von Kessel to Silvio Bertoldi, quoted in Bertoldi, *op. cit.*, p. 245. Kessel was an aide of Ambassador Weizsäcker.
2. *Ibid.*
3. Giovannetti, *op. cit.*, p. 255.
4. Konstantin, *op. cit.*, p. 227.
5. Kappler's testimony in THK, quoted in Algardi, *op. cit.*, p. 114.

6. *L'Osservatore Romano,* Mar. 25, 1944, p. 1.
7. *Ibid.* Completing the text here in full, the final paragraph reads, "Whoever is deeply solicitous about the fate of Rome and the Romans cannot but entrust himself to his own good citizenship and in the wisdom of a condition of life consonant on all levels with the religious and paternal feeling of the citizenry."

XII

1. *Raider statement.*
2. D'Annabile gave testimony in INQ, TPC, and THK.
3. Testimony of Karl Wiedner, June 11, 1948, in THK; partial transcript in *Il Messaggero,* June 12, 1948. Wiedner, one of the accused in THK, participated in an execution squad at the caves.
4. *Raider statement.*
5. *Ibid.*
6. The bloodstained sweater was seen by the author at the Via Tasso museum.
7. *Raider statement.*
8. *Ibid.*
9. *Ibid.*
10. *Ibid.*
11. *Ibid.*
12. Raider's testimony, June 28, 1948, in THK; partial transcript in *CDS,* June 29, 1948, p. 3.
13. *Raider statement.*

XIII

1. *Pers. int. ED;* Dollmann, *op. cit.,* p. 244. One must express some doubt that Wolff did not know that the reprisal was being carried out that afternoon. Nevertheless, there has never been any evidence to the contrary.
2. Dollmann, *op. cit.,* p. 244.
3. *Ibid.*

XIV

1. Testimony of Michele Usai, June 14, 1948, in THK; partial transcript in *CDS,* June 15, 1948, p. 3.

2. *Lavagnino dep.*
3. *Ibid.*
4. Quoted in Capano, *op. cit.*, Vol. II, p. 486.
5. *Lavagnino dep.*
6. Testimony of Marcella Rodriguez, June 14, 1948, in THK; partial transcript in *CDS*, June 15, 1948, p. 3.
7. *Ibid.*
8. Usai's testimony, in *ibid.*

XV

1. Kappler's testimony, June 8, 1948, in THK; partial transcript in *CDS*, June 9, 1948, p. 3.
2. The singing was heard by a passerby that afternoon who was stopped in Via Ardeatina by German guards. *Cf. Il Messaggero*, June 6, 1944.
3. TMR, p. 180.
4. *Pers. int. PT. Cf.* also Tompkins, *op. cit.*, pp. 167–171.
5. Tompkins, *op. cit.*, p. 170.
6. Testimony of Durante Domizlaff, June 9, 1948, in THK; partial transcript in *CDS*, June 10, 1948. Domizlaff was one of the accused in THK.
7. The actual order of the executions is unknown. When the bodies were exhumed, however, each cadaver was assigned a number corresponding to the *apparent* order of death, which was ascertained by the distribution of bodies–the cadavers at the bottom of the pile being the first to be killed. The remains of Domenico Ricci were given number 1. *Cf.* INQ, p. 90. It was impossible, however, to establish definitively which of the two piles of corpses had accumulated first. *Cf.* INQ, p. 39.
8. Note found at the time of exhumation; INQ, p. 41.
9. Domizlaff's testimony, June 9, 1948, in THK; partial transcript in *CDS*, June 10, 1948, p. 3.
10. D'Annabile's testimony, Sept. 20, 1944, in TPC, *Caruso proceedings*, p. 167.
11. TMR, p. 180.
12. Caruso's testimony, Sept. 20, 1944, in TPC, *Caruso proceedings*, p. 137.
13. *Ibid.*; *cf.* also *Carretta dep.*, *Caruso proceedings*, pp. 97–100. Carretta was director of Regina Coeli during the occupation.
14. Pretrial interrogation of Caruso, Aug. 9, 1944, *Caruso proceedings*,

p. 66; *cf.* also Alianello testimony, Sept. 20, 1944, in TPC, *Caruso proceedings*, pp. 168–169.

15. Kappler's testimony, in THK, quoted in Algardi, *op. cit.*, p. 114.
16. Testimony of Antonio Carella, June 17, 1948, in *THK;* partial transcript in *CDS,* June 18, 1948, p. 3. Dr. Carella was an aide of Dr. Ascarelli, the director of the exhumations of the Ardeatine victims.
17. Domizlaff's testimony, June 9, 1948, in THK; partial transcript in *CDS*, June 10, 1948, p. 3.
18. Kappler's testimony, June 8, 1948, in THK; partial transcript in *CDS,* June 9, 1948, p. 3.
19. *Ibid.*
20. Kappler's testimony in THK, quoted in Algardi, *op. cit.*, p. 114.
21. *Ibid.*
22. Kappler's testimony, June 8, 1948, in THK; partial transcript in *Il Messaggero,* June 9, 1948.
23. *Ibid.*

XVI

1. *De Gasperis statement.*
2. *Lavagnino dep.*
3. *Ibid.*
4. R. De Felice, *Storia degli ebrei italiani sotto il fascismo*, Turin, 1961, p. 523.
5. *Lavagnino dep.*
6. *Ibid.*
7. *De Gasperis statement.*
8. *Lavagnino dep.*
9. *Pers. int. CD.*
10. Troisio, *op. cit.*, p. 151.
11. *Pers. int. CD.*

XVII

1. *Carretta dep.;* testimony of Antonio delle Moracce, June 12, 1948, in THK; partial transcript in *CDS*, June 13, 1948, p. 3. Delle Moracce was attached to the registry office of Regina Coeli and was on duty on the afternoon of Mar. 24, 1944.
2. TMR, p. 180.

3. Sentence handed down Sept. 21, 1944, in TPC, *Caruso proceedings*, pp. 273–286.
4. Caruso's testimony, Sept. 20, 1944, in TPC, *Caruso proceedings*, p. 137; *cf.* also Alianello's testimony of that day and *Carretta dep.*
5. Alianello's testimony, in *ibid.*
6. Reproduction of original list with cancellations and substitutions appears in *Caruso proceedings*, facing p. 80.
7. Piscitelli, *op. cit.*, p. 249.
8. Quoted in Battaglia, *op. cit.*, p. 254.
9. Testimony of Gaetano Borruso, Sept. 20, 1944, in TPC, *Caruso proceedings*, p. 175.
10. Alianello's testimony, Sept. 20, 1944, in TPC, *Caruso proceedings*, p. 168.
11. TMR, p. 181.
12. Quoted in Capano, *op. cit.*, Vol. II, p. 479.
13. *Ibid.*

XVIII

1. Tompkins, *op. cit.*, p. 188.
2. *Ibid.*

XIX

1. Dollmann, *op. cit.*, p. 248.
2. *Ibid.*
3. *Ibid.*
4. *Ibid.*
5. Möllhausen, *op. cit.*, p. 240.

XX

1. Kappler at his trial repeatedly denied this most gruesome aspect of the massacre. But the prosecution evidence is incontrovertible: a) the spent shells from the German guns were found *between* the many layers of corpses, indicating precisely where the bullets had been fired; b) the piled bodies were recovered with their knees still bent, retaining the position in which they had died (if they had been moved they would not have been found this way). See expert-witness testimony of Dr. Ascarelli and Dr. Carella in THK; also INQ.

2. Carella's testimony, June 17, 1948, in THK; partial transcript in *CDS*, June 18, 1948, p. 3.
3. INQ, Table 18.
4. *Ibid.*, p. 39.
5. *Ibid.*, pp. 55–56.
6. *Ibid.*, p. 36.
7. *Cf.* testimony of Enrica Leonelli, June 17, 1948, in THK; partial transcript in *CDS*, June 18, 1948, p. 3; also Ripa di Meana, *op. cit.*, p. 287.
8. TMR, p. 180; *cf.* also Amon's testimony, June 12, 1948, in THK; partial transcript in *CDS*, June 13, 1948, p. 3.
9. Told to author by Ennio and Lucianna Pisciarelli, the couple noted here.
10. *Valentini statement.*
11. Quoted in *Il Messaggero*, June 6, 1944.
12. Koffler's testimony, June 11, 1948, in THK; partial transcript in *CDS*, June 12, 1948, p. 3.
13. Testimony of Attilio D'Acerno, June 21, 1948, in THK; partial transcript in *CDS*, June 22, 1948, p. 3. D'Acerno, then deputy chief of the Rome fire department, took part in the exhumation procedures at the Ardeatine caves.
14. *Valentini statement.*
15. INQ, p. 36.
16. Quoted in Möllhausen, *op. cit.*, p. 224.
17. His name is Leonardo Azzarita, president of the National Association of Italian Families of Martyrs (ANFIM), 8 Via Montecatini, Rome.
18. INQ, p. 53.
19. *Cf.* Carella's testimony, June 17, 1948, in THK; partial transcript in *CDS*, June 18, 1948, p. 3.
20. INQ, p. 46.
21. *Ibid.*
22. Quoted in Battaglia, *op. cit.*, p. 254.
23. Koffler's testimony, June 11, 1948, in THK; partial transcript in *CDS*, June 12, 1948, p. 3.
24. Möllhausen, *op. cit.*, p. 224.

XXI

1. *Giornale d'Italia*, Mar. 25, 1944, p. 1.
2. Scrivener, *op. cit.*, p. 144 (diary entry for Mar. 24, 1944).
3. *Ibid.*

XXII

1. *Pers. int. PT.*
2. Tompkins, *op. cit.*, p. 188.
3. *Pers. int. PT.*
4. *Pers. int. CC.*
5. *L'Europeo, op. cit.*
6. Trabucco, *op. cit.*, p. 190.
7. De Wyss, *op. cit.*, p. 204.
8. Troisio, *op. cit.*, p. 26.
9. *De Gasperis statement.*

XXIII

1. *Pers. int. ED.*
2. Dollmann, *op. cit.*, p. 249.
3. *Ibid.*
4. Kappler's testimony, June 8, 1948, in THK; partial transcript in *CDS*, June 9, 1948, p. 3.
5. Möllhausen, *op. cit.*, p. 239.
6. Dollmann, *op. cit.*, p. 249.
7. *Cf.* TMR, pp. 182–184.
8. Möllhausen, *op. cit.*, p. 239; *cf.* also Kappler's testimony, June 8, 1948, in THK; partial transcript in *CDS*, June 9, 1948, p. 3; Dollmann, *op. cit.*, p. 249.
9. Möllhausen, *op. cit.*, p. 250.
10. *Ibid.*
11. Dollmann, *op. cit.*, p. 250.
12. *Ibid.*
13. *Ibid.*
14. *Pers. int. ED.*
15. Möllhausen, *op. cit.*, p. 240.
16. Dollmann, *op. cit.*, p. 251.
17. *Ibid.*
18. Möllhausen, *op. cit.*, p. 240.

XXIV

1. *Il Messaggero*, Mar. 25, 1944, p. 1.

PART FOUR: *The Aftermath / March 25–31, 1944*

1. INQ, Table I. Reproduction of the notice mailed to the family of Ardeatine victim Marcello Bucchi.

I

1. Möllhausen, *op. cit.*, p. 240.
2. Testimony of Temistocle Testa, June 21, 1948, in THK; partial transcript in *CDS*, June 22, 1948, p. 3. Testa, during the occupation, was a high official of the Fascist administration for Rome.
3. Möllhausen, *op. cit.*, p. 240.
4. *Ibid.*, p. 241.
5. A. Scotland, *Der Fall Kesselring*, Bonn, 1952, pp. 24–28.
6. Möllhausen, *op. cit.*, p. 241.

II

1. *Valentini statement.*
2. *Ibid.*
3. INQ, p. 72.

III

1. Dollmann, *op. cit.*, p. 252.
2. Kappler's testimony, June 8, 1948, in THK; partial transcript in *CDS*, June 9, 1948, p. 3.
3. Dollmann, *op. cit.*, p. 252.
4. *Ibid.*
5. Möllhausen, *op. cit.*, p. 242.
6. Tompkins, *op. cit.*, p. 189.

IV

1. Florio, *op. cit.*, p. 43.
2. *Pers. int. RB.*

3. *Pers. int.* CC.
4. *Il Messaggero*, Mar. 25, 1944, p. 1.
5. *L'Europeo, op. cit.*
6. *Ibid.*
7. *Ibid.*
8. *Ibid.*
9. *Ibid.*

V

1. Scrivener, *op. cit.*, p. 145 (diary entry for Mar. 25, 1944).
2. *Valentini statement.*
3. *Ibid.*
4. *Il Messaggero*, June 6, 1944.
5. Fascist Ministry of Interior document dated Mar. 27, 1944, in *Deakin collection.*
6. *Cf.* G. Gorlu, *L'Italia nella seconda guerra mondiale*, Milan, 1959 (diary entry for Mar. 31, 1944); Committee for a Democratic Foreign Policy, *Facts from Italy*, New York, May 1, 1944; de Wyss, *op. cit.*, p. 206.
7. De Wyss, *op. cit.*, p. 206 (diary entry for Apr. 1, 1944).

VI

1. *Pers. int. GA* and *pers. int. MF.*
2. *Pers. int. GA.* In a letter to the author dated Nov. 23, 1965, Mr. Brosio stated that "I remember these matters were discussed in our meeting of the CLN's Military Junta," but he could not recall what his position was on the issue referred to here. "I was with Mr. Amendola in the Committee," he said, "and I know sometimes we agreed and sometimes we did not agree . . ."
3. *L'Unità*, Mar. 30, 1944, p. 1.
4. *L'Osservatore Romano*, Mar. 26, 1944, p. 1.
5. *Ibid.*
6. For a lengthy exposition of the Via Rasella attack and the Ardeatine massacre based on this falsification, see G. Pisanò, *Sangue chiama sangue*, Milan, 1962, pp. 47–107. This is one of numerous such neo-Fascist accounts which are still being published in Italy. A new edition of the Pisanò book, the tenth, was issued in 1966.

VII

1. *Cf. CDS,* and *La Stampa,* of Mar. 26, 1944, p. 1.
2. *The New York Times,* Mar. 26, 1944.
3. Tompkins, *op. cit.,* p. 189.
4. *Ibid.*
5. *Ibid.*
6. *Ibid.,* pp. 189–190.
7. *Ibid.,* p. 197.
8. *Ibid.,* p. 198. Tompkins told the author in *pers. int. PT* that the raid was never actually carried out because after Giglio's death there seemed to be no further point in going through with it.
9. R. Mussolini, *La mia vita con Benito, op. cit.,* p. 237 (entry for Mar. 25, 1944).
10. *Ibid.*

VIII

1. Dollmann, *op. cit.,* p. 253; Möllhausen, *op. cit.,* p. 241.
2. Dollmann, *op. cit.,* p. 254

IX

1. *Valentini statement.*
2. *Ibid.*
3. *Ibid.*

X

1. *Il Messaggero,* Mar. 26, 1944.
2. *Ibid.*
3. *The New York Times,* Mar. 29, 1944.
4. Trabucco, *op. cit.,* p. 192 (diary entry for Mar. 26, 1944).
5. Scrivener, *op. cit.,* p. 146 (diary entry for Mar. 27, 1944).
6. *Ibid.*

XI

1. Report of Mar. 26, 1944, *Critica Marxista,* Mar.–Apr., 1965, pp. 131–139.

2. *Ibid.*
3. *Ibid.*
4. *Ibid.*

XII

1. *Giornale d'Italia,* Mar. 28, 1944.
2. Quoted in R. Battaglia and G. Garritano, *Breve storia della Resistenza italiana,* Rome, 1964, p. 94.
3. *Il Messaggero,* Mar. 27, 1944.
4. *Ibid.*
5. *Giornale d'Italia,* Mar. 29, 1944.
6. Quoted in Capano, *op. cit.,* Vol. II, p. 337.
7. *Ibid.*
8. *L'Unità,* Mar. 30, 1944.
9. *Ibid.* Mr. Amendola told the author in *pers. int. GA* that he was the writer of this article.
10. Giovannetti, *op. cit.,* p. 256.
11. *Ibid.*
12. Pretrial interrogation of Caruso, Aug. 9, 1944, *Caruso proceedings,* p. 66.
13. Morpurgo, *op. cit.,* p. 240 (diary entry for Apr. 16, 1944).
14. *Ibid.*
15. Pretrial interrogation of Caruso, Aug. 9, 1944, *Caruso proceedings,* p. 66.
16. *Cf.* testimony of Amedeo Pierantoni, June 14, 1948, in THK; partial transcript in *CDS,* June 15, 1948, p. 3; Scrivener, *op. cit.,* p. 147.

XIII

1. The sources for this press conference are INQ, Document No. 2, pp. 73–74 and *l'Unità,* June 24, 1944. The former is based on stenographic notes captured by the Allies in the Rome Ministry of Popular Culture; the latter is a reconstruction by a journalist who was present at the meeting. The exact date of the press conference is not indicated, although it appears to have taken place at the end of the first week in Apr. 1944. The accounts corroborate one another, although the *l'Unità* reconstruction is in greater detail.

2. *L'Unità*, June 24, 1944, quoted in Troisio, *op. cit.*, p. 81.
3. *Ibid.*
4. *Ibid.*; *cf.* also, INQ, p. 73.
5. *Ibid.*, p. 82.
6. *Ibid.*, p. 83.
7. *Ibid.*
8. INQ, p. 74.

XIV

1. *Valentini statement.*
2. *Ibid.*
3. Scrivener, *op. cit.*, p. 147 (diary entry for Mar. 27, 1944).
4. *Valentini statement. Cf.* also testimony of Don Fernando Giorgi, June 12, 1948, in THK; partial transcript in *CDS*, June 13, 1948, p. 3.
5. *Valentini statement.*
6. Don Giorgi's testimony, June 12, 1948, in THK; partial transcript in *CDS*, June 13, 1948, p. 3.
7. *Valentini statement.*
8. Don Giorgi's testimony, June 12, 1948, in THK; partial transcript in *CDS*, June 13, 1948, p. 3; *cf.* also *Valentini statement.*
9. *Ibid.*; *cf.* also *Valentini statement.*
10. *Valentini statement.*
11. *Ibid.*
12. *Ibid.*
13. Don Giorgi's testimony, June 12, 1948, in THK; partial transcript in *CDS*, June 13, 1948, p. 3.

XV

1. *Valentini statement.*
2. Trabucco, *op. cit.*, p. 211 (diary entry for Mar. 21, 1944).
3. *Ibid.*
4. *Ibid.*
5. *Valentini statement.*
6. Don Giorgi's testimony, June 12, 1948, in THK; partial transcript in *CDS*, June 13, 1948, p. 3.

XVI

1. *Deakin collection*, Ministry of Interior Bull. No. 87 Bis, Mar. 27, 1944. This is a routine report to the Duce by the Fascist monitoring facilities of a BBC German-language transmission at 12:15 P.M., on the 27th.
2. Southern edition of *l'Unità*, Mar. 30, 1944.
3. *Cf. Giornale d'Italia*, Mar. 30, 1944.
4. *Pers. int. MF*, *pers. int. CC*, and *pers. int. GA.*
5. *Deakin collection*, Ministry of Interior Bull. No. 106 Bis, Apr. 15, 1944.
6. *Ibid.*
7. Bonomi, *op. cit.*, p. 172 (diary entry for Mar. 31, 1944).
8. *Ibid.*
9. *L'Unità*, Apr. 13, 1944.
10. Bonomi, *op. cit.*, p. 171.
11. *Ibid.*, p. 175.
12. *Risogimento Liberale*, May 5, 1944; quoted in Piscitelli, *op. cit.*, p. 338.
13. *Cf.* Morpurgo, *op. cit.*, photograph facing p. 176.
14. *Cf.* INQ, Table I.
15. Pretrial interrogation of Caruso, Aug. 9, 1944, *Caruso proceedings*, p. 67.
16. *Giornale d'Italia*, Mar. 31, 1944.

XVII

1. Quoted in Piscitelli, *op. cit.*, pp. 323–324.
2. *Ibid.*, p. 323.
3. MLI document entitled *Elenco delle principali azioni di GAP nella città di Roma.*
4. *Pers. int. MF*, *pers. int. CC*, and *pers. int. RB; cf.* also testimony of Guglielmo Blasi, June 28, 1948, in THK; partial transcript in *CDS*, June 29, 1948, p. 3. Blasi later had to stand trial as a collaborator and received a thirty-year prison sentence.
5. *Pers. int. MF.*
6. *Pers. int. CS* and *pers. int. RF.*
7. *Cf.* Piscitelli, *op. cit.*, pp. 311–312.
8. *Ibid.*, p. 335.
9. *Ibid.*, p. 329.
10. *Cf. ibid.*, p. 332; also Battaglia, *op. cit.*, p. 258.

PART FIVE: *Epilogue*

1. From the introduction to the edition commemorating the twentieth anniversary of the Ardeatine massacre of Ascarelli, *op. cit.*, p. 7.

I

1. INQ, p. 27.
2. *Ibid.*, p. 29.
3. *Ibid.*, pp. 29–38.
4. *Ibid.*, p. 40.
5. *Caruso proceedings*, p. 80.
6. *Ibid.*, pp. 3–6.
7. *Ibid.*, p. 7.
8. *Ibid.*, pp. 103–111; *cf* also dispatch of eyewitness American correspondent, *The New York Times*, Sept. 19, 1944, p. 1.
9. H. L. Matthews, *The Education of a Correspondent*, New York, 1946, p. 480.
10. *Caruso proceedings*, p. 292.
11. Matthews, *op. cit.*, p. 476.
12. A. Hayes, *All Thy Conquests*, New York, 1946, p. 109. This book about liberated Rome at the time of the Caruso trial is written in the form of a novel.
13. Capano, *op. cit.*, Vol. II, p. 422. *Cf.* C. C. Ciulla, *L'Attività criminosa della banda Koch coi particolari di villa Triste a Milano*, Milan, 1945, pp. 14–15.
14. Scotland, *op. cit.*, p. 22.
15. *CDS*, Nov. 19, 1946, p. 1.
16. TMM in *UNWCC*, Vol. 8, pp, 1–8.
17. *The New York Times*, Dec. 1, 1946, p. 1.
18. *Ibid.*
19. TAK in *UNWCC*, Vol. 8, p. 9; *cf.* also *The New York Times*, May 7, 1947, p. 10.
20. TAK in *ibid.*, p. 13.
21. TAK in *ibid.*, p. 12.
22. Kesselring, *op. cit.*, p. 355.
23. *Ibid.*, p. 357.
24. *Ibid.*

25. *Ibid.*
26. TAK in *UNWCC*, Vol. 8, p. 12.
27. *The New York Times*, Oct. 27, 1952, p. 6.
28. Bertoldi, *op. cit.*, p. 180.
29. Kesselring, *op. cit.*, p. 376.
30. *Moscow Declaration on German Atrocities*, Nov. 1, 1943; full text in *World War II International Agreements*, *op. cit.*
31. TMR, pp. 165–170.
32. *CDS*, June 8, 1948, p. 3.
33. TMR, pp. 188–203.
34. Quoted in Capano, *op. cit.*, Vol. II, p. 300.
35. *Ibid.*
36. *Ibid.*, p. 301.
37. Bertoldi, *op. cit.*, p. 240.
38. *Ibid.*, p. 242.
39. Quoted in Algardi, *op. cit.*, p. 120.
40. Quoted in Capano, *op. cit.*, Vol. II, p. 321.
41. *Ibid.*, p. 322.
42. Quoted in Algardi, *op. cit.*, p. 120.
43. *CDS*, Aug. 4, 1957.
44. *Ibid.*
45. Quoted in Algardi, *op. cit.*, p. 121.
46. Kappler's testimony, June 7, 1948, in THK; partial transcript in *CDS*, June 8, 1948, p. 3.
47. Pisanò, *op. cit.*, pp. 47–107.
48. *La Civiltà Cattolica*, 1946, *Quaderno* 2297, p. 368.
49. *Enciclopedia Cattolica*, Vol. X, Vatican City, 1953, columns 1176–1177.
50. *L'Europeo*, *op. cit.*

II

1. Hochhuth, *op. cit.*, p. 210.
2. Möllhausen, *op. cit.*, p. 221.
3. *Cf. supra*, p. 109.
4. TMR, pp. 181–200.
5. Pretrial interrogation of Caruso, Aug. 9, 1944, in *Caruso proceedings*, p. 66.
6. Caruso's testimony, Sept. 20, 1944, in TPC; *Caruso proceedings*, p. 137.

7. Alianello's testimony, Sept. 20, 1944, in TPC; *Caruso proceedings*, p. 168.
8. *Cf.* Möllhausen, *op. cit.*, pp. 162–165.
9. *Cf.* R. Leiber, "Pius XII" in E. Bentley, ed., *The Storm Over The Deputy*, New York, 1964, p. 182.
10. Piscitelli, *op. cit.*, p. 379; *cf.* also A. Hatch and S. Walshe, *Crown of Glory, The Life of Pope Pius XII*, New York, 1958, p. 179.
11. O. Halecki and J. Murray, *Pius XII: Eugenio Pacelli, Pope of Peace*, New York, 1954, p. 206.
12. *The New York Times*, Feb. 15, 1964, p. 14.
13. Tittmann's telegram to Hull, Mar. 1, 1943, in *FRUS*, p. 915.
14. Letter of Apostolic Delegate at Washington to Myron C. Taylor, Personal Representative of President Roosevelt to Pope Pius XII, June 15, 1943, in *ibid.*, p. 918.
15. Letter of Apostolic Delegate at Washington to Taylor, June 28, 1943, in *ibid.*, p. 923.
16. Tittmann's telegram to Hull, June 29, 1943, in *ibid.*, p. 925.
17. Tittmann's telegram to Hull, July 23, 1943, in *ibid.*, pp. 935–936.
18. G. B. Montini, "Pius XII and the Jews," in Bentley, *op. cit.*, p. 67. This article published in connection with the controversy over Hochhuth's play was written some days before Montini became Pope Paul VI. It was released, however, shortly after the papal election.
19. *Ibid.*
20. *Ibid.*, p. 68.
21. Tisserant's letter to the Archbishop of Paris, June 11, 1940. As a result of a search by the Nazis of the Archbishop's residence this document fell into the hands of the Germans and subsequently the Allies. It is quoted in Lewy, *op. cit.*, p. 307. In a letter twenty-five years later, dated March 4, 1965, to Saul Friedländer, author of Friedländer, *op. cit.*—a book which is highly critical of Pius' wartime policies—Tisserant said of Friedländer's work, "It is well that the whole truth be known." (Facsimile in American edition, New York: Knopf, 1966, p. v.)
22. *L'Espresso*, Dec. 19, 1965, p. 9; *cf.* also Associated Press dispatch from Rome in *The New York Times*, Dec. 7, 1965, p. 11. The first volume of 379 documents, covering Mar. 1939, to Aug. 1940, was published on Dec. 7, 1965, breaking a Vatican rule that no archive paper less than fifty years old may be publicly released. Except for interesting detail, the 550-page book contained little not already known from other sources. Entitled *Le Saint Siège et la Guerre en Europe, Mars 1939, Août 1940,* this publication deals

with the period beginning with Pius' election as Pope through the first year of the war. On Mar. 5, 1966, a volume containing the texts of 124 letters written by Pius to German Catholic bishops was published by the Vatican. These letters, some of which had already been published, cover the years from 1939 to 1944. They are said by the Vatican to show that the Pope called repeatedly on the German bishops "to leave nothing undone in behalf of the oppressed and persecuted." (*The New York Times*, Mar. 6, 1966, p. 1.) Subsequent volumes for the years 1940 to 1945 are said to be in preparation and scheduled for issuance during the next few years.

ACKNOWLEDGMENTS

I would like to thank the following persons for having contributed in one way or another to the realization of this book: Doreen Alexander, Giorgio Amendola, Rosario Bentivegna, Manlio Brosio, Franco Calamandrei, Carla Capponi, Alfonso Cascone, F. W. Deakin, Carmello De Stefanis, Eugen Dollmann, Raoul Falcioni, Mario Fiorentini, Saul Friedländer, Aaron Gerstel, Rose Gerstel, Gertrude Hayes, Rolf Hochhuth, Alan Katz, Howard Katz, Massimo Legnani, Saro Mirabella, Robert Rahtz, Ulrich Rehwaldt, Peter Ritner, and Carlo Salinari. To all of them, and many others, I am very appreciative.

Also, the following institutions: Biblioteca Nazionale Centrale of Rome, Bibliothek für Zeitgeschichte of Stuttgart, Bundesministerium für Landesverteidigung of Austria, the Gramsci Institute of Rome, Institut für Zeitgeschichte of Munich, Istituto per la Storia del Movimento di Liberazione in Italia, Museo Storico della Lotta di Liberazione di Roma, the National Archives, the New York Public Library, and Saint Antony's College.

I would like also to record a special note of thanks to my mother and father for their unwavering confidence. I am very grateful.

To my dear friend Oscar Ochs I am especially indebted. For two years, virtually day to day, he read and pondered the notes and pages that became this book. He listened, made suggestions, was uncompromising in his criticisms, but, above all, he encouraged me.

Finally, but foremost, I want to thank my wife, Beverly, whose patience and understanding were inexhaustible and invaluable. Without her, it can honestly be said, this book would not have been possible. To her and to our two sons, Stephen and Jonathan, I express my deepest gratitude.

BIBLIOGRAPHY

The principal documentary sources for this work were, in order of importance: the testimony and the final sentence handed down in the trial of Herbert Kappler; the report of Dr. Attilio Ascarelli on the Ardeatine Caves Commission (and the documents included in that report); the testimony and pretrial interrogations in the trial of Pietro Caruso; the testimony in the trial of Albert Kesselring; and the testimony in the trial of Eberhard von Mackensen and Kurt Mäelzer.

The proceedings of the Kappler trial are deposited at the Tribunale Militare Territoriale di Roma, 5/C Viale delle Milizie, Rome. For reasons best known to the Procuratore Generale of the Tribunale Supremo Militare of Italy, who is responsible for the official transcript, attempts by me to examine this material were discouraged. A day-to-day account of the testimony, however, is given in the form of a partial transcript in the Milan newspaper *Corriere della Sera* over the period of the trial, May 3 to July 20, 1948. *Il Messaggero* of Rome also carried daily verbatim reports. In addition, the trial proceedings are summarized in great detail in the 30,000-word sentence of the Military Tribunal of Rome. The full text of this document is printed in the twentieth-anniversary commemorative edition of Dr. Ascarelli's report, *Le Fosse Ardeatine* (Bologna, 1965), and in the law journal *Rassegna di Diritto Pubblico*, 1948, Vol. III, No. 2.

The pretrial interrogations and the proceedings of the Caruso trial have been published and are noted below. The proceedings of the Kesselring and Mackensen-Mälzer trials, both of which were conducted by British military courts, are on file at the Public Records Office.

Other unpublished documentary material, most of which is of a general nature, is to be found among the captured German documents which are available at the National Archives in Washington, D.C., as well as in the government archives of London and

Bonn. Of particular interest are some of those catalogued in Volumes 38, 39, and 40 of *Guides to German Records Microfilmed at Alexandria, Va.* (Washington, 1963). Among these documents are political and military reports from Rome and other centers of the German occupation forces in Italy. The great majority of the surviving Italian documents for this period are held by the Italian Foreign Ministry and the State Archives of Rome. These are all classified. Copies of some of this material are deposited at Saint Antony's College in Oxford, England, in the custody of F. W. Deakin, Warden of the College. Microfilms of some other Fascist records reporting on conditions in Rome from September, 1943, to April, 1944, are at the National Archives (Microcopy T-586, Roll 479). The archives of the Istituto Nazionale per la Storia del Movimento di Liberazione in Italia, 14 Piazza Duomo, Milan, and of the Hoover Institute, Stanford, California, contain further material.

The following is a list of published documents, books, and articles which have been helpful to me. About half deal in more or less detail with one or some aspects of the Via Rasella-Ardeatine caves episode. These are indicated by one asterisk when there is only minor mention, by two when there is more extensive treatment.

Algardi, Z., ed., *Il processo Caruso*, Rome: Darsena, 1945.**

——— *Processi ai fascisti*, Florence: Parenti, 1958.**

Allied Commission, *A Review of AMG and AC in Italy*, Rome: Allied Commission, 1945.

Amicucci, E., *I 600 giorni di Mussolini*, Rome: Faro, 1949.

Arendt, H., *Eichmann in Jerusalem*, rev. ed., New York: The Viking Press, Inc., 1965.

Ascarelli, A., *Le Fosse Ardeatine*, Rome: Palombi, 1945 (a twentieth-anniversary commemorative edition with new material, including the full text of the sentence in the Kappler trial, was published at Bologna: Canesi, 1965).**

Associazione Nazionale delle Famiglie Italiane dei Martiri, *Roma onora i martiri del II risorgimento*, Rome: privately printed, 1957.*

Associazione Nationale dei Partigiani d'Italia, *I crimini della Wehrmacht*, Rome: privately printed, 1955.*

Bacino, E., *Roma prima e dopo*, Rome: Atlantica, 1945.*

Badoglio, P., *L'Italia nella seconda guerra mondiale*, Milan: Mondadori, 1946.

Battaglia, R., *Storia della Resistenza italiana*, rev. ed., Turin: Einaudi, 1953, 1964.**

——— and Garritano, G., *Breve storia della Resistenza italiana*, Rome: Riuniti, 1964.**

——— and Ramat, R., *Un popolo in lotta*, Florence: La Nuova Italia, 1961.*

Benigno, J. di, *Occasioni mancate, Roma in un diario segreto 1943–44*, Rome: Edizioni S.E.I., 1945.*

Bertoldi, S., *I tedeschi in Italia*, Milan: Rizzoli, 1964.**

Bianchi, G., *25 luglio: crollo di un regime*, Milan: Mursia, 1963.

Bonomi, I., *Diario di un anno, 2 giugno 1943–10 giugno 1944*, Milan, Garzanti, 1947.*

Bullock, A., *Hitler—A Study in Tyranny*, rev. ed., New York: Harper & Row Publishers, Inc., 1960.

Buonaiuti, E., *Pio XII*, Rome: Universale, 1946.**

Calamandrei, P., *Uomini e città della Resistenza*, Bari: Laterza, 1955.

Capano, R. P., *La Resistenza in Roma*, 2 vols., Naples: Macchiaroli, 1963.**

Carli Ballola, R., *Storia della Resistenza italiana*, Milan: Avanti, 1957.*

Carter, B. B., *Italy Speaks*, London: Victor Gollancz, Ltd., 1947.*

Castelli, G., *Storia segreta di Roma città aperta*, Rome: Quattrucci, 1959.**

Chabod, F., *L'Italia contemporanea*, Turin: Einaudi, 1961.*

Churchill, W., *The Second World War*, Vol. 5, Boston: Houghton Mifflin Company, 1951.

Cione, E., *Storia della Repubblica Sociale Italiana*, Caserta: Il Cenacolo, 1948.

Ciulla, C. C., *L'Attività criminosa della banda Koch coi particolari di villa Triste a Milano* (pamphlet), Milan: privately printed, 1945.

Crankshaw, E., *Gestapo*, New York: The Viking Press, Inc., 1956.

Deakin, F. W., *The Brutal Friendship*, New York: Harper & Row Publishers, Inc., 1962.

De Benedetti, G., *16 ottobre 1943*, Rome: O.E.T., 1944.

Deborin, G., *The Second World War*, Moscow: Progress Publishers, 1962(?).

Dedalo, *Passo dell' oca*, Milan: Anzani, 1946.*

De Felice, R., *Storia degli ebrei italiani sotto il fascismo*, Turin: Einaudi, 1961.*

Delzell, C. F., *Mussolini's Enemies: The Italian Anti-Fascist Resistance*, Princeton: Princeton University Press, 1961.**

Department of the Army, Historical Division, *Anzio Beachhead*, Washington: Government Printing Office, 1947.

Derry, S., *The Rome Escape Line*, New York: W. W. Norton & Company, Inc., 1960.*

Dolfin, G., *Con Mussolini nella tragedia*, Milan: Garzanti, 1949.**

Dollmann, E., *Call Me Coward*, London: Kimber, 1956.*

——— *Dolmetscher der Diktatoren*, Bayreuth: Hestia, 1963.

——— *Roma nazista*, Milan: Longanesi, 1949.**

Eisenhower, D. D. *Crusade in Europe*, Garden City: Doubleday & Company, Inc., 1948.

Enciclopedia Cattolica, Vol. 10, Vatican City: The Vatican, 1939–1954.*

Enciclopedia Italiana, Seconda Appendice, Vol. 2, Rome: Istituto della Enciclopedia Italiana, 1949.**

Falconi, C., *Il silenzio di Pio XII*, Milan: Sugar, 1965.

Florio, V., *4 giorni in Via Tasso*, Palermo: IRES, 1947.**

Foreign Relations of the United States, 1943, Volume II, Europe, Washington: Government Printing Office, 1964.

Fornaro, V., *Il servizio informazione nella lotta clandestina*, Milan: Domus, 1946.*

Friedländer, S., *Pio XII e il Terzo Reich*, Milan: Feltrinelli, 1965 (American ed. C. Fullman, trans., New York: Knopf, 1966).

Fumarola, A. A., *Essi non sono morti*, Rome: Magi-Spinetti, 1945.**

Gardini, T. L., *Towards the New Italy*, London: Drummond, 1943.

Garland, A., and Smyth, H. M., *Sicily and the Surrender of Italy*, Washington: Government Printing Office, 1965.

Giovannetti, A., *Il Vaticano e la guerra (1939–40)*, Vatican City: The Vatican, 1960.

———*Roma, città aperta*, Milan: Ancora, 1962.**

Gorlu, G. *L'Italia nella seconda guerra mondiale*, Milan: Baldini e Castoldi, 1959.*

Graziani, R., *Processo Graziani*, 3 vols., Milan: Rufulo, 1948–1950.*

Guglielmotti, U., *L'Assedio di Roma*, Milan: Mondadori, 1944.*

Halecki, O., and Murray, J., *Pius XII: Eugenio Pacelli, Pope of Peace*, New York: Farrar, Straus & Giroux, 1954.*

Hatch, A., and Walshe, S., *Crown of Glory, the Life of Pope Pius XII*, Englewood Cliffs: Hawthorn Books, 1958 (memorial edition).*

Harris, C., *Allied Military Administration of Italy, 1943–45*, London: H.M. Stationery Office, 1957.

Hibbert, C., *Il Duce: The Life of Benito Mussolini*, Boston: Little, Brown and Company, 1962.*

Hitler e Mussolini—Lettere e documenti, Milan: Rizzoli, 1946.

Hochhuth, R., *Sidelights on History* (Appendix to *The Deputy*), New York: Grove Press, Inc., 1964.*

Hughes, H. S., *The United States and Italy*, rev. ed. Cambridge: Harvard University Press, 1953, 1965.

Hull, C., *Memoirs*, 2 vols., New York: The Macmillan Company, 1957–1958.

Kesselring, A., *A Soldier's Record*, New York: William Morrow and Company, Inc., 1954.**

Kirkpatrick, I., *Mussolini—A Study in Power*, Englewood Cliffs: Hawthorn Books, 1964.

Kogan, N., *Italy and the Allies*, Cambridge: Harvard University Press, 1956.

Konstantin, *The Pope*, Diana Pike, trans., New York: Roy Publishers, 1956.**

Laternser, H., *Verteidigung Deutsche Soldaten*, Bonn/Rhein: Bohnemeier, 1950.**

Levi Cavaglione, P., *Guerriglia nei Castelli Romani*, Rome: Einaudi, 1945.*

Lewy, G., *The Catholic Church and Nazi Germany*, New York: McGraw-Hill Book Company, 1964.

Lochner, L., ed., *The Goebbels Diaries*, Garden City: Doubleday & Company, Inc., 1948.

Longo, L., *Un popolo alla macchia*, Milan: Mondadori, 1947.*

Mack-Smith, D., *Italy, A Modern History*, Ann Arbor: University of Michigan Press, 1959.

Malvezzi, P., and Pirelli, G., *Lettere di condannati a morte della Resistenza europea*, Turin: Einaudi, 1954.*

——— *Lettere di condannati a morte della Resistenza italiana*, Turin: Einaudi, 1954.

Manhattan, A., *The Catholic Church Against the Twentieth Century*, London: C. A. Watts & Company, Ltd., 1947.

Matthews, H. L., *The Education of a Correspondent*, New York: Harcourt, Brace & World, Inc., 1946.**

Maugeri, F., *From the Ashes of Disgrace*, New York: Reynal and Hitchcock, 1948.**

Mellini Ponce de Leon, A., *Guerra diplomatica a Salò*, Bologna: Capelli, 1950.**

Meneghini, M., *Roma "città aperta,"* Rome: Magi-Spinetti, 1946.*

Milan, M., and Vighi, F., eds., *La Resistenza al fascismo*, Milan: Feltrinelli, 1955.**

Möllhausen, E. F., *La carta perdente*, Rome: Sestante, 1948.**

Monelli, P., *Roma 1943*, Rome: Migliaresi, 1945; rev. ed., Milan: Longanesi, 1963.**

Morpurgo, L., *Caccia all' uomo*, Rome: Dalmatia, 1946.**

Murphy, R., *Diplomat Among Warriors*, Garden City: Doubleday & Company, Inc., 1964.

Mussolini, B., *Opera omnia*, Vol. 32, Florence: La Fenice, 1960.

——— *Storia di un anno*, Milan: Mondadori, 1944.

Mussolini, R., *Benito il mio uomo*, Milan: Rizzoli, 1958.*

——— *La mia vita con Benito*, Milan: Mondadori, 1948.*

Nazi Conspiracy and Aggression, Supplement B, Washington: Government Printing Office, 1948.**

Negro, S., *Roma, non basta una vita*, Venice: Neri Pozza, 1962.**

Pallenberg, C., *Inside the Vatican*, Englewood Cliffs: Hawthorn Books, 1960.

Pietra, I., and Muratore, R., *La résistance italienne*, 3rd ed., Milan: Archivio storico del C.V.L., 1949, bilingual, French-Italian text.*

Pini, G., and Susmel, D., *Mussolini: l'uomo e l'opera*, 4 vols., Florence: La Fenice, 1958.*

Pisanò, G., *Sangue chiama sangue*, Milan: Pidola, 1962.**

Piscitelli, E., *Storia della Resistenza romana*, Bari: Laterza, 1965.**

Puntoni, P., *Parla Vittorio Emanuele III*, Milan: Palazzi, 1958.

Rahn, R., *Ambasciatore di Hitler*, Milan: Garzanti, 1951.

——— *Ruheloses Leben*, Düsseldorf: Diedrichs, 1949.

Reitlinger, G., *The Final Solution*, New York: Beechhurst Press, 1953.*

Ripa di Meana, F., *Roma clandestina*, Rome: O.E.T., 1944.**

Salvatorelli, L., and Mira, G., *Storia d'Italia nel periodo fascista*, Turin: Einaudi, 1956.**

Scotland, A. P., *Der Fall Kesselring*, Bonn: Koellen, 1952 (bilingual, German-English text).**

Scrivener, J., *Inside Rome with the Germans*, New York: The Macmillan Company, 1945.**

Secchia, P., and Frassati, F., *La Resistenza e gli Alleati*, Milan: Feltrinelli, 1962.

Shirer, W. L., *The Rise and Fall of the Third Reich*, New York: Simon and Schuster, Inc., 1960.

Spampanato, B., *Contromemoriale*, 3 vols., Rome: L'Illustrato, 1952(?).**

Stendardo, G., *Via Tasso*, Rome: privately printed, 1965.**

Tamaro, A., *Due anni di storia, 1943–45*, 3 vols., Rome: Tosi, 1948–1950.**

Tompkins, P., *A Spy in Rome*, New York: Simon and Schuster, Inc., 1962.**

Trabucco, C., *La prigionia di Roma*, Rome: S.E.L.I., 1945.**

Trials of War Criminals Before the Nuremberg Military Tribunals, Vols. 12, 13, and 14, Washington: Government Printing Office, 1951–1952.

Troisio, A., *Roma sotto il terrore nazi-fascista*, Rome: Mondini, 1944.**

United Nations War Crimes Commission, *Law Reports of Trials of War Criminals*, Vol. 8, London: H.M. Stationery Office, 1949.**

United States Office of Air Force History, *The Army Air Force in World War II*, Vol. 3, Chicago: University of Chicago Press, 1949.

Valiani, L., *Tutte le strade conducono a Roma*, Florence: La Nuova Italia, 1947.

Vaughn-Thomas, W., *Anzio*, New York: Holt, Rinehart and Winston, Inc., 1961.

Wall, B., *The Vatican Story*, London: George Weidenfeld & Nicolson, Ltd., 1956.

Weizsäcker, E., *Memoirs*, Chicago: Henry Regnery Company, 1951.

Westphal, S., *Heer in Fesseln*, Bonn: Athenaeum, 1950.

Wiskemann, E., *The Rome-Berlin Axis*, Oxford: Oxford University Press, 1949.*

Wyss, M. de, *Rome Under the Terror*, London: Robert Hale. Ltd., 1945.**

Zangrandi, R., *1943: 25 luglio—8 settembre*, Milan: Feltrinelli, 1964.

ARTICLES

"*Alcuni documenti sull' attività della banda Koch*, in *Movimento di Liberazione in Italia*," Sept., 1950.**

Alessandrini, A., "*Carlo Zaccagnini e Monsignor Pappagallo*," in *Mercurio*, Dec., 1944.**

Amendola, G., "*Le condizioni della Resistenza romana*," in *Rinascita*, Mar., 1954.*

——— and Frassati, F., eds., "*Documenti inediti sulle posizione del PCI e del PSIUP dall' ottobre 1943 all' aprile 1944*," in *Critica Marxista*, Mar.–Apr., 1965.

Caputo, G., "*La Resistenza della scuola romana*," in *Movimento di Liberazione in Italia*, Apr.–June, 1963.*

Gambari, G., "*Tre eroi*" [Montezemolo, Di Pillo, Giglio], in *Mercurio*, Dec., 1944.**

Kappler, H., article in *Incom*, Mar., 1959.**

Kessel, A., "The Pope and the Jews," in Bentley, E., ed., *The Storm Over the Deputy*, New York: Grove Press, Inc., 1964.

Leiber, R., "Pius XII," in Bentley, E., ed., *The Storm Over the Deputy*, New York: Grove Press, Inc., 1964.

——— "*Pio XII e gli ebrei di Roma,*" in *La Civiltà Cattolica*, Mar. 4, 1961.
Montini, G. B., "Pius XII and the Jews," in Bentley, E., ed., *The Storm Over the Deputy*, New York: Grove Press, Inc., 1964.
Moravia, A., "*Vita nella stalla,*" in *Mercurio*, Dec. 1944.
Onofri, F., "*GAP di zona,*" in *Rinascita*, 1945, No. 4.
Poliakov, L., "Pope Pius XII and the Nazis," in Bentley, E., ed., *The Storm Over the Deputy*, New York: Grove Press, Inc., 1964.
Tornabuoni, L., ed., "*Morire a Roma,*" in *L'Europeo*, Apr. 12, 1964.**
Wolff, K., "*Ecco la verità,*" in *Tempo*, 1951, Nos. 5–11.

INDEX

Page numbers 273 to 310 refer to the Notes on Chapters section of this book. Thus the full title of a work cited therein as *op. cit.* may be found on the first Notes on Chapters page number under the author's name.